SLOW WALKS IN AMSTERDAM

Continuing the unique travel series established with SLOW WALKS IN PARIS, short-listed for the Thomas Cook Guide Book of the Year Award, Michael Leitch has now turned his attention to Amsterdam, the beautiful city where the canal waters drift between tall town houses packed with history.

SLOW WALKS IN AMSTERDAM offers twenty gentle strolls that uncover the fascinating attractions of this ancient city, as the reader is taken to Anne Frank's house, round the little-known Western Islands, through leafy parks to irresistible cafés and Amsterdam brown bars.

Each walk is carefully planned and utterly enjoyable. Detailed route guides and specially drawn maps accompany each walk, while helpful information about public transport, currency and places to eat take the worry out of travel and enhance the pleasures of exploration.

Travellers will be able to relax and enjoy themselves as they amble along the canal banks and backstreets, through museums, markets and churches, and discover the history and charm of Amsterdam and the neighbouring towns of Haarlem, Leiden and Utrecht.

MICHAEL LEITCH spends a good deal of time travelling, both in Europe and the United States. He and his wife have two daughters. They live in Oxfordshire where he works as a writer and editor. He is currently working on SLOW WALKS IN BARCELONA.

SLOW WALKS IN Amsterdam

A Visitor's Companion

By the same author

Slow Walks in Paris

MICHAEL LEITCH

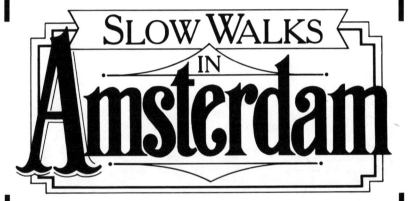

SLOW WALKS IN Amsterdam

A Visitor's Companion

HODDER AND STOUGHTON
London   Sydney   Auckland   Toronto

ACKNOWLEDGMENTS

My warm thanks to the following for their help, good company and encouragement while I was researching this book: Zoran Djapic, Rinus and Yvonne Groeneveld, Pieter Jongbloed, Daisy and Gwydwr Leitch, Yolie Mulkens, Carine van Steen and Odette Taminiau.

My thanks also to Nora Harragin for once again producing a spot-on typescript despite an unfriendly deadline.

British Library Cataloguing in Publication Data
Leitch, Michael
    Slow walks in Amsterdam.
    1. Netherlands. Amsterdam – Visitor's guides
    I. Title
    914.92352

    ISBN 0-340-51083-8

Route maps, overall map and illustrations by Alec Spark.

Published by Hodder and Stoughton,
a division of Hodder and Stoughton Ltd,
Mill Road, Dunton Green, Sevenoaks, Kent TN13 2YA
Editorial Office: 47 Bedford Square, London WC1B 3DP

Photoset by SX Composing, Rayleigh, Essex

Printed in Great Britain by BPCC Hazell Books, Aylesbury, Bucks.

CONTENTS

What to wear and carry with you; On being a good pedestrian;
The geography of Amsterdam; Transport – trams, buses,
Metro, taxis; Telephones; Money; Opening times; List of public
holidays; Clothing sizes; Watering-holes; Toilets; What's On;
Amsterdam by night; Quick Amsterdam.

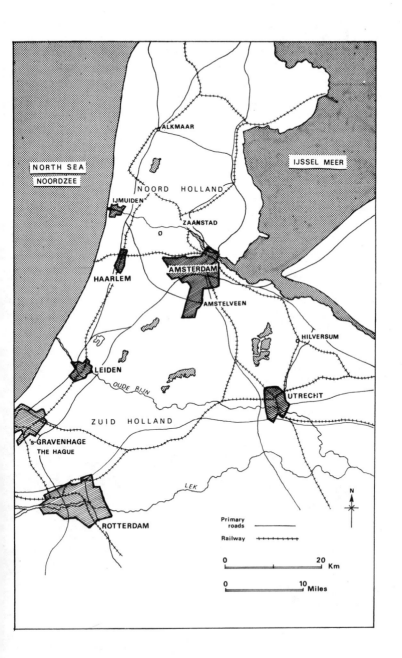

THE WALKS

Each Slow Walk opens with a Summary, then a Map and Route guide with street-by-street instructions, beginning at a tram stop. The essay which follows is suitable for reading either before you go on the walk, as a form of briefing, or afterwards as a comparison with how you found everything.

The following symbols are used, mainly in the Route sections:

▬   Special visit recommended

☂   Suitable for a rainy day

The following abbreviations are used in the Route sections:

N, NE, E, etc, to indicate directions

17C   Seventeenth century

All maps are drawn north to south.

WELCOME!

Welcome to *Slow Walks in Amsterdam*. I first visited Amsterdam in the 1960s, rushing about the place on business trips to printers and publishers, with hardly time to see so much as a canal before shooting off to the airport at Schiphol and home.

This year it has been an extraordinary pleasure to start again, spending several weeks in the city and going round it at a pace which leaves time for enjoyment and reflection. The title of this book is intended to suggest a mood, and a way of seeing, which can only be acquired by agreeing to slow down, look around, and watch how the city and its people move and behave.

Amsterdam became a perfect companion. Its natural pace is slow. You cannot hurry beside a canal, the cobblestones will see to that. People here like to have time on their hands, to sit and talk in their brown cafés, stroll the streets and go out on the town. Doing what *they* choose to do, and in the process cultivating an individuality which they know others will respect. For that is the system here.

An elderly man sits beside Prinsengracht, near the Amstelveld flower market, fishing. To add to his enjoyment of the morning, he has dragged an ancient soft armchair, upholstered in beige corduroy, out from his house and across the road to the edge of the canal. There he now sits with one leg cocked over an arm of the chair, watching his float. A tram on Utrechtsestraat crosses the bridge, a few metres away. Time passes and nothing happens. Presently a red-necked grebe arrives to fish the same stretch, tipping up to submerge and vanish, and then bouncing up thirty metres away, then diving again. Man and bird fish side by side. Half an hour later they are still there, though the man now has a bottle of beer at his feet.

Not a world-shaking sequence of events, I know. What impressed me, watching from a floating café on the other side of the canal, was that it happened in the middle of a major city, beside a tram route and barely five minutes' walk from the clamour of Rembrandtplein. In Amsterdam, bang next door to urban dash and noise, private spaces open out with a naturalness probably unmatched by any city of comparable size. What thanks we still owe to the planners who designed the great ring of canals, the *Grachtengordel*, nearly four hundred years ago.

To get to know Amsterdam, it is essential to walk. But how to go about it? Delivered at some central point, the railway station or the Dam, it is hard for a newcomer to see which way to turn. Maps offer landmarks, but do not indicate the best route between two points. How best to see the Old Side, *without* getting too mixed up in the Red Light district? And the Jordaan, famous for its markets, picturesque corners and bright boutiques – but where precisely are they, and how do you find a way through that maze of narrow streets? And those big art museums, all in a row. Is there a way of touring them gradually, avoiding pictorial indigestion?

These are some of the questions I have set out to solve in this book, devising a series of routes through Amsterdam that readers can follow in their own time. Most concentrate on one fairly small area of the city, and offer further suggestions about local cafés, restaurants and things to do in the evening. And for those who have time for a change of scene, there are two walks each in Haarlem, Leiden and Utrecht, none more than half an hour by train from Centraal Station.

With one exception (*Walk 3: City by the Sea*) you don't have to walk far on these outings, but I hope you will end up discovering much more than you may have thought was available. Amsterdam is a welcoming city. To enjoy it, you need only get your general bearings, and work out how to use the trams, and the realisation then dawns that this is one of those special places where you can do just about anything you like. I certainly hope it strikes you that way. And good luck.

Walk 1

New Side

This is the western half of the old city. Here are Dam Square and the Royal Palace, New Church and the Nationaal Monument, then the spectacular courtyards and rooms of the Historical Museum – formerly an orphanage – and the Begijnhof, a pretty and tranquil refuge for *ongehuwde dames* (unmarried ladies).

Allow 4–5 hours.

Best times Any day; New Church not open until 11.00.

ROUTE

Begin at Centraal Station. Trams 1, 2, 4, 5, 9, 13, 16, 17, 24, 25. Buses 21, 32, 33, 34, 35, 39. Metro terminus.

From Station forecourt, walk S across Prins Hendrikkade to top of Damrak. Keep to left-hand side, next to old harbour, and walk down to the former **Stock Exchange (Beurs)**. At far end of building, go round Beursplein and cross Damrak. Just past C&A, enter narrow Zoutsteeg. Continue into Gravenstraat, past shops tacked on to side of **New Church (Nieuwe Kerk)**. Walk round church (now a cultural centre) to entrance ☞; open 11.00 to 16.00, Sunday 12.00 to 15.00. *Admission*.

At exit, turn left and walk across Dam Square to far side and see **Nationaal Monument**. On left, from 1991, the new Madame Tussaud's waxworks ☞; see *Walk 2* for current details. Return to front of **Royal Palace (Koninklijk Paleis)** ☞; open June to August 12.30 to 16.00, ticket desk closes 15.40; rest of year, guided tours by arrangement. *Admission*.

Turn right at exit and walk down Kalverstraat. At No.92 turn right through archway to **Amsterdam Historical Museum (Amsterdams Historisch Museum)** ☞; open 11.00 to 17.00. *Admission, takes Museum Pass*. If this entrance closed, walk back to No.78 Kalverstraat and turn into St Luciënsteeg; entrance along on left.

Leave museum and turn down remarkable Civic Guard Gallery (Schuttersgalerij). Continue along Gedempte Begijnensloot and after about 80m turn right beneath brick archway into the **Begijnhof** ☞. Walk round the garden and look at both churches, the English and the Roman Catholic. Beyond the churches, go through tiled passageway between Nos 38 and 37, emerging in Spui. Turn right to nearby square.

Walk ends here. Nearest refreshments at Café Luxembourg or Café Hoppe next door. Trams 1, 2, 5.

Centraal Station

I like this gaudy red-brick Palace of Departure, busting out with municipal shields and allegorical reliefs in praise of shipping, trade and industry. The stone figures are grimy nowadays, grey-turning-black reminders of the soot-blown days of steam. Never mind, it is a building with guts and spirit, peculiarly Dutch, and a suitably grand arrival and departure point for more than 100,000 rail travellers each day –

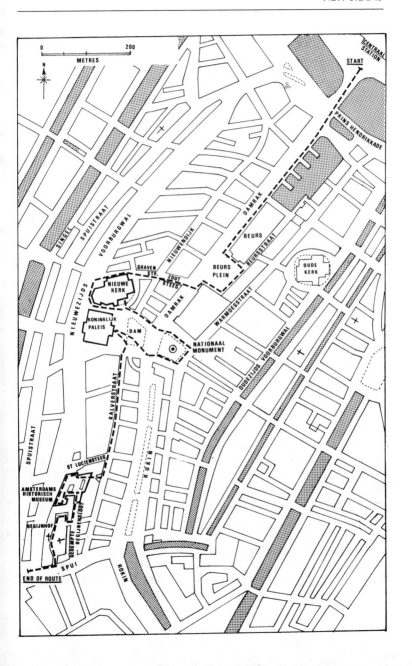

including you if you come by train from Schiphol Airport or plan a Slow Walk out of town, in Haarlem, Leiden or Utrecht.

Above the entrance, the Neo-Renaissance central block and flanking towers bristle with pinnacles and ornaments, and for your further entertainment the gilded clock in the left-hand tower is not a clock at all but a wind-rose, the single hand oscillating between the cardinal points of N, O, Z and W.

Centraal Station was designed in a so-called 'national' style by P.J.H. Cuypers, architect of the visually related Rijksmuseum, and was built between 1882 and 1889. One of its most remarkable features is the island site on which it stands, a man-made structure which rests on 26,000 wooden piles and now screens the middle part of the city from the River IJ.

Out front, the station forecourt is made less than lovely by the flocks of international scruff who perch there for hours to contemplate their rucksacks and watch the buskers and hustlers. To either side of the folk band from Ecuador, and the lone flugelhorn-player who has set up in competition, ranks of yellow trams pause at the terminus before swerving across the bridge to a peal of warning bells.

We follow the tram tracks. Past the street organ wheezing an Edith Piaf selection, then past the bright white canal cruisers in the inner harbour to Nieuwe Brug, the bridge facing Damrak.

Damrak

The long pool of Damrak was once part of the sea harbour, crammed with boats all the way back to the old Town Hall, where Dam Square stands today. Now only a few severely rusting barges flank the east side of the pool, beneath a row of still distinguished if run-down houses which mark the border of Amsterdam's Old Side, the Oude Zijde. Behind them lies the Red Light district, several acres of sleaze which we carefully glide through in *Walk 2*.

Then there is Damrak the street. There are plans to upgrade this unappealing thoroughfare, and not before time. The pavement will be widened and the blighted façades of the buildings stripped of their shoddy signboards. For many years Damrak has suffered from main station overspill, invaded by money, sex and junk-food shops which speak only the language of Wechsel, Cambio, Pizzeria, Tax Free,

Cheapest Air Fares, Venus Tempel. The shining exception to all this commercial squalor stands next to a sex cinema at No.62: Allert de Lange, probably the best bookshop in Amsterdam.

Until the upgrading is done, I suggest you keep to the far side of the road, looking out across the water for ducks, and diving grebes in season.

Flags of all nations promote the joys of canal-cruising at the boat jetties. If you fancy a pleasant hour afloat, avoid the boats filled with row on row of bus-type seating. It can be hot under those glass roofs, and for the same price you can find boats offering upholstered comfort around a table for four. It's worth shopping around.

Berlagebeurs

Ahead stands one of my favourite buildings: the old Stock Exchange or Koopmansbeurs, more widely referred to as the Berlagebeurs after its architect, H.P. Berlage. It was built in 1898–1903 and made not only a brilliant break with nineteenth-century neo-styles but also showed a dynamic way forward to the modern lines of the Amsterdam School. It looks even better viewed from the Beursplein at the far end, but best of all is the interior. Getting inside may call for a little luck and initiative, since the building is closed to visitors except for concerts and special exhibitions. Halfway along, spiky blue and gold gates guard the entrance to the box office. If they are open, go up the steps and try to slip into the former trading hall on the right. If not, try the main entrance in Beursplein. Here on the right is a new café-restaurant, the Beurs van Berlage, created in one of the old Exchange's smaller rooms and in itself a useful introduction to the architect's bold and colourful style.

In the summer months there are regular exhibitions, and at the end of August the Berlagebeurs is one of the chief indoor venues for the *Uitmarkt* (pronounced 'Out-markt'), a festival of previews for the coming arts season. Events take place from noon till midnight all the way from the Beurs through Dam Square and along the streets of Rokin and Nes. Here one Saturday afternoon I stood on a bench and craned across a sea of enthusiastic Amsterdammers for a sight of dancers from the National Ballet, suavely performing brief excerpts from their repertoire.

If you can find time to see this hall in quieter circumstances, so much

the better. It is a kind of updated medieval *Ridderzaal*, or hall of knights, enclosing a vast space with mustard-coloured steel girders reaching up to the glazed panels of the roof. The inner walls of pink and yellow brick are pierced with two rows of mysterious-looking shallow arches giving on to upper side galleries, supported by squarish pillars of speckled marble; behind them on the ground floor are the old traders' booths in polished wood, illuminated by stained-glass windows shedding a gold and amber light.

At the south end of the parquet floor, an elegant blue brick and glass enclosure once housed the *Schrijfkamer*, or Writing Room. On the north wall a frieze describes the evolution of man from naked nomad to behatted trader. Above is a memorial plaque giving thanks for the Liberation of 1945, and a row of shields (another knightly touch) bearing the names of, to yesteryear's Dutch stockbroker, the world's great trading centres: Alexandrie, B-Aijres, Batavia, Londen, New York, Sidneij.

New Church

Cross Damrak, where another street organ belts out traditional ditties. A few doors past C&A, delicious bread smells float out from the baker's shop on the corner. Turn here and delve into the narrow tapering alley of Zoutsteeg, centre of the salt trade when ships moored in Damrak and unloaded nearby. Cross into Gravenstraat, lately in the process of being heavily knocked about, leaving De Wenteltrap, a famous old brown bar, shorn of any visible means of support on one side of the building.

The reason for taking this cobbled route is to arrive beside the magnificent choir of New Church (Nieuwe Kerk) which dates from the end of the fourteenth century. Along here too is the strange spectacle of several tiny shops tacked on to the church wall. One of them, only a door and a narrow window wide, proclaims itself the 'Smallest Shop in Town'.

If you are early for the church, which opens at 11.00, drop into the Corner House coffee shop and bar, a comfortable brown room with a long bar and carpet on the tables. A few steps away, the trams clank up and down Nieuwe Zijds Voorburgwal. Opposite are two imposing buildings.

Die Port van Cleve is a famous restaurant, built in 1885–88 and synonymous in this city with a memorable blow-out constructed on foundations of pea soup and fortified by a generous helping of steak. Three great yellow awnings balloon out over the main windows like inverted tulips, and in the early evening waiters in long white starched aprons gather on the front steps to gossip, waiting for fresh stomachs to arrive and take up the challenge.

Next door is the gigantic Main Post Office building (Hoofdpost-kantoor). This grand Gothic structure, dating from 1895–99, almost out-palaces the Royal Palace which it faces across the road. In June

1990 the Post Office moved to new premises on the Singel, directly behind the old building which then began its metamorphosis into an upmarket shopping mall. The exterior is to be kept, but the switch of use should restore much-needed colour to Nieuwe Zijds Voorburgwal. This broad and in parts handsome boulevard has looked a little drab since the newspaper offices, once its heart and soul, took themselves away from the city centre.

Back at Nieuwe Kerk, follow the church wall into Mozes en Aäronstraat. The entrance to the church is next to a diamond shop attached to the wall. It is no longer a working church but a 'national and international cultural centre'. Now in the choir they have a café where you can sit and contemplate the huge marble tomb of Michiel de Ruyter, a celebrated Dutch admiral and scourge of the English in the Second Anglo-Dutch War (1665–67), who now lies where the high altar once stood.

The programme of exhibitions and events changes regularly through the year. If, as I once did, you arrive to find an art show in occupation, it is difficult to see the original church when the nave has become a maze of tall white screens from which the pictures hang. Look up, though, to the splendid timber roof and see the principal treasures of the church.

The brass chancel screen is by Johannes Lutma, a friend of Rembrandt, and was made soon after the disastrous fire of 1645, caused by an erratic workman pouring lead on the roof, which gutted the church. The building was virtually reconstructed over the next twenty years. The fine, ornately pinnacled pulpit by A.J. Vinckenbrinck also dates from this period, as does the Great Organ above the West door. The organ cases were designed by Jacob van Campen and the shutters painted by J.G. van Bronckhorst with scenes from the life of David. There are regular organ concerts in summer (see *What's On* for details).

After the French occupation of the country between 1795 and 1813, the New Church became the national church of the Netherlands. Several Dutch monarchs were invested here, the latest being Queen Beatrix, on 30 April 1980. The date chosen was the 71st birthday of ex-Queen Juliana, her mother, who abdicated in her favour. Out of respect for the former Queen, this date is still kept for the annual feast day known as the Queen's Birthday.

The Dam

Out in Dam Square, walk ahead to the gaunt Nationaal Monument, erected by public subscription in 1956 to commemorate the Second World War, and which I describe in the more appropriate context of *Walk 6: Resistance Museum to Anne Frank House.*

Around the edges of the square, there is not a great deal to detain you. Of the two big stores, the grey exterior of Peek & Cloppenburg cloaks a very ordinary shop, and De Bijenkorf, while not at all bad inside – in fact it is the best department store in the city – seems oddly short of self-confidence. It should be the Harrods of Amsterdam, but all too often its window displays are sadly short of the oomph needed to attract international visitors.

In 1991, Madame Tussaud's is due to move from Kalverstraat to much larger premises on the three upper floors of Peek & Cloppenburg, and that should brighten the square somewhat. When the move is made, readers should insert their tour of the waxworks, at present described in *Walk 2*, into this walk.

The Dam, the long rectangular space that stretches between the Royal Palace and the Hotel Krasnapolsky, is central to the life of the city. The original fishing village took root here, mainly on the east bank of the Amstel (the Old Side), and then became a fast-growing medieval town. The old Stadhuis (Town Hall) and Waag (Weigh-house) were here. Then came Van Campen's new Stadhuis (1648–55), which now is the Royal Palace. Always this square has served as a forum, for parades, executions, or just a jolly party to keep the good burghers amused.

In 1989 the *Uitmarkt*, which I have already mentioned, opened with an ambitious televised concert. On a gigantic stage in front of the Royal Palace, an orchestra that year featuring 150 saxophones honked and blared into the night. Supplementary horn-players in white T-shirts hung in lines from the upper storeys of the Rabobank and Peek & Cloppenburg, and balanced fearlessly on the roof of the Nieuwe Kafé, by the New Church.

This spectacular was shortly followed, as it is followed every year on the first Saturday of September, by the Bloemencorso, a flower parade organised by the growers of Aalsmeer. Fifty-seven extravagantly decorated floats, floral cars, carts, bicycles and tractors – sometimes you could not *see* what was underneath – rolled slowly through the Dam, past the beaming Mayor seated in the front row of the grandstand. It was the climax of a parade that had taken the vehicles through half of Amsterdam. They drew large crowds all the way, proudly showed off their amazing confections – fifteen thousand roses on one float was not all that unusual – and then they came for their final salute to the centre of everything – the Dam.

Royal Palace

The Queen comes only two or three times a year to the Royal Palace, to attend official functions. Wisely, she never stays here overnight, preferring the calm of the Huis ten Bosch in The Hague.

First impressions of the Royal Palace may be that this great baroque box is overwhelmingly large, and that the German sandstone (originally a pale cream colour) is in need of a good clean. And, up there in the tympanum, what on earth are all those figures doing, writhing like spaghetti?

The building does not speak of majesty or royalty, but then it was not meant to. When Jacob van Campen won the architectural competition, he had been competing to build not a palace but a massive new Town Hall, a Stadhuis that would reflect Amsterdam's position as the trading capital of Europe. In 1648 the nation won full independence from Spain following the Congress of Münster and the new Town Hall was to stand as a symbol of lasting peace as well as civic power.

The Royal Palace is open in the summer months, or can be visited by special arrangement. Enter by a modest door on the far right of the arcade at the front. Leaflets in several languages offer a logical route through the various chambers and galleries. It is no bad idea to begin in the video room. An English-language version is played from time to time (see clock for next showing). From the projection area, turn right into the *Vierschaar*, the High Court of Justice. This is the most impressive room in the whole building, where the marble reliefs of Artus Quellien of Antwerp are extraordinarily effective.

The *Vierschaar* was used for one function only: to pronounce the death sentence. The judges sat on a long marble bench, surrounded by allegorical reliefs of Mercy, Wisdom and Righteousness, and the figures of two women who cover their faces in shame. The blank whiteness of the marble lends the room an almost mythical atmosphere, somewhere between reality and dream, uplifted from ordinary mortal affairs into an abstract zone. It was in fact very necessary to try to distance the ceremony from the crudity of everyday life. For, while the judges passed sentence, and contemplated the figures of Justice and Prudence facing them, they were by no means alone. Through the barred windows in front of them, a great crowd on the Dam bellowed and roared, blood-curdlingly eager for a sight of their next execution. Thus was preserved the rugged Dutch tradition that justice must be carried out in full public view.

Go upstairs next to see the Citizens' Hall. This vast room is a kind of civic temple to Amsterdam's power, abundant with allegorical statues. On the floor are three inlaid marble maps of the eastern and western hemispheres and the northern heavens, their purpose to celebrate the city's dominance in the maritime affairs of trade and exploration. From here, walk through to the Magistrates' Court, notable for its massive chimney-piece painted by Ferdinand Bol and imposing equestrian portraits. Then tour the South Gallery.

In the side galleries you will come upon much evidence of the French occupation, when Louis Napoleon, brother of the French Emperor, was King of Holland. In 1808 it was he who turfed out the city's administrators and converted the building into a regal palace, and much of his imported collection of Empire furniture remains to this day. (France's hold on Amsterdam collapsed in 1813 after the *Grande Armée*'s defeats in Russia and Germany.)

Eventually you reach the front of the building and three rooms looking out over the Dam: the Burgomasters' Council Room and Chamber, and the Chamber of Justice. Here the condemned man was brought up from the *Vierschaar*, to receive a prayer for the salvation of his soul. He was then ushered through the window to take up his final place on earth, standing on the platform of a wooden scaffold, raised high above the seething crowd.

The tour continues through the City Council Room and the North Gallery, where special exhibitions are mounted. At four o'clock, the building is most emphatically closed. Lights flash on and off and officials suddenly begin to dart this way and that, sheepdogging errant visitors towards the *Uitgang* with a zeal rarely found in museums. The Royal Palace is, in more ways than one, an extraordinary building.

Historical Museum

The climax of this walk is not far away. First, turn from the Dam into Kalverstraat, a narrow, paved West European souk with many open-fronted shops where leather jackets, boots and T-shirts hang in tiers, alongside a few diamond merchants and a useful bargain bookshop, De Slegte, on the right at Nos 48–52.

When you reach No.92, turn right through an archway topped by the triple-cross arms of Amsterdam and a coloured relief, dated 1581, with rather bulbous figures of boy orphans in black and red uniforms. This is the boys' entrance to the Burghers' Orphanage, founded in 1578, which took over the site of a former convent, St Lucy's, together with its cowsheds and outhouses and an old men's home. The orphanage moved out in 1960 and the buildings were gradually, and brilliantly, converted for occupation by the Amsterdams Historisch Museum, which moved here in 1975.

If, by the way, the boys' entrance is closed, retrace your steps to St Luciënsteeg, at No.78 Kalverstraat, then walk along this alley past a row of small coffee shops and turn in at the museum entrance signalled by a collection of old gable-stones set in the walls, rescued from houses demolished in the early years of this century. The stones depict symbols of a multitude of trades and other subjects: a trowel, a hat, three moles, a goat, the Oude Schans canal, the Queen, a cooper at work.

On your way through to the museum from the Kalverstraat entrance, you pass the boys' courtyard on your left. On the far wall is a gallery, built in 1762, with a double row of lockers where the orphan boys kept their belongings. On the other side of the cloister, the old barn is now the museum restaurant, In de Oude Goliath, its interior dominated by a colossal bearded figure which from 1650 to 1862 stood in one of the city's amusement parks. If lunchtime has intervened, it would be convenient to settle here, or out on the terrace if the weather allows.

Walk straight ahead to the girls' courtyard and the main entrance. As you might expect from a museum designed just over fifteen years ago, the layout is modern, smart, makes excellent use of the original buildings and employs a range of ingenious models and audio-visual displays to sharpen our picture of the city and its growth since the thirteenth century. The result is excellent. I would include it in my list of best ten large museums anywhere.

Take Room 1 for an immediate sample of the museum's inventive approach. Here is a remarkable bird's eye-view of Amsterdam made in 1544 by Cornelis Anthonisz. Nearby, a tall steel column charts the growth in the city's population. Lights flicker up the column, illuminating the dates and figures. The count begins in 1050, but not until 1300 were there 1,000 people. By 1475 there were 10,000. By 1600 the total has leapt to 100,000, and then doubles during the seventeenth century, the city's Golden Age. Another explosion occurs between 1875 (300,000) and 1900 (550,000). By 1950 the figure has soared to 900,000. Meanwhile, next to the column, an enormous lightbox map demonstrates the chronological expansion of the city from its modest beginnings on the Dam.

The museum has twenty rooms altogether, and although you will no doubt find your own favourite exhibits, let me prepare the way by mentioning some that I especially like. Room 4: another bird's-eye view by Anthonisz, in colour, dated 1538, the earliest surviving plan, commissioned by the city governors and first hung in the old Stadhuis. Room 5: marine paintings, globes and an explorers' map which lights up to show the routes they took – Barendsz and Heemskerk, de Houtman and Keyzer, van Noort, and Henry Hudson, also the pattern of trade contacts achieved by 1600 with the furthest corners of the world. Room 7: inset in a blown-up picture of a row of warehouses, model store rooms are cut away to show some of the goods kept in them – china, lead, cloth, saltpetre, gold, pewter, coffee, tin, tea, wine, wood, spices, indigo, copper.

Upstairs, along the lengths of Rooms 8, 9 and 10, look down on the paintings in the extraordinary *Schuttersgalerij* (Civic Guards' Gallery) which we visit later. 10a: climb a spiral staircase to the Bell Room, where four seventeenth-century carillons can be summoned at the press of a button, those of Westerkerk, Stadhuis (Royal Palace), Oude Kerk and Zuiderkerk. And real bells from the Mint Tower, in 1873 sold for scrap but mercifully kept safe.

Cross by the bridge to Room 11: fine group portraits of eminent burghers, and a huge painted board with the coats of arms of the governors of the orphanage. Nearby is a study for the figures adorning the Nationaal Monument, by John Rädecker, donated in 1985 by the artist's widow.

Finally, look for the famous Regents' Room. Not obviously signposted, it is in fact next to the entrance hall. This is the restored room where the regents or governors of the orphanage held their meetings. In the small adjoining room are portraits of girls in the orphanage, walking in procession and carrying out their daily duties.

At the exit, return through the girls' courtyard and turn right into the Schuttersgalerij, at once an outdoor art gallery and a street. On the walls hang group portraits of Civic Guardsmen, members of the companies originally formed at the end of the fourteenth century to keep public order and defend the city. In about 1530 the custom began of commissioning group portraits to hang in the company halls. The practice continued until 1650, and the portraits form a priceless document of civil life in sixteenth- and seventeenth-century Amsterdam.

Many famous Dutch artists took up commissions to paint Civic Guard portraits. Among them were Frans Hals, whose biggest collection is housed at 'his' museum in Haarlem (see *Walk 15*) and Rembrandt, whose *Night Watch* in the Rijksmuseum has been called, a little rashly perhaps, 'the world's greatest painting' (see *Walk 10*).

The portraits in this gallery are great fun to examine in detail. Several groups posed at their company's annual banquet, and some of the faces indeed betray men who have dined and drunk well, while others are frozen in the act, slicing through a chicken or pensively gripping a pewter pot, no doubt wishing the wretched artist would get on with it. Most, however, are portrayed in regimented lines (the old style of group portraiture), gripping their halberds and arquebuses and staring outwards with an expression that well justifies the martial cliché – *fierce pride*.

The Begijnhof

At the far end of the Schuttersgalerij, walk down the charming lane between white-rendered houses that prop each other somehow up, and turn in at the brick archway to the Begijnhof.

'May peace prevail on earth/*Moge vrede heersen op aarde*' says a sign on a post in the central grassy patch, formerly a bleach-field. It is a most peaceful place of refuge, and preserves its dignity despite being on every tourist's map and thus visited by thousands every week.

There is nothing all that spectacular to see, the value of the place lies in its tranquillity: a cluster of retirement homes for *ongehuwde dames* (unmarried ladies) administered by Het Begijnhof foundation. The courtyard dates back to the fourteenth century, and originally was for women and girls who sought a form of convent life which left them free to leave or marry if they wished. Within the Beguinage are two churches, the English Reformed Church, built in 1607, and a Catholic church made clandestinely in 1665 from two houses for the benefit of Catholic sisters who after the Reformation had been deprived of a place of worship.

One of the nearby houses is a great rarity – 'Het Houten Huys' at No.34, built in 1460. Only two wooden houses remain in Amsterdam, this and another at the top of Zeedijk (see *Walk 7*). Fires were all too common in the medieval city, and while many buildings of similar age have survived, their timber fronts were long ago replaced by brick gables.

To rejoin the twentieth century, find the doorway between Nos. 38 and 37 and go up the steps through a tiled and vaulted passage. Emerge on Spui (pronounced 'Spy') opposite the Maagdenhuis, now part of the University of Amsterdam. Turn right to the little square, a picturesque place of cafés and bookshops, where this walk ends. The better watering-holes are next to each other – the Café Luxembourg beneath the Oranjeboom sign and the Café Hoppe, one of my favourites. You have to be lucky, or early, to claim a table on the terrace but the darkish cream and brown interior is comfortable and has an agreeable timelessness. This café is also popular for unwinding after work, and in summer the pavement is filled to the edge with gossiping City-types.

Walk 2

Old Side

Bizarre and historic Amsterdam in a unique blend, from wax figures of the famous at Madame Tussaud's to live models in the windows of the Red Light district. Stroll beside canals and 17C gabled houses in the eastern half of the old city. Visit the oldest parish church in Amsterdam, and a secret attic church beautifully preserved at the Amstelkring Museum.

Allow 3–4 hours.

Best times Any day. On Sunday and holidays Amstelkring Museum not open until 13.00; Sunday service 11.00 at Old Church (in Dutch).

ROUTE

Begin at Spui. Trams 1, 2, 5. Walk E from the square along the street called Spui. Take 3rd right into Kalverstraat and visit **Madame Tussaud's** at No.156 👁; open 10.00 to 18.00, in July–August 09.00 to 19.00. *Admission*. (In 1991 this museum moves to the Dam, see essay for details.)

Exit is at rear of building, so turn right and right into Spui, then cross Rokin and walk past Queen Wilhelmina statue into Lange Brugsteeg. Keep straight on to Grimburgwal and cross next bridge, passing House on Three Canals on left (249 Oude Zijds Voorburgwal). At next canal, Oude Zijds Achterburgwal, cross to other side and take 1st right beneath stone arch into **Oudemanhuispoort**; book market Monday to Saturday, gets under way about 11.00, packs up about 16.00.

Walk through to Kloveniersburgwal, turn left and continue to Oude Hoogstraat (4th left). Look across canal to **Trippenhuis** (No.29) with mortar-barrel chimneys and walk up a few yards to see the narrow house the Trips built for their coachman (No.26). Turn up Oude Hoogstraat to Oude Zijds Achterburgwal and turn right. Red lights strung across canal announce beginning of Amsterdam's most talked-about quarter: sex shops, clubs, video booths, live shows, girls in windows.

Cross 2nd bridge and go up Oude Kennissteeg to Oude Zijds Voorburgwal. Cross canal to **Old Church (Oude Kerk)** 👁 ; open Monday to Saturday 11.00 to 16.00. *Admission*.

At exit, turn right and walk round church in Oude Kerksplein, past entrance to Tower 👁; open June to September, guided tours on the hour, Monday, Thursday 14.00 to 17.00, Tuesday, Wednesday 11.00 to 14.00. *Admission*.

Return to canal. Turn left and walk up to **Amstelkring Museum** at 40 Oude Zijds Voorburgwal 👁; open 10.00 to 17.00, Sunday 13.00 to 17.00, closed 1 January. *Admission, takes Museum Pass*.

Turn left at exit and walk to top of canal. Turn left into Nieuwe Brugstraat. Walk ends at junction with Warmoesstraat. Nearest refreshments at De Eenhoorn, 16 Warmoesstraat (cheese shop with attractive café at rear). Trams at Damrak or Centraal Station.

From Spui

The Café Hoppe, where the previous walk ended, is a most useful place

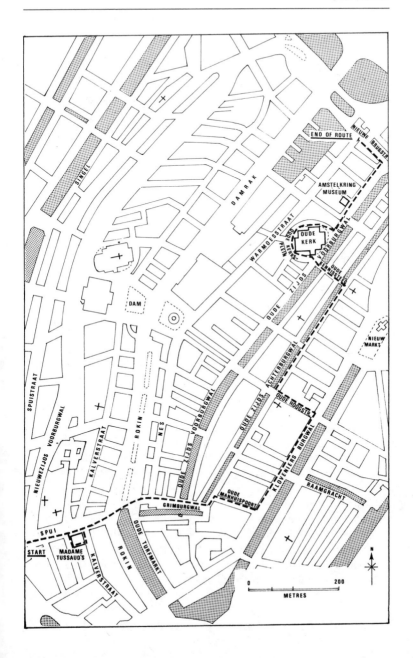

END OF ROUTE

NIEUWE BRUGSTE

AMSTELKRING MUSEUM

OUDE KERK

OUDE VOORBURGWAL

OUDE NIEUWSTR

WARMOESSTRAAT

KERK STRUK

DAMRAK

SINGEL

OUDE ZIJDS

NIEUW MARKT

DAM

ACHTERBURGWAL

OUDE ZIJDS

OUDE HOOGSTR.

SPUISTRAAT

VOORBURGWAL

OUDE ZIJDS

KLOVENIERS BURGWAL

ROKIN

NES

RAAMGRACHT

NIEUWEZIJDS VOORBURGWAL

KALVERSTRAAT

OUDE MANHUISPOORT

GRIMBURGWAL

SPUI

ROKIN

OUDE TURFMARKT

START

MADAME TUSSAUD'S

KALVERSTRAAT

0   200
METRES

N

to know, for one thing because it opens early. Many cafés and brown bars go on till two in the morning and then don't begin again until eleven. Here, though, you can pull in for an early cup of coffee, sinking into a cane chair on the covered terrace among the newspaper readers. *Het Parool* (serious, middle-of-the-road) and *De Telegraaf* (right wing) are the popular choices, also *Le Monde*. Try a Dutch paper and see how you get on.

I assume you do not speak Dutch. Few non-nationals do. But perhaps, like me, you have a little German, and that can help a lot. Dutch people are usually unimpressed by this approach, maintaining that their language is very different from German. So it is, but there are many similarities from which even a one-eyed linguist can profit. If, by the way, your coffee arrives without milk, look round for one of those plastic-capped 'baby-feeders' which are scattered round the tables: they are the communal milk supply.

Walk through the little square. The statue of *Het Lieverdje* ('Little Darling') is an essential ingredient, it seems, of every picture book about the city. For all its fame it is slender and easy to walk past without noticing (as well as fairly forgettable once you have seen it). It stands on a plinth in the centre of the square outside the Athenaeum bookshop, and was given to the city in 1960 by a cigarette company. In that decade it was taken up by the left-wing Provos as a symbol of smug bourgeois consumerism. On Saturday nights they gathered at Spui to revile the statue, start a 'happening' (remember them?) and if possible provoke the police into doing something harsh and unpopular.

Walk east along Spui. We are still in New Side (Nieuwe Zijde), but cross the invisible border into Old Side (Oude Zijde) at Rokin.

Madame Tussaud's

About fifty metres before Rokin, Madame Tussaud's waxworks museum stands three doors down Kalverstraat, to the right. I would rate it a fairly optional visit, though some of the tableaux are well done. A working knowledge of Dutch history – and their latest television presenters – would also come in handy.

After nearly twenty years in Kalverstraat, the museum plans to move in 1991 to the upper storeys of Peek & Cloppenburg in the Dam. The new site offers double the display space and, with the visitors' total already at more than 450,000 a year, Madame Tussaud's is optimistic about its future.

In the Hall of Mirrors are world leaders back to William of Orange, then forward to Churchill and Ben Gurion. Local favourites include Mr Lubbers, Queens Beatrix and Wilhelmina, Messrs Luns and Drees. Move on to where, gathered in an authentic-looking brown bar, no-one I knew stared blankly back. I think they were Dutch entertainers. Then a speed skater, then a cell-like room covered in wire mesh in which spare and *passé* heads were stored: one of Mao Tse-tung, an alternative Churchill, Fidel Castro, Richard Nixon. Past a bunch of Middle Eastern rulers in a desert tent to the Carousel exhibit.

In the next room, the names for once are spelled out: Napoleon I, who in 1806 proclaimed the Netherlands a kingdom then annexed it to his French Empire; Vondel, the most famous Dutch poet; Multatuli the novelist; Admirals de Witt and de Ruyter, and Peter the Great who came to Amsterdam to learn about shipbuilding. There is a Rembrandt room, and an ambitious Bosch room fitted with turning spheres and half-moons bearing pictorial fragments of the artist's phantasmagoria.

On to Marilyn Monroe, battling away on her famous grating in *Seven Year Itch*, with special wind effect and soundtrack. Then Mata Hari, rotating in a flimsy gown – a regular flash of wax buttocks if you care to wait. Anne Frank is in her house, then 'Pop Stars' – Michael Jackson, Boy George, David Bowie. A Boris Becker room and that's about it. A strange selection, no doubt, but, if you were curator for one day, who would you have chosen? The chief missing ingredient was, I thought, inspiration. No Chamber of Horrors, like the Tussaud's in London, nor any of the unpredictable wit that lifts the Musée Grévin in Paris above the common run. Perhaps the move to the Dam will stimulate a more bracing approach.

As I left, a girl said, 'You like to see your photo?' and handed over a print of me caught unawares by the entrance, looking crumpled and disagreeable. 'No, thank you!' Once outdoors, you find yourself in an alley at the back of the building. Turn right and right to complete a square and rejoin Spui, then carry on where you left off, crossing Kalverstraat to Rokin.

Into the Old Side

At Rokin, head past the equestrian statue of Queen Wilhelmina (1880–

1962), monarch from 1890 to 1948. Pass the twirling windmill blades at The Mill Diamond Factory and enter Langebrugsteeg. The character of the district changes immediately: we are in a narrow cobbled medieval quarter, the streets and houses uneven and curiously slanted.

Over the next bridge, the Sleutelbrug, is a much-photographed place where three canals meet and the corner house, No.249 Oude Zijds Voorburgwal, has a stepped gable on all three fronts. It is known as the 'Huis op de drie Grachten' (House on Three Canals), dates from 1610 and is now a bookshop. Across the water is another fine canal house, D' Ladder Jacobs at No.316. Designed by Philips Vingboons and built in 1655, it features Doric and Ionic pilasters, a pediment, ornate festoons and swags and an elegant pair of railed steps up to the front door. It is typical of the patrician houses in this area, which through its prosperity became known as the Velvet Canal.

Continue to the next canal, Oude Zijds Achterburgwal. The name refers to the old city wall: this canal was behind it (*achter*), the previous canal was *voor* or in front of it. Look for the stone arch leading to an alley full of second-hand bookstalls, the Oudemanhuispoort. In the covered brick arcade is a row of numbered shops, each with a tiny warehouse-like recess packed with shelves of books, and other volumes laid out on trestle tables in front. With University departments all around this neighbourhood, students are the natural targets of the booksellers, though what they sell ranges widely and there are a number of antiquarian specialists.

The large building across the courtyard from the arcade is the Oudemanhuis, built in 1754 as almshouses for elderly men and women, and since 1876 part of the University. Turn into Kloveniersburgwal and stroll along. Behind the elegant houses on the far side rises the pale stone Renaissance tower of Hendrick de Keyser's South Church (Zuiderkerk), a prominent city landmark with its red and gold clock. The narrow streets we pass recall the marshy nature of the land when it was settled in the Middle Ages: Slijkstraat (Slime Street), Rusland (Rushes Land). On the corner of Wijdestraat, look up to the handsome glazed attics of the old Proost en Brandt building, once occupied by the printing company but shortly to become the SAS Royal Hotel.

At Oude Hoogstraat, look across to the Trippenhuis at No.29, a heavy, sooty grey mansion framed by eight Corinthian pilasters and topped by two bellicose chimneys in the shape of mortars. The house was designed by Justus Vingboons and built in 1662 for two brothers of the influential Trip family which made its money out of arms manufacturing (hence the design of the chimneys). The house was built as two separate dwellings, each with its own front door but united by the monumental façade which made each half seem doubly grand. In 1815, the buildings were joined to accommodate the collections of the Rijksmuseum, which remained here until 1885 when the present museum building on Stadhouderskade was completed.

Another popular story attaches to this house. When the Trip brothers' coachman first set eyes on it, he was so stunned he declared that a house no wider than one of his masters' front doors would do him very well. He was rewarded with the extremely narrow house across the canal at No.26, 2.5 metres wide and built, it is said, from stone left over from the main house. A miracle of compression, the design still finds room for two sphinxes on top of the gable, although to fit the available space they have to tuck their rear ends around the gable's curve.

The large red-brick building on the corner of Oude Hoogstraat is Oostindisch Huis, the former headquarters of the Dutch East India Company, attributed to Hendrick de Keyser and built in 1605. It is now part of the University.

Red Light District

Things begin to get tackier. We have reached the southern border of the Red Light district and, as a prelude to the coming feast of sex shops and stout ladies in windows, a line of snack bars and souvenir joints offers its own forms of low-grade sustenance. Oddly enough, this street is directly in line with the Royal Palace on the Dam, which closes the view in the far background. Outside one of the bars hangs a warning sign: *De Laatste Pomp Voor Het Stadhuis* ('Last Pump Before the Town Hall') – not that there is much chance, around here, of perishing from thirst.

At Oude Zijds Achterburgwal, turn right before the pastry stand on the bridge. The chief business activities of this quarter announce themselves without further delay. Sex 'n drugs, drugs 'n sex. On the far side of the canal the pink fascia of the 'Cannabis Connaisseurs Club' offers 'Sensi seeds' and 'High-tech hydroculture and homegrowing equipment', and next to it is the Cannabis Information Museum.

Pass under the red lights strung prettily across the canal . . . and you have arrived. Not every house is dedicated to pornography or prostitution, though quite a lot are. At Theater 95 a sticker on the window says 'This Place is Protected by the Red Light Security Crew'. Whether the customers also benefit from this service is not made clear. Sex shops, cinemas, video booths and live shows, both straight and gay, are the principal vehicles of the porn trade.

If you are struck by an air of menace as you walk along, it seems to be normal here, part of the furniture. Something to do with the cloud of sweaty expectation which permanently overhangs these canals. As a rule, avoid eye contact with the lurking pimps, pavement hookers and prowling punters and you will stay out of their lives. Police patrol the district on foot in pairs, and by motorbike and car, and in daytime there should be no need to take more than the usual precautions for the safety of either your person or your wallet or handbag. It only remains to add that women would do better not to walk around here alone.

A word about the vices traded in this quarter. They are illegal. Neither prostitution nor drug-trafficking is officially permitted – but both are tolerated within generally understood limits. For drugs, this means that an individual may possess up to 20g of cannabis for his or her own use, and no more; harder drugs are not allowed. It may seem an ungovernable position for the authorities to control, and you have only to look about you to find plenty of battered casualties of the system.

Two years ago, the Mayor of Amsterdam decided the *status quo* was not static but slipping out of control. He clamped down on the drug traffickers and ordered the 'smoking' cafés to remove the tell-tale cannabis-leaf symbol from their windows. This was done, but then, anxious not to lose their street identity, the cafés came out in a fresh wave of psychedelic exteriors and new names rich in hallucinogenic overtones such as 'Pie in the Sky' and 'Mellow Yellow'. I was told by someone in authority that things were now reasonably stable again, though sometimes an innocent visitor became an unfortunate victim of the city's permissiveness. It was put like this:

'It's mostly all right until Mr and Mrs Jones go into the wrong café. She notices a sign advertising Space Cake and thinks a slice would go nicely with her coffee. Twenty minutes later, she and her husband are distressed when suddenly she feels most peculiar and goes all drowsy.'

In tolerating even some of the illegal traffic that goes on in Amsterdam, particularly in the Red Light district, it is clear that the burgomaster and his councillors are taking a lot of risks. You may feel that it would not work to implant such a system in your own country, based as it is on little more than loose foundations of mutual trust.

As far as I can tell, it is seen to work here because today's Amsterdammers are willing heirs of a long tradition of tolerance and respect for individual privacy. You notice this in various everyday circumstances. At the bank, the customer at the cashier's desk is left alone. The rest of the queue forms up behind a line on the floor, some two metres back, and a printed sign is there to remind transgressors to respect the privacy of other customers. Even where there is no painted line, as at the outdoor cashpoints, other customers stand back without needing to be told.

Transfer this desire to respect others, and be respected, to more complicated matters of behaviour such as taking drugs, and there is a parallel. The individual is still allotted a certain space, an area of tolerance, in which to move freely – provided he or she does not go too far.

But that is far too vague, you may say. I cannot explain it more precisely, however, beyond saying that I think it is *meant* to be vague. That is perhaps its strength. It gives people pause to reflect, to consider their responsibilities to themselves and others. If, though, someone chooses to self-destruct, there is little to stop them.

The vice district does have its occasional comic outburst, and then the raucous humour of Amsterdam surges to the surface. It may happen when, for some reason or other, a client refuses to pay the girl. She seeks help, and if the client is not quick enough, he is taken firmly by the shoulders, whirled across the cobbles and flung into the canal. Ho, ho.

Old Church

This is the first parish church of Amsterdam. The tower of the original basilica dates back to the thirteenth century. It is a hugely impressive building, notoriously cold but full of interest. Inside, walk the great grey flagstones inset with memorial stones of poets and admirals. The church is dedicated to St Nicolaas, patron saint of sailors, and among the great warriors remembered here are Admirals van der Zaan, van Heemskerck and Gillis Schey.

The Great Organ is a mighty structure, designed in 1724 by J. Westerman, and mounted on a square-columned marble base which spans the west door. In the north-west corner an exhibition shows how the church was built, and includes a large wooden model, some 4.5m (15ft) high, of a domed church planned in about 1700 for the old butter market, now the Rembrandtplein. Nearby is the grave slab of Saskia van Uylenburgh (d.1642), wife of Rembrandt. Against the north wall is the smaller Choir Organ, its case dating from 1658.

To either side of the choir is a pair of unusual stained-glass windows. Originally commissioned by the Kerkmeesters in 1654, they display the arms of the burgomasters of Amsterdam from 1578. The first window, on the south side, commemorates each burgomaster up to 1757 by which time the window was full. The second window is in the Snijderkapel, and continues the tradition with burgomasters and aldermen up to 1807. The windows are intensely colourful and worth a close look. Each man received a quarter of a window pane, and in each is recorded his shield, his name and date in office.

The Old Church is still a church, and famous too for its organ concerts (see *What's On* for details). The tower offers good views over the quarter, and guided tours leave on the hour in season (details in Route section at beginning of walk). If, though, you have time to climb only one church tower, Westerkerk is best of all (see *Walk 6*).

To reach the tower, turn right at the exit and walk round by the eighteenth-century buildings pressed against the church walls. The square itself, Oudekerksplein, is no longer, alas, a pretty place. The cafés are uniformly unattractive and, on the far side, the ladies in the front windows are not there to model the skimpy lingerie they sport. Isolated somewhat in this cobbled backwater, they beckon the passing male with rare energy. Or wink, or leer, or rap with their rings on the window.

Return to the canal and turn left. There are some fine houses to be seen on this upper stretch of Oude Zijds Voorburgwal. On the far side, No.57 was designed by Hendrick de Keyser in 1615 and is profusely decorated with masks and busts. Our final visit of this walk is to another old and quite exceptional building, the outwardly simple spout-gabled house of 1663 which contains the fascinating clandestine Church of our Dear Lord in the Attic, the post-Reformation refuge of Roman Catholics who formerly had worshipped at the Old Church.

Amstelkring Museum

The Alteration of 1578 meant not only that Catholic churches were turned over to Protestant worship, it meant that Catholics had nowhere to practise their religion. By the early part of the seventeenth century, 'underground' services were being held in all manner of rooms, attics and sheds. Around 1650 Catholics began building secret churches, and by 1680 Amsterdam had about thirty of these clandestine places of worship. Technically they were still illegal, but the authorities tolerated them on a basis of 'out of sight, out of mind'. The churches remained in use at least until 1795, when the arrival of the French brought religious freedom to the country.

Remains of several attic churches have come to light in recent years, but the house at No.40 Oude Zijds Voorburgwal is the only one to have survived intact. It was sold to the city council in 1845 and remained in use until a new Catholic church, St Nicolaas, opposite Centraal Station, was completed. The house became a museum in 1888.

The original name of the Church was 'Het Hart' (The Heart), after its founder Jan Hartman. He was a local merchant and in 1661 he began building three houses, one on the canal and two behind in the Heintje Hoeckssteeg, combining the attics of all three into a secret church.

Around 1735, as Catholics began to enjoy greater freedom, the church was enlarged and the priest, who formerly had lived in a room in the Hartman family house at the front, was able to move into the second house in the alleyway. Not until these later years did the church become known by its present title, *Ons' Lieve Heer op Solder* (Our Dear Lord in the Attic).

The Amstelkring Museum is a complex treasure, to be savoured to the full. Its brilliant achievement has been to freeze time in both the houses and the church, offering an authentic picture of domestic and religious life in the seventeenth and eighteenth centuries.

The museum offers a useful handbook which divides the tour into fourteen sections, beginning in the former entrance hall of the canal house. (Congregations entered through a side door in Heintje Hoeckssteeg.) In 'de Sael' (3), a classical Dutch living room, twisted marble columns support the great walnut chimneypiece. On the far wall is a cupboard, formerly a cupboard-bed. The brass chandelier is from another clandestine church, 'The Star'. Up narrow stairs to (5); on the grey tiled landing, look through a window to the chaplain's tiny room with bed, biretta, prayer book and rosary. Upstairs again to the church (6).

We see this delightful place of worship in its later form, after the three attic storeys had been opened up to form a single galleried space. When the church was first built, the congregation gathered on three levels and people on the upper two had to listen to the service through apertures in the floor. Up to four hundred people crowded into the church in those early days, and at least one writer has pointed out that the 'secrecy' of the services must have been pretty notional at times, what with the coming and going of the congregation and their combined voices during the services.

Seen from the altar, the church is like a ship, the organ pipes where a poop-deck might be, the four rear windows overlooking the canal like those of the captain's living quarters. The altar painting is *The Baptism of Christ* (1736) by Jacob de Wit, one of a set of three made for this church. The pulpit is most unusual, designed to revolve so that it could be stored in the altar when it was not needed.

Go up the stairway by the organ to the first gallery (7). Behind the organ is a fine collection of church silver – chalices, plate, candlesticks and ornaments for the altar. The second gallery is reached by a spiral staircase but is opened only on special occasions. Descend by the back staircase to the sacristy (9), containing a small altar with an *Adoration of the Magi* (*c*.1580), and down again to the confessional (10). In the room opposite is another display of church silver. Down more stairs to (12), and a map showing the religious situation in Amsterdam in the seventeenth and eighteenth centuries, the churches plotted on a lightbox.

Finally, see the domestic quarters – the tiled front room and the scullery at the back with an old stone sink and cupboard toilet. In the larger kitchen at (14) is a portrait of a girl dressed for her first communion. She grew up to be the last woman to live in the second of the houses in the alleyway.

To conclude this walk, turn left to the end of the canal. Ahead rises the dome of St Nicolaas Church, where the Catholics from the attic church went to worship from 1887. Turn left past the Café Montparnasse and continue to Warmoesstraat, said to be the oldest street in Amsterdam. At No.16, De Eenhoorn, they serve delicious *stokbrood* (baguettes) with cheese, ham and salami fillings. If you are with a group of people, ask for one of their large round platters, which arrive with a mouth-watering selection.

Walk 3

City by the Sea

A waterfront journey from west to east, divided into two parts. It begins near the Western Islands and finishes at the revitalised warehouses of the Entrepôtdok. Take the free ferry across the IJ to North Amsterdam. Visit the excellent Maritime Museum and a working shipyard, 't Kromhout, with its collection of historic naval engines.

Allow All day for complete walk, 3 hours for each part.

Best times Not Monday, when Maritime Museum closed. Sculptors' Collective closed Monday, Tuesday. Werf 't Kromhout Museum closed Saturday, Sunday.

TWO WALKS OR ONE?

I have divided this walk into roughly equal sections. It is quite possible to complete both parts in a single day, though timing may be a little tight towards the end because the 't Kromhout Shipyard Museum closes at 16.00, an hour earlier than most museums, and I would be sorry if you had to rush anything.

If you have time to complete only one part of the walk, the second half contains the Maritime Museum, which it would certainly be a pity to miss.

ROUTE (PART 1)

Begin at northern terminus of Tram 3 (Zoutkeetsgracht). Cross bridge to N, bear left and walk up Houtmankade, the Westerkanaal on your

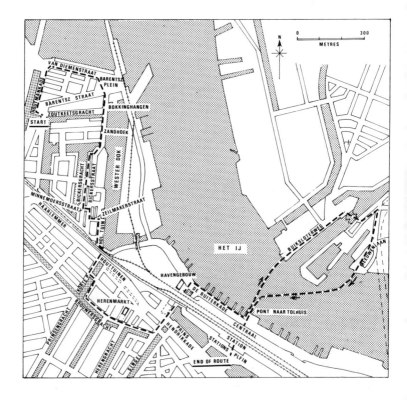

left. At the top, cross the road for views of the harbour, then turn right along Van Diemenstraat. At the Y-tech complex turn right into Barentszplein, then left at the corner of the playground and right into Bokkinghangen.

Cross bridge to Zandhoek. Cross next bridge and bear right into Bickersgracht, passing children's farm on canal. Take 2nd left into Minnemoersstraat and right into Bickersstraat, then next left into Zeilmakerstraat. At No.15, visit gallery of **Amsterdam Sculptors' Collective (Amsterdams Beeldhouwers Kollektief)** ☞ ; open Wednesday to Friday 10.00 to 17.00, Saturday, Sunday 12.00 to 17.00, closed Monday, Tuesday.

At exit, turn left then right at Westerdok into Hollandse Tuin. Follow footpath under road and railway bridge to Korte Prinsengracht. At Haarlemmerdijk, cross canal by old ship's cannon and continue to Brouwersgracht. Turn left and walk along to Herenmarkt at top of Herengracht, then keep on to Singel. Turn left past lock, and at Droogbak intersection cross busy Prins Hendrikkade and go under railway bridges. On left is **Harbour Building (Havengebouw)** with panoramic views from Restaurant Martinn on top floor.

From front door of Harbour Building, cross De Ruiterkade and walk along quayside towards Centraal Station. At **Pont naar Tolhuis** take free ferry across the IJ (pronounced 'Eye'). Two ferries work this route in tandem. As an alternative to waiting for the next boat back, you can walk round to another ferry terminal, which operates Monday to Friday only. To reach it, walk up Buiksloterweg to the double lock; cross it, bear right past the water authority building and keep on the narrow road to Meeuwenlaan. Turn right and walk past pink apartment houses to ferry. Cross the IJ again.

Disembark and cross road into **Centraal Station**. Walk through shop-lined concourse beneath platforms to front entrance. On far side of Stationsplein is VVV tourist information office. Part 1 of walk ends here. Nearest refreshments in Smits Koffiehuis down steps to jetty.

Western Islands

Old maps of Amsterdam took a very different viewpoint from those drawn up by modern cartographers. The old mapmakers looked at the city from upside down; not from north to south but from the sea. The IJ, or the 'Ya Fluvius' as they sometimes called it, was the true starting point. From this foreground the reader looked across minutely detailed rows of ships' masts in the harbour to the walled semi-circular city with its irregular grid of streets and canals, and then out to the fields beyond. Always, in the beginning, was the water. And rightly so for a city which dominated the world's maritime trade for the best part of two centuries, from about 1585 until the 1760s.

The No.3 tram delivers us at the northernmost point of its journey. An open, breezy place between Zoutkeetsgracht (Salt Sheds Canal) and the Westerkanaal, a major outlet to the harbour where barges of enormous length continually pass. Even the cat at the butcher's in Zoutkeetsplein likes the outdoor life and does most of its daytime sleeping in a cardboard box on the pavement.

The drawbridge at the end of Houtmankade is seldom still for long. As the next barge approaches, a vast thick slab of roadway and pavement, some 25m (85ft) wide and 15m (50ft) long, swivels through ninety degrees with no hint of stress, the motion as smooth as a weightlifter flexing his elbow. The barge glides through, the bridge immediately descends, the slender arms of the red/white poles guarding the roadway soar aloft, the cars and trucks grind forward. In thirty seconds it is all over.

From the pavement by the bridge controllers' box, the view across the harbour is broad and deep. The nearer wharves are thick with moored barges lolling side by side like fat cigars in a box. The yellow car ferry ploughs across the middle ground, in the distance a giant four-legged crane marks the westward route along the IJ to the Noordzee Kanaal, constructed in 1874, which runs all the way to the coastal locks at IJmuiden and the North Sea.

We turn along Van Diemenstraat, lined with warehouses on the harbour side, a bellowing throughway for heavy traffic heading between Tasmanstraat and Westerdoksdijk – names which vibrate with maritime heritage and the promise of far-off places. Times are changing now and these warehouses, having outlived their original function, are being converted into offices and science blocks. Along here is the Joseph Lam Dixieland Jazz Club – live music and dancing on Saturday and Sunday, from 21.00, and find your way home by taxi.

Moments later we are out of the traffic's roar, crossing the bridge to the calm of Zandhoek and the eastern edge of Realen Island. This is the first of the group known as the Western Islands, now an enclave where many artists have made their homes, relishing the deep spaces of the old warehouse buildings, the quiet and the village-like atmosphere that flourishes here, in a district detached from the city by the harbour on one side and the railway tracks to the south.

In Zandhoek a row of magnificent old barges stand up to the quayside, bowsprits raised high, shifting imperceptibly in the water. Facing them is a terrace of elegant black and white houses built in the second half of the seventeenth century. They display an agreeable mixture of gables – bell, step, bell, bell, spout and cornice – and share an imposing lower front, mostly windowed, which covers the first two storeys and is most attractive.

As you cross the next bridge to Bickers Island, look back at 'De Lepelaar', a pair of beautifully restored warehouses painted black with pale grey curving shutters drawn back, and steep wooden steps reaching up to the front doors. Walking along Bickersgracht you come upon a rare sight, a friendly urban farmyard. Goats, geese and hens amble and strut around a square compound, and nearby is a neat stack of rabbit hutches. It is a sort of farm-cum-zoo, intended for city children to come and visit when they can, and is maintained by people living in the neighbourhood.

Along here one morning I had my first sight of the Ladderlift, the machine that has taken some of the pain out of lifting furniture into the upper floors of Amsterdam's tall narrow houses, where the staircases are too narrow to admit your wardrobe or your bed, let alone your piano. I am assured that the old way is not about to disappear – using a pair of ropes suspended from the beam and hook in the gable, one rope to lift and the other to keep the cargo away from the wall as it slowly climbs the building. However, the Ladderlift seems a brilliant mechanical alternative. You pack your various objects in a trolley which is then winched along rails up a steel ladder. Such is the wide angle needed for the trolley-and-ladder combination, it could hardly work in narrow streets, and the trolley is not all that big. All the same, I felt I had seen the future: mechanised and effortless.

Sculptors' Collective

Halfway along Zeilmakerstraat is a long brick warehouse guarded by a

beguiling company of stone animals, nudes and garden gods. The turnout varies, depending on what they have in stock. This is the Amsterdams Beeldhouwers Kollektief, set up in 1982 by Carine van Steen, herself a sculptor, as a place for artists to work and sell what they make.

Today the emphasis is on marketing, and only a small workshop space remains. This too is due to be turned into part of the gallery, which currently occupies the front room and a new addition at the back, formerly a toy factory. More than a hundred works are regularly on show, from small medallions and 'pocket' sculptures to medium-sized portrait figures and abstracts. Collect a typewritten catalogue and wander round. They will be pleased to see you and there is no pressure to buy.

The Collective handles some forty sculptors, and changes its exhibition every two months. Its guiding inspiration is to encourage ordinary people to buy a work of art, either to keep in their home or out in the garden. The Dutch government supports such ventures by allowing art buyers to take out a loan on their purchase which they repay in instalments – and the government pays the interest on the loan. In this way, it is hoped, people will become accustomed to paying monthly sums to buy a painting or a sculpture. Later, when the first piece is paid for, they may then decide to keep up the instalments and buy a second work.

It sounds a most appealing scheme. Even without it, prices are by no means outrageous here and you may well decide to blow next month's down-payment on the car for the simple joy of possessing a bronze torso of your very own, or a pair of bacchic figures for the garden. And why not?

In a further effort to keep prices down, the gallery stocks a number of works available in editions of twenty-five. The sculptors on view are not big names, though the reputations of some are deservedly growing. Artists and their works to watch out for include bronzes and terracottas by Marianne Letterie, Geer Steyn, Thijl Wijdeveld, Saskia Pfaeltzer, Lia van Vugt, Barbara de Clercq and Peter Erftemeier; wood carvings by the promising Frans Muhren; 'female fragments' by Luut de Gelder, for all the world like newly polished archaeological finds; the singular creations of Rob Ligtvoet, and the delightful grotesques of an ex-priest, Bruno Paul de Roeck.

To the Harbour

Walk through to Westerdok. The low-cost housing around here is somewhat bleak, but this was always a practical, working-class area inhabited by specialist craftsmen. The street names commemorate the old callings: Sailmaker, Boilermaker, Blockmaker.

We rejoin city life on the far side of the bridge in Korte Prinsengracht, where the familiar pattern resumes of canal, quaysides and gabled houses. At Haarlemmerdijk, cross the bridge by the old cannon, a favourite huddling place for the local pigeons. Ahead is the fine tower of Westerkerk and, to the right, the triangular space of Noordermarkt with its church. Continue along the near or north side of Brouwersgracht. One of Amsterdam's most picturesque canals, the 'Brewers' Canal' was formerly home to twenty-four different brewers who used the canal water to make their beer.

After crossing Keizersgracht we come shortly to Herenmarkt, a small dusty square at the top of Herengracht, the 'Gentlemen's Canal', our subject for *Walk 5*. The Classical house (1615) behind the playground was once occupied by the Dutch West India Company. Later it was rebuilt for the Lutheran Orphanage but retains its old name, Westindisch Huis. In this building the decision was made, some 350 years ago, to found a settlement on Manhattan – the future New York City.

At the next canal, Singel, we turn past the lock, negotiate the heavy traffic on the main harbour road, and after the railway bridges emerge beside the large modern slab of the 1960 Harbour Building (Havengebouw). On the top floor is the Restaurant Martinn, a smart venue open for lunch and dinner, its windows offering splendid views across both harbour and city. It is not a café, but the manager assured me they won't send you away if you arrive and ask for just a cup of coffee. They would, of course, like to welcome you back one day for a proper go at the menu. In the meantime, tall buildings with good views, *and* open to the public, are surprisingly rare in Amsterdam – apart from the Havengebouw, only three church towers (summer only) and the café-restaurant at Metz & Co. come to mind, so it is well worth a quick visit.

Walk along De Ruiterkade towards the station, passing a line of piers where large cruise ships are often moored. On Pier 10, the small 1930s pavilion overlooking the water is now a restaurant, called Pier 10 and offering fine views over the harbour at water level. It is full most nights from 18.00, so reserve a day ahead. Ask for a table in the back room.

Ferry ride

At Pont naar Tolhuis we take to the water, stepping on board the free ferry for a trip across the IJ. This is one of several links with the dormitory suburb of North Amsterdam. All the world travels on this ferry – students and shoppers, a man with his dogs, a flock of cycling commuters, and passengers on the No.39 bus who remain in their seats for the brief crossing. Over on the left is the bronze-windowed slab of the Royal Dutch Shell building, its spiky top intended to represent a crown. More amusing are the gigantic loads carried by some of the barges – great funnels and cylinders and chunks of factory along with more conventional cargoes such as coal, sand and cement. The ferry noses up to the pier, down comes the ramp and we walk off.

Rather than simply wait for the next ferry back, stroll up beside the Noord Hollandsch Kanaal as far as the lock. A calm unhurried atmosphere prevails, as though we had already entered the provinces. Enormous barges are moored here, and seem to offer their owners a quite reasonable living. One skipper keeps his BMW, a 316, parked across the after-deck, intermittently shrouded by the family's washing.

From Monday to Friday a second ferry runs between Meeuwenlaan and Centraal Station. To reach it, cross the lock and continue along the narrow roadway past the water authority building and through the gardens. The two black towers are ventilation outlets for the IJ road tunnel which passes beneath. When you come to Meeuwenlaan, turn right and walk past a line of pink-walled apartment buildings to the ferry pier.

To discourage their dogs from fouling the pavement, the Dutch have issued a most unpleasant traffic symbol. You may see it as a painted sign on a lamp-post or etched into a paving stone, like the one here in Meeuwenlaan. It features a fiercely squatting dog, its attitude somehow conveying both agony and enthusiasm; next to it an arrow points to the gutter with the message '*In de Goot*'. I thought you should be forewarned: it can be a nasty moment, seeing one of these for the first time.

This alternative ferry slants across the IJ towards the great curving shed of Centraal Station, and lands close to where the first ferry set off. Cross the road, walk into the station (see *Walk 1* for history of), and continue through the concourse lined with snack bars ('*Broodjes/ Dranken/Versnaperingen*', or 'Rolls/Drinks/Refreshments'). In the front entrance hall turn and look at the large double-columned departures board. In the next hour or so, forty trains will leave for all parts of the Netherlands, some also going to Germany, Belgium and France. They will leave on time, what is more, the carriages will be clean, and an attendant will come down the train with a refreshments trolley.

Near the doors a plaque on the wall remembers W.H. Zeeman who fell here 'for Freedom' on 7 May 1945, aged twenty-two. Pictured next to the words is a broken tulip and a dove arriving, alas, too late. Many such plaques are to be found in Amsterdam. The years of Occupation were a particularly grim period, and memories of it show no sign of fading.

This first part of the walk ends in front of the station. On the far side of the forecourt is the VVV tourist information office, housed in the North-South Holland Coffee House, a charming wooden pavilion that was pulled down to make way for the new Metro but then, happily, was fully restored in 1982. Walk down the steps to the jetty and take a break in Smits Koffiehuis, overlooking the inner harbour.

ROUTE (PART 2)

Begin at Centraal Station. Trams 1, 2, 4, 5, 9, 13, 16, 17, 24, 25. Buses 21, 32, 33, 34, 35, 39. Metro terminus. Walk E and follow pavement past bus stops, bearing right to Prins Hendrikkade.

Cross to far side of Prins Hendrikkade and turn left to **Weeping Tower (Schreierstoren)** at top of Geldersekade. Continue along Prins Hendrikkade to the **Scheepvaarthuis** (No.108). Turn right into Binnenkant, past windows decorated with chains and anchors, and continue to Oude Schans. On right is the **Montelbaan Tower (Montelbaanstoren)**. Turn left into Kalkmarkt and rejoin Prins Hendrikkade. Turn right and continue to **Maritime Museum (Scheepvaart Museum)** ; open Tuesday to Saturday 10.00 to 17.00, Sunday and holidays 13.00 to 17.00, closed Monday. *Admission, takes Museum Pass.*

At exit, walk across Kattenburgerplein and continue along Kattenburgergracht. Pass East Church (Oosterkerk), then turn right across yellow and white Overhaals Gang bridge. Walk through to

Hoogte Kadijk and turn left across bridge to **'t Kromhout Shipyard Museum** 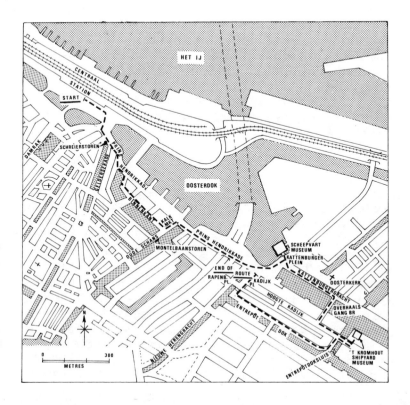; open Monday to Friday 10.00 to 16.00, closed Saturday, Sunday. *Admission.*

Leave shipyard, turn right back across bridge then left down steps on S side road to Entrepôtdoksluis. Walk across paved terrace by flats to **Entrepôtdok**, a long development of converted warehouses. Continue to end, turn right through arch to Kadijkplein.

Walk ends here. Nearest refreshments in square or, a better recommendation, across bridge at De Druif, 83 Rapenburgerplein. Nearest bus, No.22, goes along Prins Hendrikkade to Centraal Station.

Weeping Tower

In this second part of the walk, the monuments and buildings with maritime associations fall thick and fast. The harbour trade has now largely shifted to the west of the city, but here in the eastern half are many old docks and shipyards and long lines of warehouses dating back to Amsterdam's greatest period of eminence in the seventeenth century, when the United East India Company was the world's strongest commercial organisation. In those days, the route to the sea lay through the Zuider Zee, now the IJsselmeer, and the Amsterdam waterfront was much closer to the city, along the line of the Oosterdok, with the warehouses on Prins Hendrikkade facing the ships across the quayside.

We set off from the Noord-Zuid Hollands Koffiehuis, adorned with a weather vane in the shape of a three-masted ship and a sign with a cog ship, which formed part of the city's old coat of arms. On the far side of Prins Hendrikkade stands the Weeping Tower (Schreierstoren), built in 1480 and now a nautical instruments shop. It began life as a defensive tower in the first city wall, and the battlements were then above the round-arched frieze which runs beneath the present upper storey. From these battlements, if the message of a tablet of 1569 is to be believed, sailors' wives wept and waved farewell to their husbands as they departed on great voyages that might take several years and from which many failed to return.

A bronze plaque on the wall commemorates Henry Hudson, who on 4 April 1609 set sail from here in the *Half Moon* to seek a shorter passage to the East Indies. His voyage brought him to the harbour of New York and the Hudson River which is named after him. The plaque was presented to the city in 1927 by the Greenwich Village Historical Society of New York City.

Of Ships and Warehouses

Follow the road as it curves towards an extraordinary turn-of-the-century fortress, the Shipping House (Scheepvaarthuis). It stands at the place from which the first Dutch fleet sailed for the East Indies. Roughly triangular in shape, it was built in 1913-16 as an office for six Amsterdam shipping companies, and the leading edge that we now approach symbolises the prow of a ship. In style it is between late Jugendstil (Art Nouveau) and early Amsterdam School. Its strong verticals and dark brickwork give it a formidable presence, and the exterior is superbly decorated, studded with details of shipping and the sea – heads of explorers and naval heroes, seahorses, dolphins, steering wheels, chains and anchors on the black wrought-iron window bars. It is now the headquarters of the GVB, the Municipal Transport Authority which runs the trams, buses and Metro.

Turn into Binnenkant and walk to the end. Here in the calm of Eilandsgracht is a fine place to keep a houseboat. There are some 3,000 on the canals of Amsterdam and this must be one of the most desirable moorings. On the right is a much-photographed landmark, the Montelbaanstoren, originally a defensive tower built in 1512. In 1606 it was enlarged by Hendrick de Keyser who added the octagonal upper section and the openwork steeple.

We return to Prins Hendrikkade via Kalkmarkt. Across the canal is a group of black-doored warehouses, united by twin gables and a pediment bearing a coat of arms and the monogram of the Dutch West India Company. Around the corner, at No.176 Prins Hendrikkade, is a many-shuttered warehouse block designed for the East India Company, with four projecting roofs covering the beams and lifting gear in the gables.

Across the road is the largest part of the inner harbour, the Oosterdok, its most famous resident the amazing floating pagoda of the 800-seater Sea Palace Restaurant, based on an even larger one in Hong Kong Harbour. Look to the right of the pagoda and you may yet catch a glimpse of the full-scale replica of an eighteenth-century East Indiaman which was built there for a special 'Sail Amsterdam' festival in August 1990.

Maritime Museum

To reach the Maritime Museum (Nederlands Scheepvaart Museum), its name prominently displayed and already readable for some minutes, follow the road past the nineteenth-century Seaman's House and the modern block housing the Higher Seafaring School.

This sturdy building of 1655 was originally the arsenal of the Amsterdam Admiralty. Its stores furnished the nearby shipyards with rope, sails, anchors and other equipment as well as muskets, pistols and heavy naval guns. In 1971 the Royal Dutch Navy moved out and the arsenal was converted into the present museum.

A booklet with explanatory notes in English is available at the entrance desk. Cross the courtyard and enter the museum proper. Exhibits are arranged in categories – early shipping, naval warfare, yachting, navigation, and so on. It is a fine collection, thoughtfully displayed, and wherever possible uses contemporary ship models, paintings, charts, instruments and weaponry.

Close to the entrance is the marvellous Royal Barge, built at Rotterdam in 1816–18: a narrow, delicate-looking six-tonner in cream and gilt, 17m (56ft) long, at the stern a pillared canopy cloaked by red drapes. On the prow sits a gilded Neptune in his racing conch holding the reins of three chargers. Twenty oarsmen propelled the barge, and around the walls photographs show the vessel with royalty aboard, from 1841 until 1962 when it made its last journey to celebrate the silver wedding of Queen Juliana and Prince Bernhard.

Return to the main staircase by the angel figurehead, go up to the first floor and Room 1: the 'History of Boats and Navigation until 1600'. Among the ship models, astrolabes and atlases, look out for the three large bird's eye-view pictures mapping the growth of Amsterdam and dated 1544, 1597 and 1647. In the last, the west side of the city has suddenly appeared, a great belt from the 'Heere Graft' (Herengracht) to 'Lynbaens Graft' (Lijnbaansgracht), with 'Haerlemmer Poort' and the Western Docks clearly visible.

Wander as the mood takes you. Room 2 has excellent ship models of local traders, fishing boats and whalers, along with numerous globes, navigational instruments and battle paintings. In Room 3, I am particularly fond of *Battle off Gibraltar, 1607* by Cornelis van Wieringen (1622), commemorating Admiral van Heemskerck's dramatic victory over a Spanish fleet in the Bay of Gibraltar. The foreground details are fascinating: survivors afloat on a fragment of mast, or being pulled out of the water clutching an oar, or, less mercifully, being fired at in the water. The battle was an overwhelming Dutch success, and the artist has not held back from glorifying his own side's achievement. Very few Spanish ships have any prominence except for their vice-admiral's vessel which is exploding; the rest is a cloud of yellow/orange, white and blue colours.

Room 4 continues the story of naval warfare in the seventeenth century, then Room 5 is devoted to sailing for pleasure. Here is a charming full-sized touring and rowing barge, one of the many yachts used by eighteenth-century families who had a house on the banks of the Rivers Amstel, Vecht and Zaan.

In Room 7 is a huge model of a 74-gun ship of the line, *c*.1725, and next to it a wall chart illustrating the range of battle tactics its commander would have employed. Then a display of cannon, loading equipment, and grenades, mortars and handguns for short-range and close-quarter fighting. Room 8 has more guns and edged weapons, Room 9 explains navigation in the eighteenth century, and the next two rooms study the great Dutch trading companies – the United East India Company, the *Verenigde Oostindische Compagnie* or *VOC*: its shipyard in Amsterdam, money coined for the company, and its operations in Asia, where its farthest outpost was the island of Deshima in the Bay of Nagasaki, Japan. Then the story of the West India Company, in Guyana and the Antilles (Caribbean).

Exhibits continue on the second floor. The climb is worth it for the hugely impressive model, about 10.5m (35ft) long and reaching from floor to ceiling of the *Drommedaris*, a three-masted sailing ship with four square-rigged sails on each mast, three triangular sails on the bowsprit and a triangular fore-and-aft sail between the main and foremasts.

Go downstairs to the main entrance and take a stroll out to the broad landing stage. The museum has its own puffer boat which from time to time chugs visitors round the dock. Out here is a good place to see at close quarters the redoubtable stone façades of the old arsenal. Finally, the Maritime Museum has a surprisingly agreeable café-restaurant with a terrace on the dock, and a first-rate nautical bookshop with posters, postcards, models, toys, sea lanterns and other souvenirs.

Eastern Islands

On leaving the museum, cross to the Kattenburgerplein which stands on the first of the three Eastern Islands – Kattenburg, Wittenburg and Oostenburg. These islands were built in the IJ in 1658 to create space for more Admiralty buildings and shipyards. It was here, at one of the yards of the East India Company, that in 1697–98 Peter the Great of Russia came to study shipbuilding.

Walk along Kattenburgergracht-Wittenburgergracht as far as the East Church (Oosterkerk), built in 1669 in the form of a Greek cross.

After falling into sad disrepair, it was restored in the early 1980s and converted into a community centre. The outside still looks none too cheerful, but the interior is light and bright, with imposing pillars and cornices to admire above the modern furniture and fittings.

As you cross the Overhaals Gang bridge, the iron sheds and slipways of 't Kromhout shipyard come into view. After a short walk along Hoogte Kadijk, and across another bridge, we reach the entrance gate.

't Kromhout Shipyard Museum

A hundred years ago Kromhout were leaders in the new age of shipbuilding, making vessels of iron and steel powered by steam engines. In 1873 they took a revolutionary step when they switched to steam power to drive their punches, cutters and drills. Their most famous product was the Kromhout 12hp paraffin engine, a centrepiece in the small museum that now occupies the old workshop. The secret of this engine's commercial success lay in its simple design, which repaid its makers many times over by becoming the most popular power source for vessels navigating the inland waterways of the Low Countries.

This yard was once the company's headquarters. Then the order-book outgrew the buildings and production was shifted across the IJ to a larger yard in North Amsterdam. There the company developed another winner, the Kromhout semi-diesel, which inspired a new generation of marine engines.

Whether you are stirred by such feats of engineering or not, it is difficult to resist the antiquated charm of the old sheds. It remains a working shipyard, so step out to the slipways and see what they are working on: a small canal cruiser getting a refit, perhaps, or a great flat barge in for repairs, raised up and baring its broad underbelly.

I was taking notes here one day when a guy rode into the yard, jumped off his bicycle and walked up to me. In Dutch he asked:

'What is that you're writing?'

In English, and to allay fears that I was some kind of malevolent intruder, I said: 'It's in English.'

Immediately, he replied in English. 'Oh,' he said, waving an arm as he walked away. 'I thought you were from the insurance company.'

For me it was one more good example of how the Dutch move

effortlessly out of their native language into English. And not just English. This facility for 'bilingual thinking' may extend to French or German as well, not to mention the languages of non-European countries such as Indonesia, with which many are familiar.

Upstairs in the main building is a café with further exhibits in wooden display cases and on the walls posters of ships and a proudly displayed illustration of the Kromhout-Heesen Generator-Type E. Even to a non-engineer, these documents of the past communicate the enthusiasm felt here for the company's industrial heritage.

Entrepôtdok

I am in two minds about this conversion of an immense row of old warehouses into offices and dwellings. I am glad they have survived, but the great length of the overall façade – formerly the largest warehouse complex in Europe – makes them a rather chilling spectacle. More fun to live in than to look at. Each house has its own staircase and is named after a town in Belgium or the Netherlands. As we walk along the quayside, we progress in reverse alphabetical order past Zutphen, Zwolle, Zierikzee and Zaandam all the way to Arnhem, Amsterdam and Amersfoort.

Halfway along, the designer uniformity is mercifully broken by a grocer's and a café. I would have preferred more breaks, to bring back some of the buzz and human untidiness that must have prevailed when the warehouses were warehouses and the quayside was a jumble of carts and barrels, crates, sacks and boxes. The Entrepôtdok was built in 1827 as a depot where ships carrying dutiable goods put in, settled their dues and then unloaded, either here or elsewhere in the harbour.

If you began this walk beside the Westerkanaal, rather than picking it up at the halfway stage, you will have had a long day. The best place I know for well-earned rest and recuperation is across the Nieuwe Heren-gracht in Rapenburgerplein. De Druif is a small but light and airy brown café, much favoured by locals. Mind your head on the winding stair down to the toilets.

Walk 4

The Jordaan

Amsterdammers are particularly fond of this old and picturesque working-class quarter to the west of Prinsengracht, its streets and canals named after plants and flowers. Visit a local market, stroll through narrow cross-streets bright with boutiques, try out a brown bar and visit 'De Looier' indoor antique market.

Allow   3–4 hours.

Best times   Not Friday or Sunday, when 'De Looier' closed. Noordermarkt has a morning junk market on Monday, a bird market on Saturday, plus a 'farmer's market' (*Boerenmarkt*) selling organically raised produce. Westerstraat has a general market on Monday morning; Lindengracht has one on Saturday morning. Each year the Jordaan Festival begins on 2nd Friday in September and lasts 10 days.

ROUTE

Begin at Haarlemmerplein (Tram 3). Leave square at SE corner and walk down cobbled Nieuwe Wagenstraat to Brouwersgracht. Turn left and cross next bridge to Palmgracht. See almshouses at Nos 20-26 and 28-38.

Take 1st left into Palm Dwarsstraat (= Palm cross-street). Keep straight on, via Tweede Goudsbloem Dwarsstraat to Lindengracht. Cross canal to Eerste Linden Dwarsstraat and turn left at Lindenstraat to **Noordermarkt**. Visit the market and, if possible, the church ☞ ; open Saturday morning 10.00 to 12.00 and for Sunday services at 10.00 and 19.00.

Leave square at S corner and turn right into broad Westerstraat. Take 2nd left into Eerste Anjeliers Dwarsstraat. Keep straight on, via Eerste Tuin Dwarsstraat and Eerste Egelantiers Dwarsstraat, to Egelantiersgracht (despite the long street names, this paragraph covers barely 200m altogether). Turn left, cross bridge and walk down along Prinsengracht (tower of West Church ahead). Take the next right into Nieuwe Leliestraat. Continue to 3rd left (Derde Lelie Dwarsstraat) and turn down to Bloemgracht.

Turn right and walk to Post Office at end, then cross bridge on left and walk down Lijnbaansgracht. Cross busy Rozengracht and take 1st left into Rozenstraat. Take 1st right (Tweede Laurier Dwarsstraat) and cross Lauriergracht to Hazenstraat (good for boutiques).

Turn right at Elandsgracht and at No.109 on left visit **'De Looier' antique market** ☞ ; open Monday to Thursday 11.00 to 17.00, Saturday 09.00 to 17.00, closed Friday, Sunday. Walk round the maze of shops and stalls, exit and walk down Lijnbaansgracht to Looiersgracht, where at No.38 a rotating flea market is held ☞ ; open 11.00 to 17.00, closed Friday, see essay for what's on sale when.

Walk ends here. Nearest refreshments around Prinsengracht. For something a little more interesting, walk along Looiersgracht towards Spui and try brown café De Doffer at 12 Runstraat or Louis XVI-style Pâtisserie Pompadour at 12 Huidenstraat. Trams 1, 2, 5 at Spui, or 7, 10 across Lijnbaansgracht in Marnixstraat.

A Special Place

The Jordaan has a quite distinct, low-key charm that by itself is enough to draw me back there time and again. Maybe to wander with

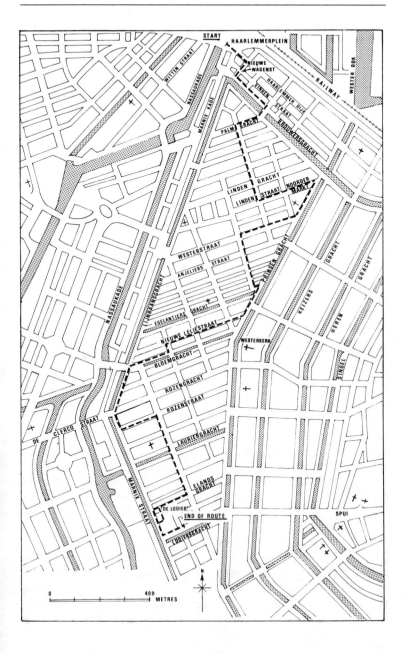

nonchalant nosiness in search of some fresh corner, maybe for a strident night in a blues café, or jolly brown bar, or for another helping of surreal accordion-opera at De Twee Zwaantjes.

In its tight grid of east-west streets and narrow crossways you will find an oddly harmonious community of students, refugees, boutique and gallery folk, almshouse dwellers, young up-and-comers, and a large wedge of working-class originals. In its time the Jordaan has been, in part, a hippy hideaway, before that an industrial workers' enclave, and before that a slum to harbour the persecuted of Europe, many of them Jews and Huguenots who moved in alongside the founding population of traders and immigrant workers who came to dig the three great concentric canals ordered by the city council in 1607.

Unlike the magnificent spacious plan devised for the *Grachtengordel*, the building of the Jordaan quarter immediately to the west was not tightly controlled but put out to speculators who flung up a dense new suburb along the lines of existing drainage ditches and pathways. Cramped and noisome, the Jordaan took on a very separate character from the rest of the city – intimate, raucous, direct, living its life at pavement level. Today it is a little smarter, a little more sought-after, but still refreshingly different.

The origin of the name Jordaan is disputed. The most plausible explanation is that it derives from the French *jardin*; certainly many streets are named after plants – Palm, Marigold, Rose, Carnation, Lime-tree, Lily and Laurel.

Northern Approaches

In outline the Jordaan is sock-shaped, bordered by Brouwersgracht in the north, Prinsengracht and Lijnbaansgracht to east and west, and Looiersgracht at the toe end. Appropriately, we insert ourselves into the sock at the usual entry-point for wearers, and then zig-zag down the criss-cross pattern of streets to the heel and toe.

At Haarlemmerplein, look across to the Neo-Classical gateway, the Willemspoort, built in 1840 as a tax collectors' office and restored in 1986 when it was converted to living quarters for students at the University. We now head down a cobbled lane to Brouwersgracht, the Brewers' Canal. Heron favour this quiet stretch, lined with houseboats, and flap over the water in search of food. At the next bridge we cross into the Jordaan district and walk along Palmgracht, a filled-in canal, to find a pair of the Jordaan's many almshouses (*hofjes*).

Two doors side by side are numbered 20–26 and 28–38. The first is marked 'Bossche Hofje' and the other bears the initials 'P.A.' beside a carving of a turnip. The latter is the symbol of the Raep Hofje, founded in 1648 by Pieter Adriaensz Raep (= turnip) for elderly women and orphans belonging to the Reformed Church. If the door is open, no one is likely to mind if you take a peek at the neat courtyard, but it may well be shut. Modern times, alas, have made it necessary to install locks on doors such as this. There are exceptions. In the centre of the city, the much larger Begijnhof is open for all to visit (see *Walk 1: New Side*) and several smaller almshouse courtyards are open in Haarlem (see *Walk 15*).

We turn into Palm Dwarsstraat and continue into Tweede Gouds-bloem Dwarsstraat, which in translation means Second Marigold Cross-street. The Jordaan is full of tiny streets about thirty metres long with triple-barrelled names. This system of naming indicates to the informed passer-by that he or she is in the second cross-street, counting from east to west, that intersects with Goudsbloemstraat. To the east, sure enough, is a street called First Marigold Cross-street (Eerste Goudsbloem Dwarsstraat). What could be clearer?

We continue over Lindengracht, though if you are here on a Saturday morning you may like to explore its general market. At the next crossing, we turn left into Lindenstraat which leads us all the way to Noordermarkt, one of the principal open spaces in the Jordaan. Ahead, the big red girders holding up the roof of the Harbour Building make a useful landmark.

Noordermarkt

The Noordermarkt is more fun when it is crowded. Choose between the junk market on Monday morning, and the cage-bird market on Saturday.

One Saturday morning I was heading for Noordermarkt via the Lindengracht market stalls. It began to rain heavily, and I dived in under the low canvas awnings stretched here and there, but not everywhere, between the double row of market stalls. Pools the size of small bathtubs were collecting in the bowed canvas roofs of the stalls and suddenly discharging in full cascade on passing shoppers. Halfway along I noticed a stall with a display of cut-price Marco van Basten bath-towels, each bearing an effigy of the great footballer wearing his red-and-black striped Milan outfit. At least, I thought, I could dry myself if it came to the worst – but what about the birds at the Noordermarkt, which I had come to see? Surely the birds would not be on show in this weather?

Well, they certainly were. A Dutch market trader is not lightly put off, and the birds were duly exhibited. In deference to the rain, cages were piled up in car boots, or stacked in a long row by the church wall, the top line of cages roofed with cardboard strips torn from flattened packing cases. Budgies and canaries are evidently popular here, but do not have it all their own way. The preference seemed to be for birds of more brilliant plumage – fierce-looking creatures with hooked bills and startling scarlet and orange crests, alongside a flurry of finches and birds of the small parrot variety, and several batches of doves – grey, black and white, and a very smooth shade of suede-brown with white. I saw, too, a load of chickens in the back of a van which shortly revved up and drove off – the deal already struck, I thought, or hope abandoned by the seller. It was still raining hard.

At the top corner of the Noordermarkt triangle is a pleasant coffee shop, larger than it looks from the outside with a long brick-walled room. It is called the Woutertje Pieterse, and is named after a character in a novel by Multatuli. He is probably the best-known Dutch novelist of the nineteenth century and is also commemorated in a statue nearby, a gnome-like double portrait of Woutertje Pieterse and the considerably taller Femke (his wife).

Across the canal at 89–113 Prinsengracht you can see the quadrangular form of a rather grand almshouse, the Hofje De Star, designed by Abraham van der Hart in 1804.

From 10.00 the Farmer's Market (*Boerenmarkt*) occupies the other half of the square. This is an updated Sixties trading post selling 'biologically grown produce'. Much emphasis here on healthy green vegetables and fruit (especially if it's rhubarb) and 'ecological' cheeses. Other stalls have wholemeal bread and rolls, fruit wines, and 'essential oils' in little flasks.

The Monday market is quite different. It deals in junk, with some stalls on the side selling cheese, fruit and vegetables. Ignore any previous suggestions you may have read that antiques are available at this market. Only the impressive age of some of these cast-outs would ever qualify them. What they sell here, operating from stalls and rugs laid out on the ground and on the bonnets of parked cars, is impossible to describe adequately at less than catalogue length. A sample, though, might include: old clothes, albums filled with badges, old records, tins of floor polish, old kettles, a baby's wicker pram, and a tray of grubby chrome-topped pepperpots, presumably from some defunct restaurant, with pepper still in them. 'Everything under five guilders!' called an aproned stallholder, perhaps unnecessarily. Shuffle on through the crowd – there is always a crowd – and if you suddenly find your feet bouncing up and down you have strayed on to the rubber tiles of, on other days, the children's playground in the middle of the square.

North Church

The best time to see inside the gaunt Noorderkerk or North Church is from 10.00 to 12.00 on Saturday morning. The huge brown brick building is in great need of restoration but is unlikely to receive any for years to come. 'Other churches are more in need,' I was told at the religious bookstall inside. As we talked, the organ softly played – the organist usually a student from the Conservatory. I looked around at the tall brick interior, the peeled-back plaster and long-gone windows, the dowdy furnishings. It occurred to me that, like a faded store selling an unfashionable product, closure might be the church's most likely fate, not resurrection. And yet it still attracts two hundred for its Sunday services, so we must hope that somehow they manage to hang on a little longer until sufficient money arrives.

The Noorderkerk is not a lovely building, but it is of great architectural interest since it was the last church designed by Hendrick de Keyser, one of the city's great seventeenth-century architects who was also responsible for the South Church (Zuiderkerk) of 1603, the nearby West Church (Westerkerk) of 1620 and, among other towering landmarks of Amsterdam, the steeple of the Montelbaanstoren (1606) and the Munttoren (1619).

For his church in the Jordaan, de Keyser chose a simple Greek cross design with massive hipped roofs and curiously un-churchlike gable ends, topped with broad balustrades. Small triangular buildings nestle in the corners of the cross. The plan is significant in that it moved radically away from the traditional Dutch Renaissance style of his earlier churches, seeking to provide a large central meeting space inside the building and to create the kind of subdued atmosphere more appropriate to the needs of Protestant worship.

Outside the entrance to the church is a challenging statue of three figures tightly bound to each other. It is a monument to the Jordaan riots of 1934, directed against unemployment and poverty in the Depression years. The inscription, *Eenheid de Sterkste Keten,* means 'The Strongest Chains are those of Unity'.

Kippers or Knickers

At the foot of Noordermarkt, turn into the broad avenue of Wester-straat. On Monday morning it could be a scene from the late Middle Ages. All along the centre of the street a double line of white canvas pitched roofs extends to a distant pinpoint somewhere near the Lijnbaansgracht. Half-close your eyes and imagine how an artist such as Avercamp or Brueghel might have painted it. And what marvellous details they would have found among the red-faced stallholders and their customers, the tomato-rolling, cheese-gawping, raw herring-scoffing, gossiping old men and wives, and the sly underworld beneath the counters, where dogs scavenge and pant among the rubbish, tracked by wide-eyed silent blond babies passing by at dog's eye-level.

At the Westerstraat market they sell clothes, food, furniture, toiletries, electrical goods and much else in no particular order. If your desire be kippers or crabs, you will find them here, or lacy knickers pegged on lines across the central alleyway between the stalls, or bolts of cloth or bottles of cleaning liquid, or lampshades or shoes – in short, this market is a primary distribution centre for the new junk which a generation later turns up on the floor of the Noordermarkt – part of a neat local trading cycle which need never end.

Once inside that narrow alleyway, the visible world becomes a narrow, apparently unbroken cone wrapped in white canvas. You may wonder if you will ever find a way out. Fortunately, they have thought of this, and there are breaks at each cross-street. We turn left and, in translation, move quickly through the cross-streets of First Carnation,

First Garden and First Dog-rose. Along here are some tempting specialist shops: musical boxes, books, prints and postcards at Muziekantiquariaat, then dolls at the house dated 1625 on the next corner. They sell not only finished dolls, beautifully painted and dressed, but spare parts as well – heads, tiny hands and feet that you can fix on and paint yourself.

You find, too, the occasional shop that has laid down and died. Ravi Textiel, an all-purpose clothes shop of the old school, had clearly been shut for weeks. Half the goods in a previously crammed window had vanished, as though eaten in the night by giant moths, leaving ugly gaps in the sagging display. The rest of the merchandise hung there still, covered in thick dust – socks, woollen baby-suits, hats and jumpers, and a tall column of decaying brassières, the white ones gone grey from neglect, the colour faded from others in orange, green and blue, all still padded out and pointed hopefully at the street, their price tags in place, though surely now doomed never to find a mistress of their own.

Nearby is an outstanding success story among the campaigns over the last twenty years to restore derelict but important buildings in the city. In Eerste Egelantiers Dwarsstraat you will see the entrance to Claes Claesz Hofje, which now extends over 23 neighbouring properties including the Anslo's Hofje in Egelantiersstraat, and contains some 60 flats, many of them bedsitters occupied by students at the Conservatory. All these buildings, some dating back to before 1620, were fully restored between 1968 and 1973, with the excellent result that a large cluster of original small houses, displaying a fine variety of neck, step and spout gable, have survived and now prosper. Just as important, they were not replaced by one of the stark geometric blocks that are also gaining a toehold in the revitalised Jordaan.

On the corner of Egelantiersgracht is Café 't Smalle, a panelled and beamed gem among brown cafés, the window panes framed with stained-glass borders, an oval picture in the middle of each pane. On the wall inside hangs one of those Victorian tear-jerkers, a cartoon of a man on the front step of a bar, clearly intent on entry. Next to him stands a forlorn little figure. 'Not again, Father!' she cries. This café is where Peter Hoppe, of the ubiquitous Hoppe Jenever, founded his distillery in 1780. The café serves, by the way, a huge range of rolls, spicy buns and helpings (*portie*) of apple cake.

Cabaret

Walk over the bridge and turn down the quayside by Prinsengracht. On the other side of the canal the red and black flag of Amsterdam flies outside the Anne Frank House (see *Walk 6*) and farther along is the elegant tower of de Keyser's Westerkerk. On this side of the water, at 114 Prinsengracht, is an extraordinary institution: De Twee Zwaantjes (The Two Cygnets), a bar-cabaret offering 'Music and Song since 1928'. An evening visit is strongly recommended, more on grounds of wonderful eccentricity than brilliance of music. Opening hours are vague, and those for music vary; try Sunday from about 18.00, or later in the evening on Friday and Saturday.

The indispensable instrument in this tiny bar is the accordion. Framed photographs on the walls show its many applications – anywhere from leading a jolly Jordaaner singsong to backing an opera. The stage, an open-fronted pulpit at the back of the bar, is reached by a short flight of steps. The performing area is large enough to take, at most, three or four humans – who would anyway need to be very fond of each other – and one accordion. Any nervous or tipsy musician who fell off the front of the stage would also be in line for a nasty header down the steps to the toilets; no doubt to delighted applause.

Some nights the music is provided by a set of keyboards. The massive instrument stands next to the bar and is one of that versatile kind which can imitate drums, guitars, birdsong, and often just goes 'Tchikka, tchikka, tchukka' in between bursts from the singer. Beside it there is just room for high-spirited jigging by elderly dancers.

Every singer who performs here has a vast repertoire of music-hall favourites, beefily rendered in Dutch, French and English. After 'La Vie en Rose', it may be 'Bye Bye Blackbird' or 'You Are My Sunshine'. What you can be sure of, *everyone else* in the bar knows the words. The insufficiently relaxed newcomer tends to be the one who sits there politely grinning instead of howling the tear-stained climax: '. . . to my Memoreeeeez!!!' Never mind. No one is looking at you, they are too busy enjoying themselves, laughing and drinking and nudging each other.

Two Indoor Markets – for Antiques and 'Rommel'

Along the next turning, at No.34 Nieuwe Leliestraat, is a good lunch stop. The De Reiger café serves *stokbrood* (baguettes) with various fillings, soup of the day and salads in a long narrow bar-room with a larger dining room beyond. The rooms have tables of stripped wood and narrow wooden floorboards, there is a polished wooden bar and gantry, and deep airy windows. Take the large table by the door, and you may be joined by the resident cat – if it's not there already. A real Jordaaner, it likes to sleep on the table, catching the two o'clock sun through the window, and will not budge unless pushed. Left to itself, it stretches and rolls over on its back, resuming its sunbath with front paws bent in *blasé* obliviousness.

De Reiger is a popular meeting point for young locals who appear always to have time on their hands; time to drop in for a chat with friends or read a newspaper, and roll a cigarette from their personal bag of Samson (*'Halfzware Shag'*). Perhaps some are students, or musicians who work at night, or actors or artists in a resting mode.

Across the street are smart casual clothes at Exota and Tulips – belts, T-shirts in imaginative shades, Dim socks and own-brand dresses. At No.129, Dat Narrenschip has an interesting window of old books and prints. Down to Bloemgracht, and a crumbling turreted corner-house rises on the far side of the canal, faintly spooky with the air of something that Charles Addams might have built. At the corner where you turn is Ve-Ka, selling everything for potters. Stroll along the pretty canal, which is one of the few to survive in this part of the city – only four out of the original eleven have not been filled in. At the far end, by the Post Office, we touch for the first time the western extremity of the Jordaan.

A little to the north, at Nos 160–163 Lijnbaansgracht, is a trio of loud blues cafés where you may like to take your pick one evening from Maloe Melo, Stip and De Kroeg. Or do as the locals do and drift intermittently from one to the other. Nothing happens before 22.30, but then you can stay till three in the morning.

The least agreeable street in the Jordaan is probably Rozengracht, the busy commercial artery which carries the trams across from Westermarkt to the Old West. We slip rapidly across and soon are walking over a bridge on Lauriergracht. On the next corner is the bright and friendly English Bookshop, well stocked with novels, poetry and non-fiction; a good and worthy place to augment your bedside reading. The customers here are mainly Dutch – not surprising, really – who apparently prefer to read British and American authors in the original.

Although the mark-up for English books in the Netherlands is high, cover prices are still cheaper than a Dutch version would usually cost, and I have heard that translations from English can be pretty indifferent. Try asking, instead, for a Dutch author in English – Multatuli, say, or Cees Noteboom, Jan Wolkers, or one of Nicolas Freeling's Van der Valk mysteries set in and around Amsterdam.

Plunge into Hazenstraat, chiefly famous for idiosyncratic fashions and décor shops. Our last calls are at a pair of indoor markets. 'De Looier' is at No.109 Elandsgracht, and extends for a whole block in a maze of narrow alleys. It takes only seconds to become entirely lost. The alleys and stalls have a scruffy air, and so does the café if and when you find it. All the same, it may feel like Harrods after the Noordermarkt. Here, among the juke boxes of a certain age and a multitude of pots and pans, you will find real antiques. 'De Looier' is strongest, it seems to me (a complete non-expert), in antique jewellery and certain types of ephemera such as brass buttons or tin toys.

Just down the road and round the corner is an unashamed and really rather friendly 'Rommelmarkt' (junk or flea market) at No.38 Looiersgracht. One of its interesting characteristics is the way it rotates its programme of junk and collectibles. It is open from 11.00 to 17.00, closed on Friday. On Monday, you will find a coin and stamp market; on Tuesday, books and records; Wednesday, junk; Thursday, second-hand clothes; Saturday and Sunday, junk, glorious junk.

The Real Amsterdam

I have this running joke with myself that what I am really searching for in this city is 'the *real* Amsterdam'. It is a joke because I am just about convinced that the real anywhere is a state of mind, not a place. It is something that happens unexpectedly, a sublime moment when you feel a surge of happiness, or love, or perfect mental balance. 'Ah,' you say to yourself, 'this is the place, the real Amsterdam!' In truth, however, it is not a place at all. It's you.

The idea is fun, though, and intriguing. Let's go on. Suppose 'the real Amsterdam' *were* a place, somewhere that contained the power to please or inspire not just a single person but several, or even a hundred. If so, where is it? Let me make a suggestion.

High on the list of desirable Amsterdam moods must surely be the gentle but satisfying melancholy induced by a half-lit brown café. It would be somewhere like De Doffer perhaps, in Runstraat – one of the stopping-places recommended at the end of this Slow Walk. By the door, dusty velvet curtains are suspended from a pole on brass rings. The bar stools, chairs and tables are of dark wood, chipped and scarred, of indeterminate age, the ceiling yellowed by the tobacco smoke of half a century. Candles in bottles are the light source, and most are unlit. Soft West Coast jazz is on the player; from the back room comes the chink of billiard balls. Outside it is mid-afternoon and raining, so no hurry to leave, just watch the people passing by, a cyclist gliding through with a raised umbrella in one hand. The barmaid looks across. *'Alstublieft. Een Pils.'*

Many other brown cafés are capable of inducing similar moods. My choice would include Reijnders and Eijlders, off Leidseplein (*Walk 11*); De Reiger and 't Smalle (*this walk*); Café Hoppe (*Walks 1, 2*), De Druif (*Walk 3*) and Gijsbrecht van Aemstel (*Walk 5*).

Walk 5

Herengracht

A stroll along the 'Gentlemen's Canal', passing many of the finest merchant houses in Amsterdam. Includes the nearby Round Lutheran Church and the Cat Boat, the Theatre Museum and a visit to the Willet-Holthuysen Museum, a seventeenth-century house preserved as it was lived in by its last occupants, the nineteenth-century art collector Abraham Willet and his wife Louise.

Allow 4–5 hours.

Best times Not Monday, when Theatre Museum closed.

ROUTE

Begin at top of Nieuwe Zijds Voorburgwal. Trams 1, 2, 5, 13, 17. Walk back towards 'Sonesta' sign, forking right into top of Spuistraat. Turn 1st right into Kattegat. The **Round Lutheran Church** is on left; see poster outside for details of Sunday concerts at 11.00.

Walk up to Singel and turn left. House at No.7 is smallest in Amsterdam. Look across to **Cat Boat** (De Poezenboot), a shelter for the city's stray cats, moored opposite 40 Singel; open to public 13.00 to 14.00.

Go to top of Singel, turn left into Brouwersgracht and walk along to **Herengracht**. Cross to W (even-numbered) side of canal and walk down it on this side. (See essay for notes on types of gable, architects, etc.)

On other side of canal see warehouses 't Fortuijn and d'Arcke Noach at Nos 43-45 (built *c*.1600). **Theatre Museum** is at No.168 (built 1638) ☞; open 11.00 to 17.00, closed Monday. *Admission, takes Museum Pass*. See Bartolotti House (1622) at Nos 170-172.

At crossing with Raadhuisstraat, see contrasting styles of the Berlage house at No.184 (1898) and the Van Gendt building at No.194 (1896), and the traditional eighteenth-century house at No.211.

Cross canal and continue along odd-numbered side. See interesting group of houses at Nos 265–271 and the turreted *Proeflokaal* at No.319, a seventeenth-century revival built in 1889.

No.366, a neck-gabled house by Philips Vingboons, now houses the **Bible Museum**; open 10.00 to 17.00, Sunday and holidays 13.00 to 17.00, closed Monday. *Admission*.

After the crossing with Leidsegracht and Beulingstraat, many houses are of later date and considerably larger. See No.450 by Vingboons (1663) and No.462 by Adriaan Dortsman (1670), and note various opulent façades and balustrades, e.g. at Nos 438, 446, 456, 458 and 460.

At the crossing with Vijzelstraat we meet the twentieth century: the vast ABN fortress at 30-34 Vijzelstraat (1926) and the shops and flats by Rutgers at 511-513 Herengracht (1928).

Call finally at the **Willet-Holthuysen Museum** at No.605 ☞; open 11.00 to 17.00. *Admission, takes Museum Pass*. At exit, turn left to bridge, where Herengracht meets River Amstel. Walk ends here. Nearest refreshments: escape view of Muziektheater by turning left and 1st left and walking up to **Rembrandtplein** and the terrace of your choice; best interiors at the Opera and Café Schiller. Trams 4, 9, 14.

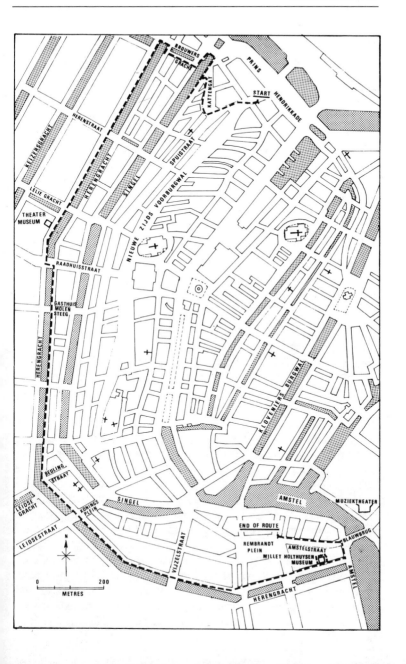

Coffee Concerts

The nearest tram stop is a little way from the top of Herengracht, but there are several attractions – some might be better called oddities – to entertain us as we go. In Kattegat are two important old buildings, and the first of these is a restaurant! You could hardly get more 'old Dutch' than De Zilveren Spiegel, Amsterdam's oldest restaurant – two tottery step-gabled houses built in 1614, with an extra windowed storey above the ground floor (very picturesque) and quaint half-shutters above.

We come next to the Round Lutheran Church. Designed by Adriaan Dortsman, built in 1668–71 and rebuilt in 1822 after a fire, it is now part of the Sonesta organisation and since 1975 has served as a cultural centre, making its name with a varied and consistently good programme of Sunday morning *Koffieconcerten*. Check the poster by the front steps for details, or look them up in *What's On* (under 'Sonesta Koepelzaal'). Concerts begin at 11.00 and last for an hour or more. They usually get a full house – the concerts having taken over, perhaps, from going to proper church – and it is as well to arrive by twenty-to, bag a seat and then go back to the foyer for your cup of coffee.

Cat Boat

Continue along Kattegat to the Singel canal. A house on the left, at No.7, is the smallest in Amsterdam, scarcely wider than its front door. The Cat Boat (De Poezenboot) is about 50 metres further along, on the other side of the canal, moored facing 40 Singel.

I know cats do not appeal to everyone, but we have four at home and I am quite sure they would happily spend the rest of their days on the Amsterdam Cat Boat should anything happen at our end to curtail their daily Whiskas. If they did go, they would find themselves sharing the main cabin of a chalet-style houseboat with a couple of dozen 'abandoned and destitute' cats, sleeping in wicker or plastic baskets ranged around the room or lounging outside in a wire enclosure overlooking the canal, and enjoying a mixed diet of meat, biscuit and day-old chicks.

The Cat Boat takes in strays – said to number 50,000 in Amsterdam – has them neutered and gives them a home. So many cats are brought in, the organisers have now opened a second boat and a small farm near Hoorn where 150 aged cats live out their time. You can go on board and join the cats, each day between 13.00 and 14.00. Predictably, some will

snooze through your entire visit, but several will want as much fuss and contact as you can give them. Afterwards, a donation is appreciated. It costs a lot to feed this crowd and the vets' work must also be paid for.

The Gentlemen's Canal

A short walk along the pretty Brewers' Canal (Brouwersgracht) brings us to the head of Herengracht. Go round by the bridges to the even-numbered side, next to No.2.

Our walk takes us the full length of the canal, travelling through a series of bends to complete about two-thirds of a horseshoe around the inner city: total distance is about 2.5km (1.5 miles).

The Herengracht is one of three concentric canals laid out from around 1612 to cater for the housing needs of a rapidly swelling population (30,000 to 139,000 between 1570 and 1640). The master plan of the *Grachtengordel* (canal girdle), with radial streets cutting across the new canals, was drawn up and supervised by Hendrick Staets, the municipal carpenter – a position of great authority at a time when all buildings in Amsterdam had to stand on wooden piles sunk into the marshy ground.

The narrow, expensive building plots along the Herengracht, Keizersgracht and Prinsengracht were snapped up by merchants who built tall, steep-roofed town houses which could double as warehouses. They had storage space in basements and in the attics, which contained up to three storeys. Although the original canal houses date from the seventeenth century, nearly all have been altered and many replaced in the nineteenth and twentieth centuries.

The canal houses of Amsterdam are famous for their decorative gables. The first types were the Pointed or Spout gable (*c.*1620–1720), which followed the profile of the city's old timber houses, and the simple Step gable (*c.*1600–65). The medieval timber façades were gradually replaced by brick, and in the Classical period after 1625 the brickwork was faced with sandstone.

Later, from 1638, came another gable type, the Neck, resembling a head and neck, which continued until 1770 or so. Bell gables, with a smoother, flowing outline, belong in the period 1660–1790. Later still, from 1670, came the Flat, Plain or Italian style, with a straight cornice, sometimes decorated with a balustrade.

These basic shapes evolved during the building of the Herengracht, developed and refined by architects such as Hendrick de Keyser (1565–1621), Jacob van Campen (1595–1657), Philips Vingboons (1614–78) and Adriaan Dortsman (1635–82).

From where we now stand, several of these types can be seen. Look back across Brouwersgracht for Step, Neck and Bell gables. On this side of Herengracht are several in the Plain or Italian style. Walk down on this even-numbered side. Opposite, at Nos 43–45, are two famous old Spout-gabled warehouses De Fortuijn and d'Arcke Noach (Fortune and Noah's Ark), dating from around 1600.

At Nos 77 and 81 are two step-gabled buildings, the former a house, the latter a warehouse, designed by Hendrick de Keyser in the Flemish or Artisan Mannerist style.

Our next call is at No.168. Meanwhile, keep an eye out for modern abuses. The columned pavilion on top of the corner house at Blauwburgwal (Nos 105–107) is one of the more gross examples. And something quite extraordinary has been happening to the top of No.123.

At ground level, look out also for your own safety. Not so much from cars roaring up behind – though they too need watching – as from the lethal Order of the White Lights. These are drivers who start up somewhere ahead of you and then suddenly go into reverse and hurtle backwards to the next road crossing to beat the one-way system.

Theatre Museum

No. 168 Herengracht was originally a confectionery, and then in 1637 a new owner, the city-magistrate Michael de Pauw, commissioned Philips Vingboons to design a new front to the house. He produced a large-windowed façade in white sandstone topped with Amsterdam's first neck gable. Since 1959 the building has been the home of the Theatre Museum (Nederlands Theater Instituut).

The two ground-floor reception rooms are dazzlingly decorated in late Louis XIV style, the work carried out between 1728 and 1733. In the front room, large murals in oil on canvas (Amsterdam being too damp for frescos) tell the story of Jephthah and his daughter (Judges 11). Isaac de Moucheron was responsible for the landscapes and Jacob de Wit for the figures and the ceiling. The back room is devoted to the Virtues – Love, Generosity, Abundance, the Fates, Hope,

Temperance, Prudence, Faith and Courage.

In the other front room is a large model of Amsterdam's first theatre, the Schouwburg on Keizersgracht, built in 1637 and burnt down in 1772. In those early days the main audience had to stand in the auditorium. Only the regents and respected burghers were allowed seats in the upper galleries.

At the back of the museum a permanent exhibition, 'On and Back Stage in Eighteenth-century Dutch Theatre', surveys types of scenery used and techniques of presentation. Great fun because you can take part, operating sets from a control panel: raise the backcloth, make the sea roll and press a button to ignite a flash of lightning. To one side is a long tube on a pivot to be swung up and down with both hands – a primeval rain machine. In another back room, next to the café, are charming Nymphenburg porcelain figures of characters from the *commedia dell'arte*.

The museum stages special exhibitions upstairs, and has a library, bookshop and video collection.

Towards Golden Bend

Next to the Theatre Museum is the Bartolotti House. Designed in 1617 in red brick and stone by Hendrick de Keyser, who gave the broad façade an ornately stepped gable, the house was magnificently renovated in 1971.

The next crossing, with Raadhuisstraat, contains a fascinating mixture of styles. The view is dominated by the powerful curve of the arcaded Utrecht Gallery, a long row of shops bearing the Berlage influence and designed by A.L. van Gendt in 1899. Facing it is the Berlage corner-house at No.184, and on the other side of the Herengracht is a modest traditional house with an eighteenth-century neck gable.

After the crude mass of the Bank Bilson at Nos 206–214, built in 1914 in a Neo-Classical style that looks resolutely backwards in time, look for the attractive mixture between Nos.265 and 271 – a seventeenth-century revival dating from 1882, a tall tower of 1900, a real old stepped gable and a 'dwarf' house, also seventeenth-century.

At No.319 is an attractive spout-gabled and turreted *Proeflokaal* (tasting house), built in 1889. No.323, however, is 'Neo-Vingboons' of

1940, and made of a rather unpleasant plum-coloured brick. Nos 364–370 are real Vingboons, dating from 1662, with dignified pedimented gables and festoons.

In the middle of this last group is the Bible Museum. I would rate it an optional visit, in view of all that is yet to be seen on our walk. It has clear and well-presented displays on the work of the Dutch Bible Society, the spread of Luther's Bible, archaeological finds in the Land of the Bible, Jewish daily life and sacred objects, and models of temples in Jerusalem. Information and educational material are available on request.

At 380–382 Herengracht is an imitation French Renaissance château *cum* city mansion, designed in 1890 by A. Salm – easily the *Grachten-gordel*'s most luxurious residential project of the nineteenth century. Beyond it stands a pleasantly varied group of seventeenth-century houses, on single and double plots, all with pedimented neck gables and modest decorative flourishes.

Time Out

Refreshment stops have been thin on the ground so far – though you will always find somewhere if desperate, such as the disappointingly austere café on the corner of Raadhuistraat. Something altogether better awaits at No.435, De Gijsbrecht van Aemstel. Beyond the tiny terrace lies a warming brown interior and a menu offering lots of snacks and tasty dishes: Soups, Saté (pork fillet), Fried Mussels in Garlic Butter, Croquettes, Dutch Meat Balls, Stuffed Mushrooms with Crabmeat and Cheese . . . Having ordered, look round at the décor: the collection of suspended objects – models of a farm cart and a spinning wheel, copper pots; the wheel-shaped 'lanternabra' by the window and the low barrel lightshades suspended on long chains; the junk of ages lined up on shelves for your inspection. Steps lead to further rooms at the back – up to restaurant tables and down to a small sitting room with sploshy leather couches and toilets off. Gijsbrecht van Aemstel, by the way, was a thirteenth-century lord and early Amsterdam hero, celebrated in a play by Vondel, written in 1637.

The Upper Crust

We are now at the intersection with Koningsplein and Leidsestraat, in the elbow of Herengracht, an area known as 'Golden Bend' after the splendiferous houses it contains, built for bankers and burgomasters. Elegance, alas, is not a word you would apply to many of them. Corporate or civic grandeur has become the overriding concern. Plots are consistently more than double the width of the standard seventeenth-century canal house. Imported stone has taken over from brick, to be applied with rustication or channelled joints. The front door occupies the centre of a five-windowed frontage, and is reached by an elaborately railed pair of steps.

All of these elements have occurred in houses we have already passed. In Golden Bend the concentration of them is far greater, almost oppressive. One can over-generalise, however, and miss somewhere like No.475, a finely proportioned house of 1730 in Louis XIV style. The flat sandstone façade terminates in a straight cornice above a small-windowed attic storey, crowned by a pair of curved balustrades.

On the other side of the canal, No.450 is by Philips Vingboons and dates from 1663. Try to forget the top-floor extension, added in 1922. Beneath it is a classic stone house in the Plain style. The approach is similar to that of Adriaan Dortsman who in 1670 designed No.462. This house has a particularly pleasing front door, reached by a single sweep of steps and topped by a strong sculpted balustrade. The theme is repeated in the roof balustrade which bears sculptures of Welfare and Trade, concepts very dear in Amsterdam, then the world centre of bourgeois capitalism. Look for other balustrades on Nos 438, 446, 456, 458 and 460.

Further along the canal, Dortsman built a more modest house on similar lines for himself – the fruit of a profitable spell of speculative building in which he enjoyed the partnership of Jan Six, burgomaster and patron of the arts.

At the meeting with Vijzelstraat, overpowering modernity engulfs the view. The shops and flats by Rutgers (1928) have a chunky elegance, and De Bazel's monster, now the ABN building (1926), is handsome and challenging but has clearly landed from another planet, where everything is twice the size.

On the left at the next bridge is Thorbeckeplein, with F. Leenhoff's 1874 bronze statue of the statesman Thorbecke looking out over the canal. The Herengracht comes to an end shortly, in the stretch beyond the low flat steel bridge which carries Utrechtsestraat from one side to the other. Further imposing houses to look out for are No.502, since 1927 the mayor of Amsterdam's official residence, and Nos 520, 527, and 539. Our final call is at No.605, to see how the interior of a wealthy family's house looked towards the end of the nineteenth century.

Perhaps pause first, for a cup of coffee or what you will, either at The Bread Mill coffee shop or at the brown bar 't Trefpunt opposite. Both offer wide-angled views of canal and bridge life, the latter often dominated by spectacular traffic jams. It only needs one delivery truck to park in the vehicle lane behind the tram stop for immense chaos to break out. As the delivery men vanish northwards into the narrows of Utrechtsestraat pushing trolleys laden with boxes of videos and washing machines, cars pile up behind, veer impatiently across the tram track and, in no more than a minute, all movement in either direction is frozen. Behold then, with simple joy, the faces of the perspiring drivers, and smile sweetly at the passengers suspended in time on board the No.4 tram.

Willet-Holthuysen Museum

The house was built in 1689 in the final extension that joined the Herengracht to the River Amstel. Ownership passed through several families until 1858, when it was inherited by Sandra Louise Geertruida Holthuysen. Three years later she married Abraham Willet, who with his wife's encouragement built up collections of glass, ceramics, silver and paintings, and an extensive library. When she died childless, in 1895, Mrs Willet left the house and its contents to the City of Amsterdam, on condition that it be preserved and opened to the public as the 'Museum Willet-Holthuysen'.

The museum opened in 1896 but for a long time had little appeal to citizens with no interest in the recent past, whose own furniture was little different from that on show. It was even the butt of a sly local joke: that it was one of the only places in Amsterdam, apart from Kalverstraat on a Whit Monday, where a man could meet his mistress without being noticed. Since then many rooms have been restored, and almost a century has passed since Mrs Willet lived in the house. Its appeal is altogether different, and it has become a popular calling-place for visitors to the city.

It is large but not particularly grand. It has good but not outstanding furniture, and much is made of Abraham Willet's collections of Delftware, glass, and Dutch porcelain from Weesp, Loosdrecht, Amstel and The Hague. What is most fascinating, however, is the air of rather stuffy, well-scrubbed melancholy that overhangs many of the rooms: we feel that 'Victorian' Mr and Mrs Willet are not far away. The first curator of the museum may well have experienced similar vibrations, for he apparently had the poor taste to write a gossipy novel about the Willets' unhappy home life, culminating in her sad death from cancer in a house overrun by cats.

We go in at the tradesmen's entrance beneath the main steps. The beamed and tiled eighteenth-century kitchen in the basement is full of interesting old copper utensils, china cupboards, an ancient water-purifier and an ornate wooden high-chair.

Upstairs in the long high-ceilinged hallway, one of the best pieces is a tall eighteenth-century longcase clock, made by Albert Vreehuis of Amsterdam and decorated beneath the clockface with ships rocking back and forth and indications of the season, date and position of the moon.

The front room on the right (facing the front door from inside) is decorated in the Neo-Classical Louis XVI style, with much marquetry and Oriental panelling. Through double doors to the rear is a 'ballroom'. A painting on an easel, by Willem Steelink Jnr, shows how the room looked in 1882, in the Willets' day. The heavy gilded chandelier is missing from the painting, and presumably was taken down for receptions and balls. Any dancer more than 1.75m (5ft 9in) tall would have been lucky to avoid catching a nasty headache from it. The other front room has a fine painted ceiling, clover-shaped in a gilt frame, the work of the Amsterdam artist Jacob de Wit who also decorated the Theatre Museum. Alas, it is not original to the house, having been imported from No.250 Herengracht. The walls, in common with the blinding mauve of the Theatre Museum's woodwork, are partly painted in a violent blue and partly covered in bright blue velvet, of a type known as *velours d'Utrecht*.

In the sumptuous Louis XVI dining room the table is laid for six with a beautiful china centrepiece. Although additions and embellishments have been made to some rooms, this is an original Willet concept, furnished by them in the 1860s, the first decade of their marriage.

The garden has suffered from a renovation in 1972 which gave a tightly organised eighteenth-century look with low hedges murderously clipped in scroll patterns. The small room which overlooks the garden is much better: a pleasant pavilion crammed with porcelain, the view guarded by two portly cupids representing Trade and Abundance.

The first floor was where the family slept. No beds stand here now, the space being given over to Abraham Willet's fine collections: glass in the front room, and in the back room silver boxes, flasks, ink pots and all kinds of eighteenth-century necessaries. The paintings here, of very variable quality, are probably from the studio of Jurriaan Andriessen, a wallpaper painter. None could be worse than the mawkish St Bernard dog, by Wouterus Verschuur (1812–74).

Turn left at the exit. A plaque on the wall of No.619 records that Jan Six, burgomaster of Amsterdam and friend of Rembrandt, lived here. Our walk ends by the banks of the Amstel, before the grating façade of the Muziektheater. Flee quickly along smelly Amstelstraat, vulgar in a different way, to a terrace in Rembrandtplein.

Walk 6 ⚒

Resistance Museum to Anne Frank House

Aspects of the city in the Second World War, as revealed in a former synagogue, now the Museum of the Dutch Resistance, and the house on Prinsengracht where Anne Frank lived with her family in a secret apartment from July 1942 until August 1944. A chance also to climb the tower of the Westerkerk, the tallest in Amsterdam.

Allow   5–6 hours.

Best times   Not Monday, when Resistance Museum closed, or Yom Kippur (Day of Atonement). On Saturday, Sunday and public holidays museum does not open until 13.00.

ROUTE

Begin at Victorieplein. Trams 4, 12, 25. Bus 15. Walk S along Rijnstraat and take 1st right into Lekstraat. **Resistance Museum (Verzetsmuseum)** is on left at No.63 ☞; open 10.00 to 17.00, Saturday, Sunday and public holidays open 13.00 to 17.00, closed Monday. *Admission, takes Museum Pass.*

At exit, return to Rijnstraat and take Tram 25 to Dam. Walk to the **Nationaal Monument** ☞. Continue W across Dam Square into Paleisstraat, keeping Royal Palace on your right. Cross Nieuwezijds Voorburgwal, turn right and left into Raadhuisstraat. Keep straight on to Westermarkt. The **Westerkerk tower** is to your right ☞; open 1 June to 15 September, Tuesday, Wednesday, Friday, Saturday, guided tours on the hour 14.00 to 17.00. *Admission.*

The **Anne Frank House** is just N of Westerkerk at No.263 Prinsengracht ☞; open 09.00 to 17.00, Sunday and public holidays open 10.00, in summer (June to August) closes 19.00, closed Yom Kippur. *Admission.*

Walk ends here. Nearest refreshments at De Kalkhoven, on far side of Westermarkt (283 Prinsengracht). Trams 13, 14, 17. Bus 21.

Resistance Museum

The German raid on Rotterdam in May 1940 was devastating and conclusive. About 900 defenceless inhabitants were killed. The Germans threatened to move in like manner on other cities and the Dutch supreme commander surrendered. Queen Wilhelmina fled with her family and the entire government to London. The Netherlands was an occupied country. In place of formal war, the Dutch turned to resistance.

This museum, located in a former synagogue, tells the story of how the Dutch resisted. Not all took up active, illegal resistance, in fact the number of those that did was initially small – about 25,000. At the opposite end of the spectrum, many thousands collaborated with the occupying power. A few had been members of the minority Dutch Nazi Party (NSB) led by Anton Mussert; many more capitulated before the demands of Dr Seyss-Inquart, Hitler's supremo in the Netherlands, and became collaborators. The in-betweeners, the great majority, supported the resistance in spirit but saw their main task as getting on with everyday life and surviving the war. The braver ones resisted in

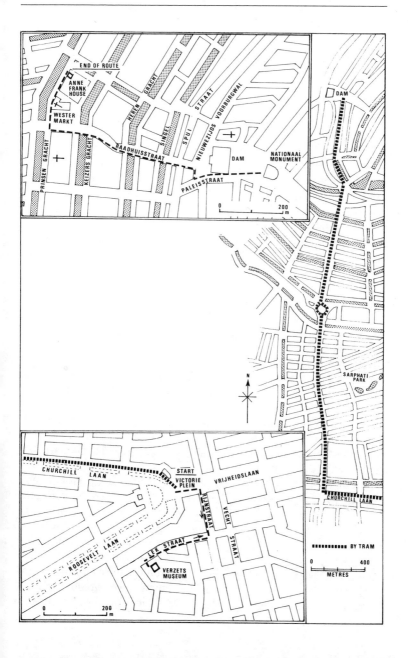

unspectacular but telling ways. Their efforts too are recorded in the museum.

The permanent exhibition is arranged in two parts. The black partitioned corridors deal with the first period of the Occupation (Sections 1–17) and the other sections (18–40) cover the period of increasingly active resistance up to the end of the war in Europe.

The first phase shows the Germans turning the screw. Abolition of political parties; banning of anything to do with the royal family, the House of Orange; anti-Jewish measures and the first round-ups; the protest strike of February 1941, and the German reprisals; repression of creative artists and performers, doctors, university teachers, and former members of the Dutch armed forces; the protest strikes of April–May 1943 and further savage reprisals; persecution of the Jews, who were rounded up and deported to the death camps of Auschwitz and Sobibor. In 1940 there were 140,000 Dutch Jews; 104,000 were killed by the Nazis.

When deportation began, in July 1942, it provoked a new form of resistance. Jewish families went into hiding. As many as 25,000 Jews went underground. An escape route to Spain was organised, and some Jews were rescued from the transit camps. As the war continued, more and more groups had to go into hiding – Jews, students, ex-soldiers, people avoiding the Germans' compulsory work scheme (*Arbeitseinsatz*), and active resistance workers. By 1944 there were about 300,000 people in hiding – the *onderduikers*.

People hid in attics and basements, behind false doors and double walls. In the country they hid in sheds and hen-houses, in boats concealed in the rushes, in dug-outs in the woods. Non-Jews tried to find jobs on farms and some managed an almost-normal existence, but they always needed a place to hide from German checks and round-ups. In the eyes of the occupiers they were non-people, with no ration card and no identity pass.

Forgery became a big underground industry. Secret organisations came into being to help those in hiding, act as their bankers, and form attack squads to steal documents and sabotage German stores. There were further strikes, betrayals and bitter reprisals, culminating in the Hunger Winter of 1944–45 after all food supplies to the western Netherlands were cut off. Then came Allied weapon drops, the rise of an underground army, and the long slog to Liberation.

As can be imagined, each phase of the Occupation is thoroughly documented with photographs, posters, diaries, letters, Jewish badges, passes, arms and radio equipment – also press-button slide shows and radio broadcasts. The museum fulfils a special role as a centre for those who lived through the war, and also as a source of information for young people who want to find out what is meant by 'the Dutch Resistance'.

The exhibits convey an attitude that is remarkable for its forbearance. There is no self-pity, and no attempt to seek out scapegoats. 'This is what happened to us,' is the overwhelming message, 'and this is how we dealt with it.'

Tram Ride to the Dam

The No.25 tram turns past the sturdy statue of the architect H.P. Berlage in Victorieplein, then runs between the long, long rows of 1930s housing in Churchill-laan. This broad avenue was originally conceived by Berlage as part of his *Plan Zuid* (1917) for the southern extension of the city: a kind of garden suburb project in which 75 per cent of the buildings would be for working-class housing. After Berlage's death, the building of the New South (Nieuw Zuid) was entrusted to the Amsterdam School architects Michael de Klerk and Piet Kramer.

Not all the housing in the New South is as monotonous and austere as this part of Churchill-laan. In the narrower streets behind the boulevards, especially those of Apollolaan and Stadionweg, are stylish mansions and apartments, and smart shops on Beethovenstraat.

It was to this part of the city that Otto Frank, Anne's father, brought his family when in 1933 he decided that life in Frankfurt-am-Main was becoming too hazardous for them. They settled into a house in Merwedeplein, off Churchill-laan, and remained there until July 1942. By that time their past had, as it were, caught up with them. After two years of the German Occupation, Amsterdam had become a highly dangerous place for Jews.

Otto Frank had a herbs and spices business which he ran from No.263 Prinsengracht. During the early months of 1942, he began converting the two upper floors and the attic of the Annexe to the rear of the house. Furniture and household utensils were brought over in discreet batches from Merwedeplein. Entrance to the secret apartment was sealed by a hinged bookcase.

The tram rolls on, then at Ferdinand Bolstraat turns right into the Old South (Oud Zuid). In the working-class quarter known as 'De Pijp' (the Pipe), after its tall lines of red-brick tenements, we pass the end of the Albert Cuypstraat market (see *Walk 13: Beer and Diamonds*).

Across the canal from the Heineken Brewery is the Weteringcircuit, where on 3 April 1945 twenty people were shot by German troops, and their bodies left lying in the open for twenty-four hours. The long isolated wall on the right by the gardens is a memorial to them. It bears these lines of verse:

een volk dat voor tirannen zwicht
zal meer dan lijf en goed verliezen
dan dooft het licht . . .
(a people that yields to tyrants
shall lose more than life and goods
the light goes out . . .)

Nationaal Monument

National Remembrance Day is 4 May. On that day in 1956 Queen Juliana dedicated the Nationaal Monument in the Dam. It consists of a white 22m (72ft) obelisk backed by an arc of wall. It was designed by J.J.P. Oud and the sculptures are by John Rädecker. In the obelisk are eleven urns with earth collected from places where Dutch soldiers fell, and a twelfth with earth from Dutch war cemeteries in Indonesia.

The centrepiece of the sculptures is a group of naked chained figures, one in an attitude of crucifixion – the victims of war. Above on a shelf stands a mother with her baby – peace. On the lower side shelves are naked men with fierce dogs – resistance. It is a forbidding piece of work, and was no doubt meant to be. Its strident message is: 'Never again!'

Westerkerk

As a respite from war, we climb the tower of Amsterdam's favourite church. Since 1985, Hendrick de Keyser's West Church has been undergoing substantial restoration and is due to reopen in summer 1990.

The church was built in 1620 in the Dutch Renaissance style and follows the lines of the South Church (Zuiderkerk), also by de Keyser. The tower is 85m (279ft) high, the tallest in Amsterdam, and is topped by an Imperial crown, which in 1489 the Archduke Maximilian of Austria, later the Holy Roman Emperor Maximilian I, allowed the citizens of Amsterdam to add to their coat of arms.

Rembrandt is buried in the church, commemorated only by a plaque on the north wall. Severely out of pocket at the time of his death, as he was for much of his life, he was buried with two others though no one quite knows where. The hope is that when the church floor is redone, they may find him.

The ascent of the tower rises through six floors to the balcony – 160-odd steps in all, taken in mercifully easy stages. The longest climb is up two winding stone flights to the first floor. Here you can see the circular opening in the floor through which the great bells were hauled, the largest weighing 7,000kg (7 tons).

Wooden steps lead to the second floor, where the old carillon player is kept, a kind of basic organ at which the carillonist sat pulling down wooden handles to sound the bells. The church's new carillon is mechanically operated and programmed each year with a new melody. There are carillon concerts on Tuesday at 13.00. Also here is the old wooden wheel used for swinging the bell on to the clapper.

Continue upwards by ladder to see the great oak frame that holds the bells. It stands clear of the outer walls to save the tower from collapsing through vibration. Even so, no one dared give the word to ring the heaviest bell, the seven-tonner. Not only the biggest bell in this church, but the biggest bell in Amsterdam, it has never been heard.

A final briefing from the nimble guide prepares you for the summit. The balcony has a high stone balustrade. You can walk round it if feeling brave, or stand trembling in the opening. The first view is east, to the Royal Palace. Then, making a clockwise tour, you see the Rijksmuseum, suburban towers in the west, then the harbour, Centraal Station and St Nicolaas Church, and across to the other famous towers of the Old Church and the South Church.

This tower was used by fire-watchers. On sighting a fire, the watchman at the top rang a bell to warn people below, then signalled to them with flags to indicate where the fire was and what kind of fire. Citizens then ran to the scene and formed a bucket chain from the canal.

Anne Frank House

The story of what happened in this house is best read in Anne Frank's own diary – which has now been published in fifty countries, selling approximately thirteen million copies and figuring widely in school and college syllabuses.

The house is now in the hands of the Anne Frank Foundation, formed in 1957 when developers proposed demolishing the Annexe, which had stood empty for a long time. It was saved and opened as a memorial to Anne Frank, her family and the others – the Van Daans and Mr Dussel – who lived with them in the secret apartment for more than two years, until August 1944 when they were betrayed.

The Anne Frank Foundation provides a simple but clearly explained illustrated leaflet which shows the house in cross-section, with numbered captions about the principal rooms, together with a summary of events and an account of the Foundation and its work.

To amplify some of the main points of the tour, you go up a double flight of narrow stairs to a video room (1), then continue past the hinged bookcase (2) into the Annexe. In the next room, measuring about 3.6m x 2.7m (12ft x 9ft), where Mr and Mrs Frank and their elder daughter Margot slept, is a model of the cramped living space on the third floor.

In Anne's narrow room (4), measuring 4.5m x 2.1m (15ft x 7ft), which she shared with Mr Dussel, she pinned up pictures from magazines – Greta Garbo, Ray Milland, Deanna Durbin, the English Princesses Elizabeth and Margaret, and Ginger Rogers. Here Anne wrote her diary. She was aged thirteen when she first moved here. From the nearby washroom a steep stairway leads up to the Van Daans' room (6). You see the shell of the stove, the sink and cupboard beneath, and next door the tiny room of their son Pieter, and stairs leading to the attic.

Walk across a post-war 'bridge' to a long gallery of photo-boards. These describe the story of Anne's first years, the family's move to Amsterdam and the house in Merwedeplein. Then came the Occupation, and the persecution of the Jews. The Frank family prepared to go into hiding, and on 6 July 1942 vanished from the everyday world.

The Anne Frank House now attracts half a million visitors a year, and in the summer months this gallery can become so packed with shuffling bodies it is difficult to hold your concentration. But persevere.

The display continues with details of daily life in the Annexe – not using the water-tap or the toilet between 09.00 and 17.30 because not all the office staff working downstairs knew they were there. Four 'outside' people helped the Franks: Mr Koophuis, Mr Kraler, and the typists Miep and Elli, who brought them black-market food or food purchased openly with food-stamps obtained by the Dutch underground.

On 4 August 1944, German police and Dutch accomplices arrived by truck. They went straight to the bookcase and shouted: 'Open up!' It was over. On this photo-board is a copy of the transport list of the prisoners carried on the last train to leave Westerbork transit camp for Auschwitz. Among the names are those of the Frank family – Margot, Otto, Edith Frank-Hollander (Anne's mother) and Anneliese. We then read what happened to them. Margot and Anne died of typhus in Bergen-Belsen in March 1945. The family was virtually wiped out. Otto was the only survivor. After the Liberation he returned to Amsterdam and there Miep handed over Anne's papers, including her diary.

Otto decided the diary should be published, and it first appeared in 1947 under the title *Het Achterhuis* ('The Annexe'). It was translated into English and published in 1952 as *The Diary of a Young Girl*. In this room you can see the diary open at the page for 8 July 1942, in which Anne describes the day she learned that the family must go into hiding.

Downstairs, and something of an anti-climax, is an exhibit with additional background on the rise of Nazism, the war and the Occupation of the Netherlands. Much of this is more effectively described at our first port of call, the Resistance Museum.

Turn left at the exit and head for De Kalkhoven at No.283 Prinsengracht on the other side of Westermarkt. Here in this oasis of level-headed Dutch placidity, popular with local card-players, they have a large choice of refreshments. In addition to tea, coffee and beer, there is a double row of barrels behind the bar, labelled *Citroen, Cognac, Brandewijn, Oude Jenever* . . . Now may be the time to sit back and reflect on what you have seen.

Walk 7

Old Jewish Quarter

Before the Second World War this was Western Europe's most important Jewish centre. Walk includes Nieuwmarkt and the Waag (Weigh-house), the De Pinto House, the Rembrandt House Museum, Portuguese Synagogue and Jewish Historical Museum.

Allow 4–5 hours.

Best times Not Saturday, when Portuguese Synagogue closed, or Yom Kippur (Day of Atonement). On Sunday and public holidays Rembrandt House Museum not open until 13.00.

ROUTE

Begins at Centraal Station. Trams 1, 2, 4, 5, 9, 13, 16, 17, 24, 25. Buses 21, 32, 33, 34, 35, 39. Metro terminus.

From station forecourt, walk S towards Damrak, cross Prins Hendrikkade and turn left towards Barbizon Palace Hotel. Enter Zeedijk and follow bend into Chinese quarter, taking 2nd left into Stormsteeg. At the canal, Geldersekade, turn right to Nieuwmarkt and the **Waag**. Cross to SE corner. Take a look inside the Metro station (see essay for details).

Continue along St Antoniesbreestraat. To the right in Nieuwe Hoogstraat take the passage by the Metro entrance (Zuiderkerkhof) and walk through to the courtyard of the **South Church** (Zuiderkerk).

Return to St Antoniesbreestraat through the arch on E side of courtyard. Opposite is the **De Pinto House**, now a public library. Turn right to bridge leading across to Jodenbreestraat. There the second house on the right, with maroon shutters, is the **Rembrandt House Museum (Rembrandthuis)** ☞ ; open 10.00 to 17.00, Sunday and public holidays 13.00 to 17.00. *Admission, takes Museum Pass.*

At exit, turn right and cross road. Turn left under large modern building and walk along Nieuwe Uilenburgerstraat as far as the **Boas Factory**, a restored diamond-polishing works. Return to Jodenbree-straat and turn left to Mr Visserplein. Cross to far side and in adjoining J.D. Meijerplein see the 'Docker' monument and the **Portuguese Synagogue** ☞; open 10.00 to 12.15, 13.00 to 16.00, closed Saturday. *Admission.* On W side of square are the New Synagogue and the Great Synagogue, now part of the **Jewish Historical Museum (Joods Historisch Museum)**, entrance round corner in Nieuwe Amstel-straat ☞ ; open 11.00 to 17.00, closed Yom Kippur. *Admission, takes Museum Pass.*

At exit, turn right to Mr Visserplein, then left to flea market in **Waterlooplein**, next to the new Town Hall and Opera House complex (Stadhuis/Muziektheater); market open daily 10.00 to 16.00.

Walk ends in market. Nearest refreshments at Groot Mokum, on corner by Zwanenburgwal, surrounded by market stalls. Trams 9, 14.

Zeedijk and Nieuwmarkt

Great efforts are being made to rid Zeedijk of its sleazy reputation. The houses and shops are being thoroughly restored and the old cobbled

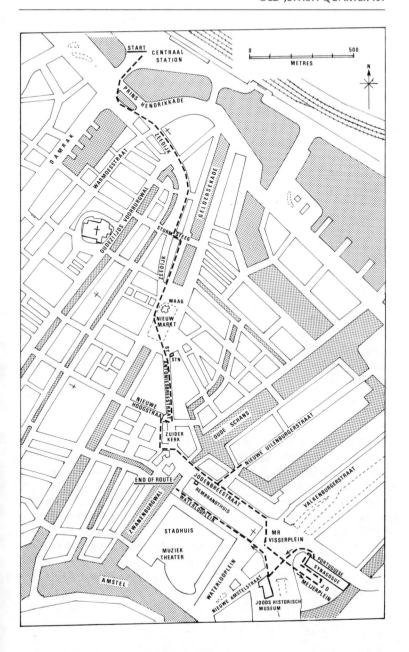

roadway has been relaid with flat paving stones. The black-fronted house at No.1, built in 1550, one of only two surviving timber houses in Amsterdam, looks especially smart, and De Vergulden Poort on the corner is a most attractive place to buy your wines and spirits.

Zeedijk's main problem is geographical. It snakes round the back of the Red Light district and cannot quite escape from it. In the narrow cross-streets to either side, the red lamps glow; an occasional junkie staggers about, and you are more likely to be offered drugs on this street than any other. Then suddenly you are in a Chinese quarter, every building a red-lacquered restaurant, grocery or catering shop. You still never quite know what to expect in Zeedijk.

Turn through Stormsteeg to the canal, Geldersekade, and walk along to Nieuwmarkt. The large turreted building ahead is the Waag, the old weigh-house, which was to have been transformed into 'the grandest café in Amsterdam' by none other than Philippe Starck, who in Paris designed that poser's paradise, the Café Costes. Then the project ran out of money and was shelved.

The building has a varied past. Originally a gate in the medieval city wall, the St Antoniespoort, it was built in 1488. In 1617 it became the public weigh-house; quite separately, the upper floor served as the meeting rooms for various guilds – the Painters, Bricklayers, Smiths and Surgeons. The Surgeons' entrance was through the door in the east turret, above which you can still see the inscription 'Theatrum Anatomicum'. Here in their dissecting room they held their anatomy lectures, those famous annual occasions which Rembrandt commemorated in two guild portraits: *The Anatomy Lecture of Dr Nicolaes Tulp* (1632, Mauritshuis, The Hague) and *The Anatomy Lecture of Dr Jan Deyman* (1656, Rijksmuseum, Amsterdam). From 1932 until 1986 the Waag housed the Jewish Historical Museum.

Each Sunday in summer there is an antiques market in Nieuwmarkt, from 10.00 to 17.00. Cross to the south-east corner of the market-place and take a look inside the Metro station. Next to the escalator and down on the platforms are memorials to those parts of the old Jewish Quarter which were demolished to make way for the Metro. A demolition ball crunches into an old brick wall. Large photo-montages remind the traveller of the neighbourhood's past – from the old anatomy lectures at the Waag to the violent police evictions of 1975 that were the only way finally to make people leave their homes before they were pulled down.

It makes for an odd spectacle – the city berating itself in public for having resorted to terror methods, using tear-gas and water cannon to enforce its unpopular Nieuwmarkt Reconstruction Plan.

This plan tore an enormous hole through the ancient quarter, in which refugee Jews had made their home since the end of the sixteenth century. The district is bounded roughly by Nieuwmarkt, the Amstel and Nieuwe Herengracht, and the first group to arrive were the Sephardic Jews, from Spain and Portugal, who had fled north to escape the Inquisition. From 1620 a new and larger influx came to Amsterdam from Germany and eastern Europe – the Ashkenazic Jews. By 1900 some 60,000 Jews lived in this area, alongside about 40,000 non-Jews. Denied entry to traditional crafts and trades by the guild network, they established themselves in the fields of diamond cutting and polishing, sugar refining and tobacco products.

The German Occupation of 1940–45 destroyed Jewish culture in this quarter. It became a sealed ghetto, from which the inhabitants were steadily transported to the concentration camps. Of Amsterdam's 80,000 Jews, 70,000 were put to death, most of them at Auschwitz and Sobibor. After the war, the Jewish Quarter fell into decay, and remained that way until the radical redevelopment programme of the 1970s.

St Antoniesbreestraat was almost entirely renewed. The replacement buildings strike me as shoddy and graceless – cheap apartment blocks with nasty aluminium balcony-fences on the arcade side and spindly tiers of crow's nests on the other side, far inferior to the old gabled houses which have survived nearby at Nos 64 and 72.

At the corner with Snoekjesteeg, strong spicy smells billow from the open front of Willem van Eijk's Brood-Banket, selling buns, pastries, rolls, croissants, and apple and almond cakes. Across the road, take the little passage called Zuiderkerkhof which leads to the churchyard of Hendrick de Keyser's South Church, a masterpiece of Dutch Renaissance architecture built in 1603. The church building is now a centre for urban renewal; the tower is open 1 June to 15 October, Wednesday 14.00 to 17.00, Thursday and Friday 11.00 to 14.00, Saturday 11.00 to 16.00, and there is a carillon concert each Thursday between 12.00 and 13.00.

On the church wall a grim plaque reminds us that 'from February to August 1945 this church served as the municipal registry of deaths. In the last year of the war more people – the victims of hardship, hunger and German violence – died in Amsterdam than could be buried. Here was their temporary resting-place.'

Walk up to the stone gateway which leads through to St Antoniesbreestraat. Directly ahead is the finest building in the street, the De Pinto House at No.69. In 1680 it was the property of Isaac de Pinto, descended from a family of Portuguese Jews who fled Lisbon in 1492. He decided to convert the house into one of the most luxurious in the city, with fine painted ceilings and extravagant wrought ironwork on the window grills. It might well have been pulled down in 1975 along with the rest of the street, but was saved after an energetic campaign by conservationists. It is now a public library.

It is difficult to imagine the scene in 1975, but I have a photograph in front of me that offers a quite bizarre view of St Antoniesbreestraat. Taken from the tower of the South Church, it looks down on the De Pinto House which stands by itself in an otherwise flattened street. Facing it there is nothing at all, only pale earth and a few stones: it is like a wartime photo of a bombed city, after the rubble was cleared.

On the right of the photograph the long new warehouse building on Jodenbreestraat has appeared, and we now head in that direction. On the way, cross the bridge by the lock at St Antoniessluis. To the left is Oude Schans and de Keyser's Montelbaanstoren, one of the prettiest stretches of water in this part of the city. To the right the waterway is the Zwanenburgwal; on the quayside stands a line of clothes stalls, a tributary of the Waterlooplein market, the last rack of second-hand dresses almost touching the bridge. In the middle of the road, a truncated column mounted on the back of a marble turtle is a memorial to the old demolished quarter. The turtle represents Time, which has crept on, leaving hardly a stone of what formerly stood on these streets.

Rembrandt House Museum

The painter lived in the maroon-shuttered house at Nos 4–6 between 1639 and 1660. It was opened as a museum in 1911 and contains about 250 of his etchings, and drawings and paintings by his masters and pupils.

A helpful booklet (copies in English) explains the techniques of etching and describes a logical tour of the house from bottom to top. From the black-and-white tiled entrance hall turn into the Sydelcaemer to see three states of Rembrandt's etching *The Three Crosses* (1653), two of his *Christ presented to the People* (1655) and three portraits of 1647, including Jan Six (of the Six Collection, see also *Walk 10*). In a small second room, where an old press stands in the middle of the floor, step-by-step pictures illustrate the etching process.

In the Back Parlour (Agtercaemer) are self-portraits, including one with his wife, Saskia Uylenburgh (1636). The two versions of his 1651 portrait of Clement de Jongh, a print dealer and publisher, show the vastly increased depth between states I and V, as the etching needle, the drypoint, and the burin, an engraver's instrument, worked into the copper plate.

Upstairs to the Middle Room (Tussenkamer), where many of the artist's series of beggars and vagabonds are displayed – *The Barrel Organ Player, The Skater, The Rat-catcher, The Blind Fiddler* – all wonderfully expressive despite their tiny size. In another etching, numbered B174, Rembrandt portrayed himself as a beggar. Here too are self-portraits and a series of female nudes remarkable for their realism and at the time controversially received by critics who felt he had betrayed the ideals of beauty.

On the second floor, Rembrandt had his studio in the front room. The first of the rooms contains his famous biblical subjects, and the so-called *Hundred-guilder Print* which shows *Christ Healing the Sick*. Also here in a glass case is the *Piedra Gloriosa*, a mystical tract in Spanish with four etchings by Rembrandt. The tract describes the coming of the Messiah and was a source of inspiration to persecuted Sephardic Jews. Rembrandt evidently had a special affinity with the Jews living in this neighbourhood, and many local faces found their way into his biblical etchings.

J.D. Meijerplein

Cross Jodenbreestraat and follow the road that passes under the new building, the Nieuwe Uilenburgerstraat. At the beginning of the seventeenth century this was the poor quarter where large numbers of foreign immigrants settled, including many Ashkenazic Jews, in a maze of alleyways that spread across the neighbouring 'islands' of Uilenburg,

Marken and Rapenburg. No need to go very far, the most impressive building is just on the right: the huge Boas factory, built in 1879 to house a diamond-polishing works which at one time had more than 350 polishing machines and was a major employer of local Jews. Deserted for many years, it was recently taken over by the Gassan Diamond House who plan to restore it to a place of eminence among the diamond showplaces of Amsterdam.

Continue along Jodenbreestraat, in another age a busy Jewish shopping street, and find a way across the nightmarish traffic patterns of Mr Visserplein (named after a burgomaster sympathetic to the Jewish cause). The walled-up underpass is a sign of our disorderly times. Once offering the easiest and safest method of crossing the square, it was taken over by muggers and drug-addicts to such an extent that it had to be abandoned.

On the far side is the large central expanse of Jonas Daniël Meijerplein. On 22–23 February 1941 the German chief of police ordered a mass round-up of young Jewish men in retaliation for a mild piece of resistance a few days earlier in an ice-cream parlour. Four hundred and twenty-five Jews were arrested and brought here, then driven away. It is said that all of them later died in the concentration camps at Buchenwald and Mauthausen. On the 25th, the Dutch responded with a general strike. The 'Docker' (*Dokwerker*) monument in the square, by Mari Andriessen, commemorates the strike, and is remembered each year with a march-past. In recent years it also served to press the cause of Russian Jews unable to leave the USSR.

When the bridge over the Nieuwe Herengracht is raised, strange messages in mysterious script are revealed. Half-close your eyes and Dutch words appear. No one seems to know much about them – except that they are good for keeping frustrated motorists occupied.

Portuguese Synagogue

When the first Jewish refugees arrived in Amsterdam, they were obliged to worship discreetly in private houses. As conditions relaxed in the seventeenth century, thanks more to the economically motivated City Fathers than the Elders of the Protestant Church, it became possible to build synagogues. The present Portuguese Synagogue (or *Esnoga*) dates from 1671–75; balustraded in the style of a grand mansion, it was designed by Elias Bouman, who also built the De Pinto House (De Pinto was an Elder of the Synagogue).

To enter, walk round to Mr Visserplein and the low buildings which enclose the front courtyard. The door is kept locked, but rattle the handle or knock and it will be opened. In the synagogue, photographs are strictly forbidden. The devout community, which runs the affairs of the synagogue, took a stand about this because visitors were taking what they considered to be disrespectful pictures, using their place of worship as a background for snaps of people not properly dressed for the occasion. It was apparently a heated issue at the time, culminating in a choice between no pictures or no visitors.

The Portuguese community now numbers about six hundred, and they come from forty-five families. After the Second World War the Jewish population of Amsterdam was reduced to about 10,000; it is now 22,000 and rising, though scattered more widely than before. A video explains the history of the *Esnoga*, and details of the seventeenth-century interior which has remained intact, and there is always someone on hand to answer questions.

Jewish Historical Museum

This important museum occupies a complex consisting of four Ashkenazic synagogues, skilfully linked by a bridge and passageways. After the Second World War the synagogues were in a sorry state, and in 1954 the complex was sold to the City of Amsterdam. The Jewish Historical collection was meanwhile inadequately housed in two rooms at the Waag. In 1974 the decision was taken to transfer the museum to the synagogues on J.D. Meijerplein. The conversion of the old complex was brilliantly achieved, and the new museum opened in May 1987.

The route, indicated on the entry ticket, begins in the domed New Synagogue. This was the last of the four synagogues to be built. The display introduces the origins of Judaism and shows how the Jewish community settled in the Netherlands, achieving civil equality in 1796. It documents the war years from 1940 to 1945. In place of the Ark, destroyed in that period, hangs a large emotive painting by Hans Mes, *The Struggle between the Powers of Good and Evil, the Triumph of Justice*!

Continue through the Gallery, used for temporary exhibitions, to the

Obbene Sjoel, built above a ritual butcher's behind the Grand Synagogue. The latter is the oldest public synagogue in Western Europe, built in 1670–71. It was designed by Elias Bouman and the plan and elevation resemble Protestant churches of the day. As the Jewish community grew, so more synagogue space was needed; a third synagogue, the Dritt Sjoel, followed the Obbene Sjoel, and then the New Synagogue was added in 1752.

In the rooms and galleries you will find an impressive assembly of robes and ritual objects, paintings and photographs of everyday life in the Jewish Quarter, among the diamond workers and street traders. A famous local character in Vissteeg was 'Crafty Coba' the fish-seller, popular despite her reputation for blowing air through a straw into the fish to make them look plumper. A special exhibit traces Jewish life in Russia: the slow growth towards a new identity that was harshly suppressed after 1922 – 'smothered by new political dogma and socialist realism'.

Waterlooplein Market

On the way to the sprawling open-air market are two noteworthy buildings. In its present form the Mozes en Aäron Church is a Neo-Classical building of 1837–41, its wooden towers inspired by those of St Sulpice in Paris. It now serves as a youth club, but its origins go back to the seventeenth century, when, as a house on Jodenbreestraat, it was converted into a secret Roman Catholic church.

At right-angles to the Mozes en Aäronkerk, and closing the east side of Waterlooplein, is a fine old group of houses with two spout gables and a central trapezium-shaped gable with a balustrade; designed in 1610 by Willem de Keyser, they now house the Architectural Academy.

Walk down through the market stalls to the canal and take a break, weather permitting, on the breezy terrace of the Groot Mokum café. From here a panoramic view of your recent walk unfolds. From left to right above the market stalls are the tower of the South Church and the St Antoniessluis; behind the apartments ahead lies Jodenbreestraat, running along to the Mozes en Aäronkerk on the far right.

At ground level the market stalls offer unrelenting racks of second-hand blouses, shirts, jackets, jeans, a glut of stressed leather jackets, waistcoats and waiter's jackets; new socks (I hope they are new);

scarves, sunglasses, belts, trilby and baseball hats, and yet more jackets. A bookstall finally breaks the rhythm of this rambling museum of what Amsterdam used to wear – and still does, if you look at some of the customers wandering by.

Walk 8

Along the Amstel

Amsterdam is the Dam on the Amstel. Take a riverside stroll from Rokin to Muntplein, visit the Water Levels Exhibition and continue past the Skinny Bridge and the Sluices to the IJsbreker Café.

Allow   2–3 hours.

Best times   Not Sunday morning or Monday, when Allard Pierson Museum closed.

ROUTE

Begin at junction of Rokin and Spui. Trams 4, 9, 14, 16, 24, 25. At the equestrian statue of Queen Wilhelmina, cross to E bank of River Amstel and turn right into Oude Turfmarkt. At No.127 is the **Allard Pierson Museum** (Archaeology) ☜ ; open 10.00 to 17.00, Saturday, Sunday and holidays 13.00 to 17.00, closed Monday.

Continue along Oude Turfmarkt and cross bridge to Muntplein. Bear left into street called Amstel and follow river to Blauwbrug. Cross here and visit the **Water Levels Exhibition** in passageway between Stadhuis and Muziektheater, next to Metro entrance. Return to river.

Walk past Amstelhof on E bank. Continue past **Skinny Bridge** (Magere Brug) and Sluices to Theater Carré. At next bridge, Hogesluis, cross road and turn left and 1st right into Prof. Tulpplein and walk past entrance to Amstel Hotel. Follow pedestrian walkway under Toronto Bridge (Torontobrug) to Weesperzijde. **IJsbreker Café** is at No.23. Walk ends here. Nearest tram, No.3, crosses next bridge (Amstelbrug).

Alternatively, continue to Amstelbrug, cross to W bank and turn left along Amsteldijk to **City Archive (Gemeente Archief)**. Worth a visit if special exhibition showing; open 08.45 to 16.45, Saturday 09.00 to 12.15, closed Sunday. On far side of building, turn right into Tolstraat. **NINT Museum of Technology** is on right at No.129 ☜ ; open 10.00 to 17.00, on Saturday, Sunday and holidays 12.00 to 17.00. *Admission.*

Extended walk ends here. Nearest refreshments opposite at café of Cinetol Library, or continue along unenchanting Tolstraat and take Tram 4 back to city centre (Rembrandtplein, Muntplein, Dam). See also suggestions for 'Other Walks'.

At the River's End

The practice in this city of filling in waterways to make more roads has brought the Amstel to an abrupt end, divorced by a long stretch of concrete from the Dam that formed the original town of Aemstelle-damme. Strictly, this section is the Binnen Amstel, the inner river, a canal-like expanse contained within the city walls since late-medieval times, narrowed by quaysides as the needs of the merchants grew. Only beyond the Blauwbrug, two bends away, does the Amstel become its original self, a broad rolling river.

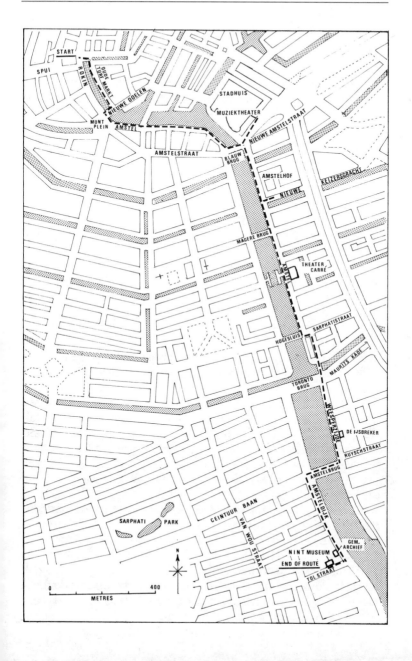

We begin at the equestrian statue of Queen Wilhelmina (1880–1962), grandmother of the present Queen Beatrix, who ruled this country through two world wars – though exiled in London from 1940 to 1945 – and finally abdicated in 1948 in favour of her daughter, Queen Juliana.

The more interesting side of the river is on the east bank along the Oude Turfmarkt, the old peat market. We turn past the sheds of the boat station and soon arrive outside a hulking Neo-Classical former bank, built in the 1860s and now the home of an archaeological museum.

Allard Pierson Museum

This is the archaeological collection of the University of Amsterdam. It is not the national museum, which is in Leyden (see *Walk 18*), but it contains an important collection of antiquities gathered from the sites of early Mediterranean cultures. The museum was founded in 1934 and moved here, into the old premises of the Netherlands National Bank, in 1976.

Collect an information sheet in Dutch and English and go up to the first floor. Rooms 1 to 4, devoted to Egypt, set the style of the museum with an eye-opening display of funerary objects: mummies, coffins, and objects from daily life buried with the dead which they might then make use of in the after-life – fishhooks, arrowheads, models of birds, cats, and crocodiles, and decorative seals and amulets. Around the walls are texts in Dutch and English, so identification is not a problem. (On the second floor, however, the texts are as yet mainly in Dutch.)

Continue through rooms covering the Near East, Cyprus, Crete and Mycenean Greece. The museum is particularly known for its Coptic collection, usually in Room 7, including Coptic clothes and artefacts from the sixth century AD. More than half the second floor is occupied by the Greek collection, with other rooms devoted to the Romans and the Etruscans. Look in, too, at the study collection – an impressive mass of vases, pots and shards.

Muntplein to Blauwbrug

The Oude Turfmarkt was the scene of a famous conservation battle in 1953, when the Nederlandse Bank's plans to develop the street, and demolish several historic houses, were thwarted by public opposition.

The houses in question, now departments of the University, include No.145, designed in 1642 by Philips Vingboons and featuring a three-tier pilaster façade and an elevated neck gable.

Across the road is the brisk department store of Vroom & Dreesman, and Hendrick de Keyser's Munttoren or Mint Tower (1619), originally part of a medieval city gate, the Regulierspoort. De Keyser added the elegant steeple with its octagonal lantern and openwork orb. Between 1672 and 1673 coins were minted here, and the name 'Mint Tower' has stuck.

Cross to this side and turn left into Amstel. On the far side is the opulent sweep of the Hotel de l'Europe, its waterside terrace and inviting basket chairs – the type that always make me think of waiters wearing gold or green epaulettes and carrying a silver tray. Look up the next canal, Kloveniersburgwal, to the pretty iron lifting bridge next to the Doelen Crest Hotel. The hotel stands where the old Civic Guards met for drill and arms practice. Rembrandt's *Night Watch* was first hung here, in the meeting hall of Captain Frans Banning Cocq and his company, also known as the Guards of the Kloveniersdoelen.

Across the river, which now begins to broaden out, is an attractive row of houses, including a black spout gable and a red-brick bell gable. Shifting right, the eye can no longer ignore the greatest blot on the Amsterdam cityscape: the glorified back-to-back, in bright orange-red brick and nerve-grating white marble, which houses the Muziektheater and the new Town Hall (Stadhuis). The buildings are the result of a municipal merger between two previously separate projects. Completed in 1986–87, they are much reviled and commonly known as

the 'Stopera', which was also the name of the unsuccessful campaign to prevent them being built. The Muziektheater is the home of the national opera and ballet companies.

We approach the monster. We do this only because it contains something we want to see. Our way to it lies across one of Amsterdam's favourite bridges, the stone and cast-iron Blauwbrug (1884), inspired by the flamboyant majesty of the Pont Alexandre III in Paris but carried out with rather more restraint. Look at the sculptures on the central piers – medieval boats with fish – and the lampholders in red Swedish granite, topped by the Imperial crown of Amsterdam in that unmistakable shade of custard-yellow.

Water Levels Exhibition

The above is not its proper name, but I cannot think of a better title. *They* call it the Amsterdam Ordnance Datum, which conveys absolutely nothing until it is explained.

It has to do with the country's special need to live on harmonious terms with the sea, the level of which is in many areas above that of the land, producing the odd statistic that some 60 per cent of today's population live below sea level.

To keep out the sea, the Netherlands are protected by more than 3,000km (1,864 miles) of dunes and dykes. The Amsterdam Ordnance Datum was established three hundred years ago to provide a common measure for all building projects. Its zero point corresponds with the average high watermark of the Zuider Zee, now the IJsselmeer, and is used internationally as a standard gauge for measuring altitude and water levels.

The exhibition is in the covered passage between the Muziektheater and the Town Hall, and was opened in 1988. There are three elements. The first and most obvious consists of three tall glass columns flanked by blue and white measuring rods. Two of these represent the current tide levels of the North Sea at IJmuiden (at the far end of the North Sea Canal) and Flushing (Vlissingen) in the south. The third column represents the level reached during the disastrous floods of 1953, when the waters surged 4.55m (15ft) above the zero point.

To see the zero point, go down the iron staircase next to the water columns. The bronze knob on the concrete pillar at the foot of the stairs marks the exact zero level. Stand next to it and half of you is below sea level. While you are down here, walk through to the next room in this basement section and you will find a series of stereoscopic views of land reclamation and dam-building projects.

Return upstairs to the passage and have a look at the third element, the cross-section relief on the wall. Seen from the north, it shows the country from the Zuider Zee on the left to the North Sea on the right, cross-cutting through city buildings, the airport and the Metro to demonstrate their relative altitudes. Look beneath the buildings and you can see that they are supported on rows of piles driven into the ground. In medieval times these were of wood and rested on the upper layer of sand. Today they are of concrete and reach down through the next layer of clay/peat to rest on a more solid lower sand layer.

The zero level runs across the country at the level of the sea and the tops of the canals. The jumbo jet pictured at the airport is 4.5m (15 ft) below sea level, and the Metro a good deal further down. Many of the buildings in East Amsterdam are also impressively low-lying, roughly 5.5m (18 ft) below sea level. It is a fascinating panorama and, if you are interested, you can buy an excellent poster entitled 'Nederland/ Waterland' in the nearby bookshop, the Stadsboekwinkel. This illustrates a similar cross-section, shows the changing shape of the country since 500 BC and explains how windmills were introduced to pump water out of land reclaimed from the sea.

Amstel to Weesperzijde

The second half of this walk is a gentle stroll along the river bank. Pause first on the far side of the Blauwbrug for a sight of the amazing grass boat, a sort of South Sea raft moored alongside the sturdy barge *Viktor IV*. At the next canal, the Nieuwe Herengracht, you may see an everyday feat of extraordinary seamanship as a barge captain swivels out of the main stream of the Amstel and, with no visible effort or reduction in speed, inserts the great vessel through the narrow canal opening, beneath the white lifting bridge.

Next comes the long frontage of the Amstelhof, a seventeenth-century old people's home (*Oude Mannen- en Vrouwenhuis*). Built in 1681–83 with thirty-one bays, it had the broadest frontage of any building in the city. On the far bank is a terrace of large mansions which includes, at No.128, the baroque home of the Six Collection (see *Walk 10*).

Upstream is the restored Skinny Bridge (Magerebrug), a cherished symbol of Amsterdam's maritime past, funnelling the river traffic through its central span. Along on the left, between the Skinny Bridge and the Sluices, is the Theater Carré. Originally designed as a circus building, in 1887, it is now a popular venue for big musical productions. Step inside the foyer and see what's on.

At the next bridge we must briefly dive inland to skirt the gigantic Amstel Hotel (1863–67) which, alas, looks somewhat dingy now, a vast acreage of pale yellow brick distinctly at odds with the braided flunkies who swarm around the main entrance in Prof. Tulpplein, levering their prosperous clientele in and out of taxis and limousines.

A sudden burst of graffitied concrete indicates our route beneath the Torontobrug, and after a few seconds in the subpontine murk we are delivered to the spacious gardens of Weesperzijde, flanked by grand waterfront houses.

At No.23 is the IJsbreker Café. Its mirrored turn-of-the-century feel has been diluted with modern additions, and fades off sharply to one side of the room. Along a corridor here resides the IJsbreker's *alter ego*, a contemporary music centre that puts on occasional concerts. Programmes are available in the café.

Our walk ends here. I considered battling on down the quayside to see the Berlage Bridge and return via Amstel Station. Try this by all means, though there is not a great deal to see on the way, and it means walking a good bit further.

Another option is to cross the next bridge, the Amstelbrug, and visit the step-gabled Neo-Renaissance building at No.66 Amsteldijk, crowned by an ornate steeple. This houses the City Archive (Gemeente Archief), which from time to time has special exhibitions on the history of Amsterdam. It is not a museum, but if you would like to look through their vast store of old photographs, someone at the desk will ask you to sign in and direct you upstairs to the photo-archive on the third floor. Here you refer to a key map on the wall to select an area of the city which interests you, then go to the numbered filing cabinets, wherein are hundreds of files of photographs, arranged in alphabetical order by street. Something, perhaps, for the specialist.

Others with a scientific bent – or with children in need of amusement

– may like to turn the next corner and visit the NINT Museum of Technology at 129 Tolstraat. It has neither the grandeur nor the artfulness of London's Science Museum, but there are many chances to press buttons and see things work. The exhibits cover a broad range of everything that I, for one, have never understood, beginning with the principles of physics and continuing with metals, how car and truck engines work, how houses are built, chemistry . . . Then upstairs to automation, microcomputers, light, energy and photography. Readers who do not share my bewilderment could well spend an enjoyable hour here.

Other Walks

If you have half a day to spend, several other walks are easily reached from here by tram. From Van Woustraat, take Tram 4 to Victorieplein (*Walk 6: Resistance Museum to Anne Frank House*). From Ceintuurbaan, take Tram 3 to Concertgebouw and begin *Walk 12: Modern Art and Vondelpark*. Or stay on Tram 3 to Haarlemmerpoort and spend the rest of the day in the Jordaan (*Walk 4*).

Walk 9

Botanical Gardens and Zoo

An exotic day out in the parklands of the inner city. Wander beneath towering ferns and palm trees, and admire the athletic swimming action of the polar bears. Visit the Hortus Botanicus and the Artis Zoo, and the progressive Tropenmuseum which documents life in Third World countries.

Allow All day.

Best times Any day except 1 January, 30 April, 5 May, 25 December, when Tropenmuseum closed. On Saturday and Sunday, Botanical Gardens not open until 11.00.

ROUTE

Begin at Plantage Parklaan. Trams 7, 9, 14. Walk to crossing of Plantage Parklaan and Plantage Middenlaan. At entrance gates to Wertheim Park, cross Plantage Middenlaan and bear right to **Botanical Gardens (Hortus Botanicus)** ☞ ; open 1 April to 30 September 09.00 to 17.00, on Saturday and Sunday 11.00 to 17.00; 1 October to 31 March 09.00 to 16.00, Saturday and Sunday open 11.00 to 16.00. *Admission*.

At exit, turn right and continue across Plantage Parklaan to next traffic lights. At 24 Plantage Middenlaan is a famous Jewish memorial to those who were deported, in the former auditorium of the **Hollandse Schouwburg theatre** ☞ ; open 10.00 to 16.00, Saturday, Sunday and holidays 13.00 to 16.00.

At exit, turn right and left into Plantage Kerklaan. Entrance to **Artis Zoo** (Natura Artis Magistra) is 80m on right ☞ ; open 09.00 to 17.00. *Admission*. Stroll through the grounds, with perhaps a lunch stop at the attractive lakeside restaurant/cafeteria. When it's time to leave, avoid doubling back to the front entrance by going out through the gate (marked *Uitgang*) next to the Aquarium (36 on the Zoo's plan) and a giant white model of a prehistoric reptile. This brings you on to Plantage Middenlaan. Turn left, cross bridge over canal and Sarphatistraat to old gateway, the Muiderpoort. Twin towers of **Tropenmuseum** are straight ahead. Entrance to museum is not at front but 100m round corner to left ☞ ; open 10.00 to 17.00, Saturday, Sunday and public holidays 12.00 to 17.00. *Admission, takes Museum Pass*.

At exit, turn right and take a stroll by the lake in Oosterpark. Walk ends either here (Trams 9,14) or after a visit to the street market in **Dapperstraat**. To get there, cross Linnaeusstraat and go along Eerste van Swindenstraat. From Monday to Saturday this general market buzzes with life, 10.00 to 16.00. Nearest refreshments all around, though cafés a little basic. Trams 6, 10 at N end market; turn right to the Pontanusstraat stop in Zeeburgerdijk.

Plantage District

In the eastern part of the city the canal girdle terminates in a spacious green suburb filled with parkland and large villas. The first green space we come to is Wertheim Park. Here on the corner of Plantage Parklaan and Plantage Middenlaan the entrance gates are guarded by two winged

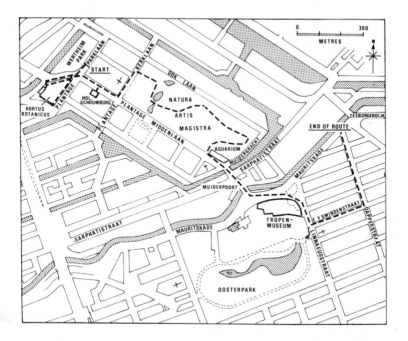

sphinxes wearing studied smiles and each balancing a heavy iron lantern on its head. Across the road is the long brick frontage of the Botanical Gardens (Hortus Botanicus).

Botanical Gardens

The entrance to the gardens is currently at the far end of the building. Great plans are afoot to build a 'new Hortus', but at the time of writing funds were two million guilders short and work could not begin. If and when it does, there will be a vast new complex with a water garden, greenhouses and restaurant. It seems an excellent project, particularly since some of the present greenhouses are suffering visibly from old age and decay.

As things stand, buy a ticket at the window, collect a brochure (in English, with plan) and wander the paths at will, stepping over hoses which are prone to snake suddenly in an unforeseen direction, tugged by invisible gardeners. The Hortus Botanicus was first of all a pleasure garden, laid out in 1682 for the benefit of people living in the Plantage district. It served also as a herb garden, used for growing medicinal herbs, and its greenhouses became an invaluable home for hundreds of 'new' exotic plants brought to Amsterdam by the merchantmen of the East India Company.

If you begin by turning left at the entrance, the way goes past a small round pond to the narrow footways of a neat hemispherical plot and on to a restful water garden in the corner. The main block to your left (B on plan) is named after Hugo de Vries, director of the Hortus from 1886 until 1918 and one of the most famous professors at the University, which took over responsibility for the gardens from 1877.

A rich supply of garden plants almost guarantees that something spectacular will be on view throughout the spring and summer months, and a noticeboard on the wall of the Orangery (M) lists the plants in flower. Two considerable and unfading attractions are the Indian House (G) and the Palm House (F), the latter containing a 400-year-old cycad (palm-fern) that is probably the oldest potted plant in the world.

In these huge glazed pavilions palm and rubber trees abound, a marvellous heritage of the Far Eastern expeditions. High upon a wall the luscious yellow blooms of *Allamanda Cathartica* glow in the warm damp atmosphere, surrounded by gigantic, jungle-high banyans. Enormous furry catkins poke fingers across the flagged pathways. In the Palm House, fabulous species rear up to the roof and great leafy fans spread everywhere; a Rousseau tiger would love it in here. On some plant labels the lettering has been worn away by an assiduous watering programme, but I can firmly recommend the erect spiky crown of *Lataria Contaroides*; the heavy gnarled trunk of *Cycadaceae Cycas rumphii*, strapped and tied to a steel girder; the swooping towers of *Strelitzia nicolai* and *Schroefpalm Pandanus furcatus* with its forked base, and the huge sweep of the oldest inhabitant, the cycaspalm mentioned earlier, and countless other bamboos, banana plants and cinnamon trees.

Close the door on all that fertile warmth and take the short path to the Tropical Houses and the spectacular lotus tank, but not alas the Propagation House which is closed to the public. Timing your dash through a garden sprinkler, head for the last cluster of buildings – the Fern House and the end-to-end Succulent Houses, and emerge by the Orangery, now a café with an outdoor terrace.

Hollandse Schouwburg

Many Jewish people lived in the Plantage district, and in September 1941 the Hollandse Schouwburg (Dutch Theatre) in Plantage Midden-laan was made over to the Jewish community as a place to perform their own plays before their own audiences. Persecution of the Jews in Amsterdam was already well advanced by then, and in June 1942 a new and horrific phase began. The theatre was turned into a transit centre for Jews on their way to Westerbork, from where trains carried them to the concentration camps at Auschwitz and Sobibor. As many as 50,000 Jewish prisoners passed through the theatre, waiting for days on end in cramped and sordid conditions. Straw mattresses were laid on the floor of the auditorium and iron racks set up in front of the stage for the prisoners' remnants of luggage. The coffee room became a sick bay and special 'S' prisoners (penal cases) were herded upstairs in the gallery.

After the war, the theatre was presented to the city on condition that a memorial chapel be built within its walls. It was decided to go further and turn the whole of the site into a memorial ground. Most of the building was in poor shape and was pulled down, preserving only the façade and the pieces of the old stage walls which now stand at the far end of a cloistered garden, formerly the auditorium. In the centre of the stage area a tall basalt column stands on a base in the form of the Star of David. On the wall behind it is an inscription: 'To the memory of those who were taken away from here.'

More impressive still is the small *chapelle ardente*, on the left of the front hall. An eternal flame burns in a bronze bracket. Nearby are three headstones, symbolising father, mother and child; the earth in which they are set was brought from Israel, together with a group of subtropical plants. The inscription on the wall, in Hebrew and Dutch, is from Psalm 119: 'My soul melteth for heaviness: strengthen thou me according to thy word.'

Artis Zoo

We move on to the largest park in the Plantage district, occupied by Natura Artis Magistra, or Amsterdam Zoo. A zoological garden has stood here since 1838, and very well stocked it is. They even have a planetarium, which, as the English handout indigestibly puts it, 'presents spectacular shows revealing the secrets of the universe that once gave birth to the world we live in'. Rather too much for me, I am afraid, especially before lunch. I resolve to concentrate on the zoo.

The guidebook is in Dutch only, but possibly worth getting if only for the coloured plan on the back cover which clearly shows where everything is. The animals, of course, are listed in Dutch too, but it should not strain your anyway fast-improving grasp of the language to work out what *olifanten* are, or *pelikanen* come to that, or *kangoeroes*.

Watoessis are not such a pushover, though you will not be shocked to find they are water buffaloes and, furthermore, live quietly in the same enclosure as a gang of *kamelen*, and another of *struisvogels*, or ostriches.

A digression about the ostrich. About two months after my first visit to the Zoo, I went for dinner one evening to a smart designer café in Overtoom. The waiter and I were running down the menu when we came to *Struisvogel*. 'What is that?' I asked, failing to link the word with the inhabitants of Enclosure 2 at the Zoo. 'It's a bird,' he said. 'It doesn't fly but it has long legs and runs very fast.' It seemed an unusual description for a dish on a restaurant menu, and I thought about it for a moment. 'Is it like an emu?' I asked. 'No,' he said, 'it's not an emu.' 'Oh,' I said, and tried again to picture my putative dinner moving rapidly along a jungle path somewhere in Africa. Stamping the earth with great horny feet, no doubt. Yes, I began to see it in my imagination, but at the same time the word 'ostrich' failed to form in my brain. What *was* it? Being hopelessly literal-minded, I had to be able to name it before I could order it. 'It's very nice,' added the waiter helpfully. 'Tastes like chicken.' 'It's no good,' I said at last. 'I can't think what it is. Give me the salmon.'

The restaurant at the Zoo is most pleasant: a new high-roofed conservatory, with pillars in cream-painted steel and a double terrace facing the flamingo pool. Next door, in the children's playground, the biggest queue has formed at the backside of a gigantic blue owl. When it is their turn, customers penetrate its interior by means of a ladder, and then helter-skelter down from its ears to its feet. Then infallibly, like clockwork toys, dash round the back for another turn.

Looking at my coloured plan, I was intrigued by No.49: an L-shaped building listed as *Broedmachine*. Mistaking *broed* for *brood*, I wondered why anyone should wish to hold bakery demonstrations in a zoo. I then realised that *broed* means 'brood', and No.49 is a breeding house, with indoor enclosures for the very young and larger outdoor pens for older, more mobile animals, most of which are aquatic birds. In one of these a brood of tiny razorbills, born sixteen days ago, huddled under lamps and waited for the strength to stand up and waddle into the shallow dip of water at the end of their enclosure. Currently the most mature birds were some slightly older Carolina ducks, already darting about quite fast on relatively huge webbed feet. Step inside the building, a wooden chalet, to see the real tinies: tottering about on fragile legs or just born the day before and snoozing in fluffy piles in one corner of their unit.

Stroll into the eastern section of the Zoo to find the llamas, zebras, antelopes and others; a shriek of macaws in military green plumage, housed next to a bunch of curly-horned moufflons; a very pretty red panda, cleaning its paws. At about this spot one day I became aware of an outbreak of harsh barking, then noticed that everyone was walking towards the sound. I followed. We arrived at the Malayan bears, but too late for the incident, whatever it was. All the bears looked irritated, far too long-haired for the hot July weather, and one of them was panting like a steam locomotive. What had he been up to?

Do make a point of striking out for the north-east corner of the park, to see the polar bears (*IJsbeeren*). On the way, enjoy a few minutes of nose-scratching calm in the gorilla house. The polar bears are full of variety and occasional vigour. While one basks on a rock, another is beating up a car tyre, jumping on it and thumping it, while another swims by himself in the pool. The bear swims beautifully, eyes closed, without effort. Looking down on him you see his great rear legs kick in a lazy breaststroke rhythm, his wet back sleek as a plaice's belly.

On the Zoo's colour plan, helpful umbrella symbols indicate several places where you can take shelter when it rains: with the gorillas, for instance, or in the palatial aquarium (36 on plan).

We exit through a gate next to the aquarium, on to Plantage Middenlaan, and turn left. This saves a considerable walk back through the main entrance. The aquarium stands at the south-eastern corner of the Zoo, next to a large white model of a rearing prehistoric reptile (one of a set made in 1953 by B. Bollee, Keeper of Reptiles).

Tropenmuseum

Walk to the bridge and cross the Muidergracht, its banks surprisingly overgrown, and keep straight on through the old gateway, the

Muiderpoort, a Classical domed structure of 1770 now serving as offices for the International Bureau of Fiscal Documentation. We want the building ahead, the Royal Tropical Institute, and in particular the ethnographical museum in the east wing.

The Tropenmuseum is laid out in a magnificent hall with a high glazed dome. On the main floor and in the surrounding galleries are some ten separate exhibitions illustrating daily life in Third World countries: in towns and villages in Africa, Latin America, Oceania, the Middle East and North Africa, Southern Asia and South East Asia. Other rooms are devoted to themes such as clothing, music, dance and technology.

On the main floor you may well find a large-scale special exhibition. A recent subject was the Yemen, dominated by an ambitious walk-in re-creation of a mud-walled souk or market-place. At the far end, turn right up the stairs to Southern Asia. On a wall a large photograph of Rajiv Gandhi says, in effect, 'Welcome' to an Indian city slum, a shanty town of timber, sacking and matting, an open-fronted corner shop selling sweets in glass jars and English cigarettes, onions and lentils weighed out on primitive iron scales. Look in at the grimly inadequate sleeping rooms and kitchens, and pass on to a life-size exposé of rural India: thatched huts, wooden carts outside, a primitive corn-grinder, a potter's workshop. Then a display on Hinduism.

The method is repeated around the galleries, and is extraordinarily persuasive. What the Western tourist may once have seen as quaint and picturesque (and some may still do so) – a lemonade seller's stall from Surinam, for instance, made with solid wooden wheels – is here a clear symbol of rural poverty.

It is a pity the museum is not better supported. When I go there I find more mannikins sitting it out in their desert tents than Western, or Eastern, spectators.

To Market

To take the weight off your feet, turn right at the exit and stroll into Oosterpark. Stretch out on the grass by the broad lake, where dogs bathe with gusto. Finally, but not on Sunday, walk through one of the broad side streets facing the park, such as Eerste van Swindenstraat, and at the next crossing mingle with the mild uproar of Dapperstraat market. Turn left between a double row of white canvas-roofed stalls conveying an atmosphere of medieval Europe tinged with tropical inserts. Among all the conventional fruit and vegetables, clothing, shoes and cleaning materials are specialists in cheese, seafood, pickles, prams and cots. In the morning the market is not fully in action before 10.00; after that time and until 16.00 it is well worth slipping down here if you need some more T-shirts, say, or an auxiliary pair of socks.

Local refreshment stops are not very distinguished-looking, but this is a plain working street unmarked by frills or boutiquerie. De Grote Plan, to the right on the corner of Commelinstraat, might be the best bet. Continue to the north end of the market and turn right to the nearest tram stop. Across the bridge ahead is the De Gooyer windmill (1814), no longer working but a handsome fixture on the eastern skyline.

Walk 10 ☂

Rijksmuseum and Six Collection

The Golden Age of Dutch art is the guiding theme of this walk. Explore the Dutch rooms in the Rijksmuseum, then browse among the antique shops of Nieuwe Spiegelstraat on your way to the excellent Six Collection, displayed in the former home of burgomaster Jan Six, friend and patron of Rembrandt.

Allow 5–6 hours.

Best times Tuesday to Friday, starting at 10.00. Six Collection closed Saturday, Sunday and public holidays, Rijksmuseum closed Monday. See also full opening times of Six Collection, below.

ROUTE

Begin at entrance to **Rijksmuseum** ☞. Trams 6, 7, 10; also 1, 2, 5 (Leidseplein) and 16, 24, 25 (Wetering Plantsoen). Buses 26, 65, 66. Museum open 10.00 to 17.00, Sunday and public holidays opens 13.00, closed Monday. *Admission, takes Museum Pass.*

Go upstairs to bookshop and information desk, and there ask for an invitation card to visit the Six Collection. Remember to take your passport.

Turn right to the *Night Watch* room (224) and then tour the other Dutch rooms, from No.223 down to No.201, which brings you back to the bookshop hall. See essay for suggested forays to other parts of museum.

At exit, cross Stadhouderskade and Museumbrug over Singelgracht to the **antiques quarter** in Spiegelgracht and Nieuwe Spiegelstraat. Continue past antique shops up to Keizersgracht and turn right. Keep straight on across Vijzelstraat, Reguliersgracht and Utrechtsestraat, crossing at some point to N side of canal.

At the River Amstel turn left. The **Six Collection** ☞ is at No.218. Ring the bell at the pavement-level door, marked 'Art Promotion Amsterdam'. Collection open Monday to Friday, 1 May to 30 October 10.00 to 12.00 and 14.00 to 16.00, 1 November to 30 April 10.00 to 12.00 only, closed Saturday, Sunday and public holidays. Guided tours last about 45 minutes, so in summer visitors should be there not later than 15.00, in winter not later than 11.00-11.15 – which gives you not much more than 40-45 minutes in the Rijksmuseum; rather a squash, but just possible. In summer, of course, you have between 10.00 and 16.00 to make your way round in proper, unhurried, Slow Walk tempo.

Walk ends here. For nearest refreshments, turn left to Amstelstraat and left to Rembrandtplein, where currently the best cafés are the Opéra and the Schiller. Trams 4, 9, 14.

Rijksmuseum

When built, in 1877–85, the steep roofs and pyramidal towers of the new national art museum were criticised for being too French. In place of Dutch Renaissance, the architect P.J.H. Cuypers had produced his own version of sixteenth-century transitional Gothic.

If the architect's own Catholic convictions, coupled with an admiration for the French Gothic Revivalist, Viollet-le-Duc, had

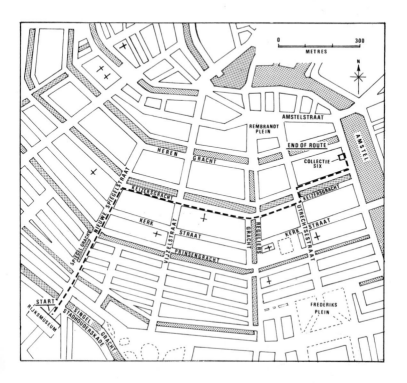

principally led him down this route, the museum does have other French origins. It was King Louis Napoleon, the French Emperor's brother, who in 1808 consolidated various collections in the Royal Palace to form a national museum. Later, as the donations and acquisitions grew, the museum was transferred to the Trippenhuis (see *Walk 2: Old Side*) where it remained until the new purpose-built museum on Stadhouderskade was completed. More recent demands for extra gallery space have been met by filling in the two central courtyards of the original building.

Go in at the entrance on the right-hand side of the tunnel and walk upstairs to the bookshop and information desk and ask for an invitation card to visit the Six Collection. A passport will be needed for proof of identity.

The Rijksmuseum is said to possess about seven million works of art, of which 5,000 are paintings. They range in time from the Middle Ages to the late nineteenth century. There is a huge amount to see, and to visit all the rooms is really more than can be done in a day. In any event, not all the rooms will be open. This museum suffers more than any other in Amsterdam from a long-running restriction on the number of staff it can employ, and many rooms are open for only half a day, either in the morning or afternoon. The rooms devoted to Dutch painting are kept open, but if you are frustrated in your efforts to see some other section the best thing to do is telephone the museum in the morning (73-21-21) and ask when that section will be open.

For this walk I propose a tour of Dutch painting in the seventeenth century, returning to the bookshop hall via Dutch art in the fifteenth and sixteenth centuries. After that, and before we set off across town for the Six Collection, I briefly describe three other routes through the Rijksmuseum. Between them they visit most of the other rooms, and you may like to come back to them another day.

Dutch Art in the Golden Age

Let's go straight to it, the Champion of the Rijksmuseum: Rembrandt's *Night Watch* (1642). Arrows point to it from the bookshop hall, and there at the far end of the Gallery of Honour it occupies a prime position, gazed upon by thousands each day. It is a very large canvas, measuring 359cm x 438cm (141in x 172in), and its full title is 'The Company of Captain Frans Banning Cocq and Lieutenant Willem van Ruijtenburch, known as "The Night Watch".'

The picture is a high peak in the art of the group portrait, far removed from the earlier 'team photo' method of lining up companies of civic guardsmen. In this treatment, one of six commissioned for the hall of a musketeers' practice range known as the Kloveniersdoelen, Rembrandt pulls his central figures forward. The captain, in black costume with red sash, orders his lieutenant, in dashing yellow, to let his civic guard march out. It is possible that a great occasion is being commemorated: scholars still argue about this, but there is a good case for associating the picture with the arrival in Amsterdam of Marie de Médicis, in September 1638, when this company was on duty at the Haarlemmer Gate.

Behind the officers, muskets and long arms criss-cross the

background, energising the picture space. The guardsmen take up lively positions, many of these based on illustrations in a drill manual, Jacques de Gheyn's *Manual of Arms*, which first appeared in 1608.

On the other walls of this gallery (Room 224) are other civic guard portraits, made for the Kloveniersdoelen by Van der Helst, Flinck and Von Sandrart, and which lack Rembrandt's dynamism. The room to the left contains documentation about the *Night Watch*. Here a copy of the original painting shows that it was even larger in its first form – approximately 440cm x 500cm (173in x 197in) – and was cut down, mainly on the left side, when it was removed in 1715 to a smaller wall in the Stadhuis (Town Hall).

Now turn back for a few moments to the head of the Gallery of Honour, the avenue leading to the *Night Watch*. Several illustrious Rembrandts are grouped here, but all too easy to miss. They include one of his famous anatomy pictures, *The Anatomy Lecture of Dr Jan Deyman* – the feet of the eviscerated subject poking forward at the viewer. Nearby are the *Self Portrait as the Apostle Paul* and the glowing *Jewish Bride*, one of Rembrandt's most moving works.

Our general direction is through Rooms 222 to 201, travelling in reverse order but remaining in the seventeenth century for much of the way. Moving among such riches, I must be very selective or this walk will turn out twice the length of any other. After Rembrandt my own favourite artists are Johannes Vermeer – his magically real *Kitchen Maid* and *Young Woman Reading a Letter*, and the exquisite *Little Street* – and Pieter Saenredam – his brilliantly composed church interiors. I find Frans Hals always stimulating, and derive much pleasure too from topographical paintings – old views of Amsterdam and Haarlem, painted by Gerrit Berckheyde and others. You will no doubt have your own preferences, and in the following paragraphs I will limit myself to noting some personal highlights.

Room 222 has a fine collection of Dutch interiors, including *Binnenhuis* by Pieter de Hooch, Van Brekelenkam's *The Tailor's Workshop* and Vermeer's *Kitchen Maid*. Continue to a group of maritime paintings, among them Jan van de Cappelle's brightly lit and microscopically detailed *The State Barge Saluted by the Home Fleet*. In Room 217 are Van de Velde's *Landscape with Family Group*, and 'social' portraits such as Adriaen van Ostade's *Fish-seller*, showing the fish-wife about to lay her knife on a plump member of the cod family.

Turn right into Room 218 where a glass case in the middle of the room contains an artist's box from the mid-seventeenth century. In Room 219 is Berckheyde's view of the *Bend in Herengracht at Nieuwe Spiegelstraat* (there is a smaller version in the Six Collection) and Jan van der Heyden's *Martelaarsgracht*. In Room 215 are some brilliant portraits: Bartholomeus van der Helst's benign *Andries Bicker* and the glaringly overweight *Gerard Bicker*, and his study of the pale and sickly *Princess Maria Henrietta Stuart* who gamely holds on to an orange. Ferdinand Bol, in *Portrait of Elisabeth Bas*, depicts a shrewd elderly lady who, though she has evidently seen much in her life, is inclined to be generous about most of it. Also here is Rembrandt's *Portrait of Maria Trip*, so full of light and depth.

Room 214 has marvellous works by Pieter Saenredam: the *St Bavo Church, Haarlem* and his *Town Hall, Amsterdam* – in which he wrote across the shop fronts, 'Pieter Saenredam first drew this from life in all its colours in the year 1641 and painted it in the year 1657'. In his *Interior of the St Odulphuskerk at Assendelft*, he is at his most geometrical, assembling an utterly satisfying construct of verticals and horizontals, subtle boxes of colour – cream and yellow walls and woodwork in biscuit brown.

Continue to Room 211, and more Rembrandts: *Joseph Telling His Dreams*, *Self Portrait at an Early Age*, *Portrait of Saskia van Uylenburgh*, *Rembrandt's Mother*, *The Holy Family*, *The Stone Bridge*. In the adjoining rooms (210-209) are works by Frans Hals. Here is his *Merry Drinker*, a clear-cut image but suggesting the fuzziness of the inner man through the erratic spikes of his moustache and beard, and the right hand that prepares to wave a greeting, or clutch at air. Here too are Hals's brilliant psychological studies of *Nicolaes Hasselaer* and *Sara Wolphaerts Van Diemen*. In Room 208 is the large civic guard group, by Hals and Pieter Coode, of *The Meagre Company*.

Look into the small circular room at the end (207), containing miniatures and very small paintings: Jan Brueghel I's pair of landscapes, no more than 15cm x 23cm (6in x 9in) but highly detailed and moody in greens and blues; Hendrick Avercamp's *Enjoying the Ice*, sure proof that golf began as *kolven*, a target game in which the players hit balls along the ice to a marker post; and the astonishingly precise, tiny oval *Portrait of a Woman*, attributed to Willem Duyster.

From here the route lies through the medieval rooms (204–201). A work that stops me in my tracks is the seven-panelled series by the Master of Alkmaar, *The Seven Works of Charity* (*c*.1500). Another painting of much charm is the Master of Brunswick's *The Birth*. These small galleries also contain works by Geertgen tot St Jans and the Master of the Virgo inter Virgines.

Other Rooms
Sculpture and Applied Art 12C–20C

At the far end of the bookshop hall, walk through Rooms 238 to 260, emerging finally in the *Night Watch* room. This tour begins with medieval religious objects, made of wood and stone for church furniture and decoration. You may also meet the attendant in here who fancies his singing voice and exploits the high vaulted ceiling with sudden Neo-Gregorian booms, interspersed with some curiously apt whistling. Sometimes he sits opposite a group of bronze tomb figures from Antwerp.

There are tapestries of lords and ladies at play, and in Room 243 look for the finely executed figures on an organ case from Utrecht. In Room 245, see the Saxon or Frankish polychrome and gilt groups of figures – *The Last Supper* and *Christ with Mary and Martha*. By Room 248 the number of secular objects has greatly increased, and thereby also the variety of things on view. Here, for example, are beautifully coloured Italian plates from the sixteenth century, made in Venice, Urbino, Faenza and other centres. The next rooms display Dutch furniture and tapestries from Brussels. Signs in Room 251 point right to the Treasury and left to Delftware.

The Treasury is nearby – a crowded display of jewellery, crystal and corporation silver. The Delft collection begins at Room 255 and is outstanding – marvellous blue and white plates and all manner of domestic objects made in Delftware, from a bird cage to a candelabrum. See the amazingly tall pair of nine-storey tulipholders, tapering like pagodas with holes for tulip stems at the corners of each layer. Go through to the cupboard-like space where the polychrome ware is exhibited, and look for more pieces in Room 257. In the next rooms are sculptures by Artus Quellien and furniture designed by Philips Vingboons for a mansion on the Singel. Finally, after the solid Dutch furniture of Rooms 259-260, look into Room 261, the display based on a

Chinese room assembled in Leeuwarden in the seventeenth century.

Dutch History

This section occupies the ground floor of the East wing. It is a mixed bag of rooms and the explanatory texts are in Dutch only. There are, however, some outstanding exhibits.

Begin at Room 101 – ancient and medieval periods – notable for some fine painted panels. Look for *Zielenvisserij* ('Soul Fishing'), by A. van de Venne, satirising religious quarrels during the Twelve Year Truce (1609–21). Rival boatloads of Catholic priests and Protestant clergymen compete for souls floating in the river.

Room 102, occupying one of the courtyards of the original building, purports to deal with everyday life, but really is a random collection of portraits, maps, weapons, cannon and ship models, and a fascinating view of a Dutch trading post in Bengal (1665). Further rooms study naval battles, naval heroes, statesmen, royalty and courtly life, and Dutch trading achievements in China and Japan.

Room 110 is devoted to a gigantic, rather staid painting of the *Battle of Waterloo*, by Willem Pieneman. Wellington, commanding the Anglo-Dutch forces, is in the centre with his officers, Lord Uxbridge prominent in hussar's uniform. On the left, the Prince of Orange is gently stretchered off, having been shot in the shoulder. Among other exhibits in the room are Napoleon's flintlock pistols and briefcase.

On the way out, at Room 114, see the bells from St Nicolaas Church, Utrecht (1550). These actually work, and the final wind-up of the mechanism is fascinating to watch. At four or five minutes to the hour, the big bell rings, and just before the half-hour the little bell takes its turn.

Meissen Figures and Dutch Painting 18C-19C

This extended trek through the western half of the ground floor came about because I wanted to see the Breitners, far away in Room 149. They turned out to be disappointingly dull and dingy. However, on the way to them and back, there is much to see.

From the West entrance, go along the vaulted passage to the back and through the door marked 'Sculpture & Applied Art'. Turn right and left past the chalices and candleholders (181), the snuff and other ornamental boxes (180) to tapestries, eighteenth-century furniture (179) and on via more tapestries to Room 175. Here is a large model of a canal house on the Herengracht. This is not the famous Dolls' House room, which we come to later (Room 162). Follow the numerical sequence down to Room 171 where – a highlight for me – you will find large Meissen birds made around 1730–50 in white and brilliant colours – pheasants, parrots and bitterns – and a Meissen monkey flanked by two French ducks on gilded bases. Also here and in Room 170 are delicate Meissen figures of lords and ladies, Harlequin and Columbine, 'Pagoda' figures and a *Temple of Venus*.

At Room 167, pass the magnificent red-gold grandfather clock and go down the steps and through to 'Painting 18–19C'. The way leads along a narrow gallery (135) to Room 136, dominated by a huge Cornelis Troost painting of the *Regents of the Almoners' Orphanage in Amsterdam*. Keep straight on to the rear landing, decorated with grey-green cabinets of Chinese porcelain, and turn left into Room 142. The Breitners are in the next room (149).

George Hendrick Breitner (1857–1923) was the leading Dutch Impressionist, and his views of Amsterdam are much reproduced. However, in his attempts to capture the Northern light of Amsterdam he worked within a narrow range of greys, browns and dull reds, which in his winter scenes especially make for gloomy viewing. In *Bridge over the Singel at Paleisstraat,* attention is daringly focused on the large foreground figure of the girl in the spotted veil, but alas she is too dark to fulfil her central role. His equally famous view of *The Damrak in Amsterdam* also seems unduly weighed down by blocks of dark colour. His *Young Girl in Kimono* is altogether brighter and, I think, more successful, executed in a more Manet-like style.

Other contemporaries to look for are Isaac Israëls (*Two Girls in the Snow* and the near-abstract shop-window of *Etalage*) and Jan Toorop (*The Sea*).

Return to the 'Chinese' landing through the parallel galleries of Rooms 147 to 144. Some fairly dull landscapes – Dutch painting certainly went into decline after the seventeenth century – are interspersed with brighter contributions from Matthijs Maris and Johannes Weissenbruch.

Asiatic Art

Downstairs from the 'Chinese' landing is a small set of rooms (12–23) devoted to the art of Indonesia, Japan, China and India. Some rooms are not numbered but the tour is simple and brief. In Room 16 see the marvellous T'ang tomb figures of camels and horses with riders. Other highlights are the bronze statue of the god Shiva (17) and the early Chinese ceramics and porcelain in the last rooms. An exit here leads to Hobbemastraat at the rear of the museum.

Dolls' Houses

On the way back from the 'Chinese' landing, go through the long gallery (135) and turn right at Room 166 to find the Dolls' House room (162). People of all ages clearly love these large and beautifully modelled houses – which were not made for children but to give adults an entertaining picture of patrician houses around 1700 – and queue to climb the step ladders and peek in at the upper storeys.

As an alternative to walking back the way we came, take the stairs from this room to the first floor. At the top, turn right and you are in the *Night Watch* room. At the far end of the Gallery of Honour are books, postcards and souvenirs. If you must have a Rijksmuseum T-shirt, now is the moment. The range of postcards is thinner than it should be.

For the record, I have omitted the following rooms: Foreign Artists (Room 225); Applied Art 18C–20C (Rooms 24–35); Prints and Drawings (Rooms 128–133).

Spiegel Quarter

The antiques quarter was founded close to the Rijksmuseum by dealers quick to see the potential in waylaying art lovers on the road from the city centre to the museum. Today the streets of Spiegelgracht and Nieuwe Spiegelstraat have the highest concentration of antique shops of any city in the world. Paintings, ceramics, furniture, glass, jewellery, old books, prints and coins – some dealers specialise and some offer large mixed collections.

If refreshment is needed after your exertions in the Rijksmuseum, look no further than the Café Hans en Grietje at No.27 Spiegelgracht: a light and airy bar and back room decorated all over with posters, even on the ceiling. Antiques begin next door at Old Prints (very reasonable for a small souvenir), then furniture and lush décor at Stodel and A. van Veen, followed by Oriental art and ethnographical finds at Aalderink.

I enjoy nosing about here. Even when I am not looking for something, it is fun to speculate, choosing which improbable object I would spirit home if someone else were buying. Would it be a high-backed white garden seat, decorated with a Maximilian crown and the triple-cross shield of Amsterdam; a two-foot high Madonna and Child in polychrome wood; or an antique clock at Stender? The story they love to broadcast here is that many a local collector bought his first antique in the Spiegel Quarter – and was hooked. The range of pieces supports the claim, even though the lack of prices in many shops hints at a need for deep pockets to join the game. However, an antique bird cage with a painted wooden songbird on the perch may not be out of reach, or a handful of stylish old wine glasses.

We break away from further temptation at Keizersgracht, and after crossing busy Vijzelstraat walk along past the Van Loon Museum (see *Walk 11*). Then cross the steep bridge over pretty Reguliersgracht; away on the left stands the green figure of the statesman Thorbecke, framed by trees. On the corner opposite, the houses lean at an extravagant angle. Along here one day a firm of caterers had just erected a gigantic tent spanning two barges moored side by side in the canal. Tables for five were being urged into place beneath the orange and white striped canopy – a grand floating party for two hundred guests was on the way, in the most delightful venue anyone could wish for.

After Utrechtsestraat we are nearly there. Cross to the north side and turn left at the River Amstel. Sound the bell of the baroque brick house at No.218 and begin looking for your invitation card.

Six Collection

This treasure-house of Dutch art is still owned by the Six family, who as Huguenot refugees quit France and settled in Amsterdam in the early seventeenth century. They moved to this house in 1915. The tour covers only the first floor, or *bel étage*, and is strictly controlled. Visitors are not allowed to wander away from the guide, who ushers you round with good humour and courtesy.

Most prized of the paintings is Rembrandt's portrait of *Jan Six*, the burgomaster and collector, which hangs in the Front Living Room. It was an experimental picture, not commissioned but done to repay a debt. The two men were friends, though after Six had lent Rembrandt a considerable amount of money, which he did not see again, bad feeling developed between them. The face of Jan Six is caught in a reflective mood, perhaps to show the inner calm of the man, while the coat and the hands are painted in a sketchy, impressionistic manner, suggesting an outward bravura closer to Six's public image.

All the portraits in the house are of immediate family or are traceable to more distant branches. They include Rembrandt's portrait of *Anna Wijmer*, Six's mother, and Frans Hals's portrait of *Dr Tulp*, who married into the family. More recent portraits include *Jan Six VIII*, painted in 1943. (To complete the story of the lineage, Jan Six IX died in 1989, and Messrs X and XI moved into the house towards the end of the year.)

Of the other first-rate paintings, there are two Ter Borch miniatures in the Front Living Room, and, in the Back Hall, where business meetings were held, Pieter Saenredam's interior of the *Buurkerk in Utrecht*. At one time the Six Collection also possessed Vermeer's *Kitchen Maid*, which it sold to the Rijksmuseum.

Many other treasures will catch the eye: a delicate folding writing table, the fan-shaped brooch worn by a sitter in one of the family portraits, Roman glass, coconut cups and pineapple and berry glasses – even, on a more everyday level, a brass-footed pole used for lowering a bucket into the canal to collect water for washing the front steps.

On leaving, sign the visitors' book. A quill pen is provided.

In search of refreshment, return to Keizersgracht and try your luck in Utrechtsestraat – the Club Café Bonjour on the corner, for example – or continue along Amstel then Amstelstraat to Rembrandtplein, and let the Opéra or Café Schiller look after your needs.

Walk 11

Rembrandtplein to Leidseplein

Two popular squares for café and night life. Visit also the Thorbeckeplein, the Fodor Museum (modern art), the Van Loon Museum, the Floating Flower Market, the top-floor café at Metz & Co for splendid all-round views, and wander down Leidsestraat, the street where Amsterdammers say you can buy everything you don't want.

Allow 4–5 hours.

Best times Not Sunday or Monday morning, when Metz & Co closed. Museum Van Loon, opposite Fodor Museum, is a fine 17–18C canal-house but is open only on Monday, 10.00 to 17.00; perhaps worth a separate visit.

ROUTE

Begin at **Rembrandtplein**. Trams 4, 9, 14. Walk round square past gardens and statue of the artist. At SW corner, enter Thorbeckeplein and walk down past row of oddly comical nightclubs to statue of the statesman, overlooking Herengracht.

Return to Rembrandtplein and at NW corner turn left into Reguliers-breestraat. See Amsterdam's most famous cinema, the **Theater Tuschinski** at No.26, an Art Deco treasure; open from 14.00. Browse for domestic bargains at Hema – anything from socks to cheese-slicers – and walk up to Muntplein. See the old **Mint Tower** and walk S to Vijzelstraat. On the right-hand side is the Carlton Hotel, an impressive Rutgers building (1926).

Cross the Herengracht, walk to the Keizersgracht and turn left. At No.609 visit the **Fodor Museum** ☞; open 11.00 to 17.00. *Admission, takes Museum Pass*. If a Monday, visit **Museum Van Loon** on opposite side of canal at No.672 ☞; open 10.00 to 17.00. Ring bell. *Admission*.

Return along Vijzelstraat to Muntplein and turn left along Singel beside the **Floating Flower Market**. At next bridge turn left to Koningsplein, and cross the Herengracht to Leidsestraat. Walk along to Leidseplein, looking at shops. Specially recommended: a visit to **Metz & Co**, 455 Keizersgracht. Take the lift to their 6th-floor café-restaurant for views to all parts of Amsterdam.

Walk ends in **Leidseplein**. Nearest refreshments all around, though the first choice of many would be the Art Nouveau/Jugendstil café of the American Hotel; see essay for other suggestions. Trams 1, 2, 5, 6, 7, 10.

Rembrandtplein

This square has two contradictory images, passed down through generations of picture books and tourist brochures. One image portrays a quiet intimate, leafy park in which students and street philosophers gather on the grass in front of the Rembrandt statue, framed by hedges and shrubs. The other image is of a brash and noisy piazza, a night-life centre nearly on a par with Leidseplein and the Red Light district. But how can it be both?

It seems to be a question of focus:, of what the photographer leaves

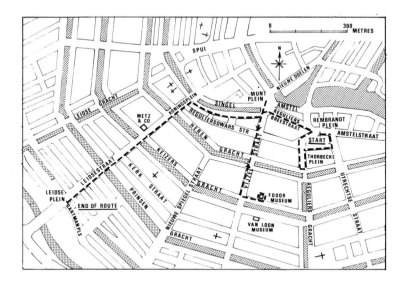

out. If, somehow, you arrived with your camera on the roof of the Amsterdam-Rotterdam Bank, on the east side of the square, you could then take two very different pictures: the peaceful inner garden, and a full panorama showing the garden surrounded by café terraces, trams, snack and souvenir stalls, and buildings debased by screaming signboards.

There is a historical explanation. The square was the medieval butter market, a popular venue for travelling fairs. The butter market ceased in the middle of the nineteenth century and a small park was laid out in the square, its centrepiece Royer's statue of the painter, completed in 1847. Since then, two distinct squares have lived amiably together, one inside the other.

I find Rembrandtplein a rather cheerless place. Thousands, however, use it for their daily rendezvous, to drink coffee and beer, eat pizzas at Pinocchio and ribs at the New Orleans Ribhouse. Best of the cafés are l'Opéra and Café Schiller, the latter a vaguely tropical tearoom fronting the foyer of the Hotel Schiller, which is decorated with stained glass and dark portraits and views of Amsterdam painted by Frits Schiller, who formerly owned the café.

Thorbeckeplein

A circumnavigation of Rembrandtplein brings you eventually to Thorbeckeplein, a smaller rectangular space with a handsome outlook over the Herengracht at the far end. Here the statue of Johan Rudolf Thorbecke (1798–1872), a Liberal statesman and three-times prime minister, faces away from the topless bars and striptease clubs which have taken over the square.

These clubs do not attempt, in general, to match the obscenity of those in the Red Light district. They are middle-ranking titillators, operating at a Folies Bergère level in terms of skin revealed and acts performed. A fresh-faced quartet called Rambo, top-hatted and mesh-stockinged, seem nice girls really – typists from Osterley, perhaps. Another artiste, Tamara, is an exotic dancer of the old school, vampish like Theda Bara. Watch out, though, for mercenary bar-girls who say: 'But I *only* drink champagne.'

Perhaps the nastiest thing about Thorbeckeplein is the repertoire of cocktails at Mister Coco's English Pub – a frightful list offering the likes of 'Orgasm', 'B-52' and 'Chemical Warfare'. (My nearly grown-up daughters tell me there is nothing at all unusual about this style of naming explosive drinks.)

On Sunday afternoon, between 12.00 and 18.00, an art market occupies the middle of the Thorbeckeplein. It has some of the simplistic attractions of all art markets that are mostly geared to the passing tourist – flower paintings, jewellery, glittery toques *à la* Twenties, portraits in twenty minutes. Elsewhere, though, are pieces of a higher standard. The potter with his open-air kiln turns out neat small bowls and amusing figurines. A sculptor sells Bosch-like images in steel, with evocative titles like 'The Man Upstairs' and 'The Devil Shaking Hands with the Angel'. You may even find a spiky little pen and ink sketch of Amsterdam that you like, and for a very reasonable price.

A Cinema with a Difference

Reguliersbreestraat is the narrow thoroughfare joining Rembrandtplein and Muntplein. It mixes amusement arcade fun with sex cinemas and the calming domesticity of Hema, and contains one of the most outstanding pieces of architecture in Amsterdam. This is the Theater Tuschinski, an Art Deco cinema built in 1918–21, now owned by Cannon who run it as a six-screen complex.

It is a twin-domed palace of escapism, the soaring verticals of the frontage decorated with schematic friezes, metal flagstaffs, stained glass, curly iron lamps and four downward-pointing alligators which guard the bronze side doors. To see beyond the front lobby you need a cinema ticket. The cinema opens at 14.00, and the room to see is Tuschinski 1, where they show their biggest film of the week. Ask for a seat in the balcony, where spectators sit in a steeply-raked set of desk-like tiers and look out over the whole marvellous extravaganza. At the Tuschinski, the intervals are just as good as the movies.

Along the road is Hema, the Dutch Woolworths/Prisunic. Browse here for high-street bargains: *Herensokken, Kindersokjes, Dames-mode, Be'has, Wekkers.* * At the back they sell bread, wine, cheese, delicatessen and good Dutch biscuits (*Koekjes, Zoutjes* = sweet and cocktail biscuits). Downstairs to household goods – kitchenware, gadgets, tools, paints and stationery.

Muntplein

On the whole a discouraging place for pedestrians, the Muntplein is given over almost entirely to trams and other traffic which converge here from eight points of the compass. De Keyser's Mint Tower (1619) is the centrepiece. He added the elegant steeple and openwork orb to the top of a medieval city-gate. When the French occupied Utrecht in 1672 and 1673, this building became the Dutch mint. The base of the tower now contains a change shop and a china shop whose repertoire includes kitsch model canal houses – the handiwork of Jean-Pierre Gault who has done the same for houses and 'typical' streets of Paris and the French provinces; if anything, the Dutch versions are even more gooey and sentimental than the French.

The square contains other noteworthy buildings. H.P. Berlage's balustraded castle at No.2 (1895/1911) is seen as a worthy predecessor to his famous Stock Exchange (Berlagebeurs, see *Walk 1*), but modern advertising signs and out-of-tune shopfronts make it difficult to appreciate the dignity of the original. Look at the arcaded Carlton Hotel (1926) at the top of Vijzelstraat, by G.J. Rutgers – a great ship of a building just recovered from a heavy refit.

*Men's socks, little socks for children, ladies' fashions, bras (short for *Bustehouder*), alarm clocks.

Detour – for Art's Sake

We turn down Vijzelstraat, along the length of the Carlton Hotel and then beside the enormous Nederlandse Handelmaatschappij (1919–26) by K.P.C. de Bazel. Between them, these two buildings occupy the best part of two blocks, and the latter, now the ABN bank building, was especially criticised when it went up for dwarfing adjacent canal houses. Its variegated brick and stone give it an unusual freckled appearance, and the staggered façade keeps the eye interested; even so, the final verdict must be that it is far too big.

Fodor Museum

The sandstone house at No. 609 Keizersgracht was built in 1861–63 and converted into an art gallery for the collector C.J. Fodor. As a gallery building it is excellent: white and full of light, which on the ground floor flows through a glass wall on the garden front. Upstairs are three large white rooms, also ideal for showing the contemporary art in which the museum specialises.

This is the gallery to see work by the latest generation of Amsterdam artists. Exhibitions change regularly, and international exchanges are also arranged. Check *Uitkrant* for details.

Taller Foundation

Next door to the Fodor Museum, at No. 607 Keizersgracht, is an avant-garde arts foundation. The word Taller means 'workshop' in Spanish, and the foundation began life in Montevideo, Uruguay in 1963, launched by Armando Bergallo and Hector Vilche. It transferred to Amsterdam and specialises in art shows and musical theatre productions. In the main downstairs room is a permanent exhibition of paintings, sculptures and models by members of the Taller group.

You are welcome to look round, and maybe ask at the desk about forthcoming projects. In the garden are several polychrome works by Bergallo, including a fiery *Angel* (1985) and a white *Pietà* (1986) streaked with brilliant acrylic colours.

Van Loon Museum

If it is Monday, cross the canal to the first of a pair of severely beautiful grey stone houses designed by Adriaan Dortsman and built in 1671–72, soon after the city's three great concentric canals – the *Grachtengordel* – were laid out.

The painter Ferdinand Bol was the first tenant. Complaining that he was paying rent for a stable block which had not been built, he sued the owner, Jeremias van Raey. Van Raey shortly went bankrupt, and for two hundred years the house passed through a series of owners who suffered either from severe lack of money or domestic misery. In 1884, after another bankruptcy scandal, the house was bought by Hendrik van Loon and it is now owned by the Van Loon Foundation. Between 1964 and 1973 the house was restored as closely as possible to its state in the late eighteenth to early nineteenth century.

It is one of the finest canal houses to which the public have access. A sympathetic air of faded grandeur prevails, spiced by hints of dubious commercial activity. The Van Loons are an old and powerful Dutch family, and the Foundation possesses a remarkable collection of more than fifty family portraits. In the front hall are paintings of Willem van Loon and his wife. In 1602 he was one of the co-founders of the Dutch East India Company, and the family coat of arms features three 'blackamoor' heads, usually taken to be the emblem of a successful slave trader.

In the Dining Room to the left of the hall, two tables for four are laid for dinner with eighteenth-century Amstel porcelain, huge tureens at the ready. A fake door in the panelling hides a dumb waiter. Portraits decorate the walls, as they do in the Drawing Room, the Red Room and the Garden Room. This charming room has peacock-patterned wall panels and tall curved double doors to the garden. In the Staircase Hall, look for the family names Van Hagen and Trip ornately worked into the copper balustrade. Under the occupation of Dr Abraham van Hagen and the heiress Catharina Trip, between 1752 and 1771 (though she died after five years), the house was almost completely redecorated.

Go up to the landing and visit the most spectacular rooms in the house. The 'Sheep' Bedroom has fine wall hangings with sheep discreetly placed in groups beneath trees, and among foliage and tropical flowers; the hangings were printed in Nîmes, France, from eighteenth-century blocks. The bed and chairs are Portuguese, also eighteenth-century, and said to have been made for a bishop. The hangings in the 'Bird' Bedroom are also from Nîmes, and picture exotic birds and monkeys. The room has a 'blue' marble fireplace and was once a library. Look for brass keyholes in the walls, in reality hinged panels behind which the books were stored. Among the large portraits is one of Louise Borski, wife of Hendrik van Loon Snr (1831–1901); nearby stands the green velvet dress she wore for the sitting.

The Painted Room is named after the panoramic wall paintings – Italian views on a grey-green background – which were brought to the house in 1970 from a castle in Drakestein owned by the Sander family, who lived here in the eighteenth century. To accommodate the panels, doors had to be cut into them. Hendrik Sander was responsible for the Corinthian columns in the Master Bedroom, decorated in 1771–76, and it is his monogram which appears on the fireplace, above the door and on the ceiling.

Go out finally to the garden, negotiating the ornamental hedges, and look at the extraordinary coach-house at the far end, dressed up as a Neo-Classical temple.

Floating Flower Market

Back at Muntplein, turn left into that perennial attraction, the line of stalls projecting over the Singel canal that makes up the Floating Flower Market. Wonderful, enticing displays of cut flowers, sprays, dried flowers in buckets and bouquets hanging from the walls. The whole country is, of course, mad about flowers, and a regular sight of any Dutch afternoon is that of a girl – not always a girl, but usually – cycling home with a bunch of flowers laid across the handlebars.

If you go to the bulbfields between April and May, you are soon reminded that the flowers dearest to Dutch hearts are daffodils, tulips and hyacinths. Here in the floating market you will surely find them too, and just about everything else – tubers, seeds, trays of gigantic Superamaryllis, shrubs and hedges already given the topiary treatment, palm trees, dwarf conifers for rock gardens and balconies, banked-up trays of petunias, geraniums, pansies, African marigolds, dahlias. A sign advertises: 'Bulbs with Health Certificates!' This does not mean that other bulbs are unhealthy, only that visitors planning to export Dutch bulbs may need to produce an official certificate before they can import them into their own country.

Leidsestraat

At the next bridge, we veer left and follow the tramlines through Koningsplein, across Herengracht and into the narrow head of Leidsestraat. This is the more elegant half of a shopping thoroughfare that runs down to Leidseplein. The fact that it has no pavements should not delude pedestrians into thinking they have the place to themselves, apart from the odd tram. Not at all. The road space here is continually fought over by trams, bicycles, scooters, delivery vans, taxis, stray cars which have no business there, and by the dawdling regiments of shoppers and visitors who throng it from breakfast to sundown.

The shops here deal in middle-of-the-road goods of the Laura Ashley-Athena Gallery-souvenirs genre. A cut above these is Metz & Co, on the corner of Keizersgracht: a high-quality furniture store with a café-restaurant offering some of the best all-round views of the city. Press '6' in the lift and rise immediately to the penthouse: split-level, lavender walls, pink columns, pale grey carpet. Sit by a window on a very thin-legged chair at a thin grey-white marble-topped table. Try the InterMetzo, a post-Modernist snack of tiny 'English' sandwiches of smoked salmon, gorgonzola and chicken, plus three wee cakes and two chocolate pastilles topped with white dragées. The whole lot goes down in about twenty seconds.

Or look for something bigger. Being a Dutch house, they have all the bulky dishes too: from the menu it is impossible to distinguish the hearty fare from the emaciated, though you should be safe with a Tournedos, Veal piccata or InterMetzo burger.

But we have come to see the view. There are four choices of aspect, the better ones looking north-west over the red-roofed houses of the *Grachtengordel* to Westerkerk and the Jordaan; and south-west along the line of Leidsestraat to the tower of the American Hotel, and across to the blue-tiled roof of the Rijksmuseum. Look down to the tram stop on the bridge and see the elegant long roof shape of the trams themselves, gliding like narrow barges through the scene. And see the automatic artistry of the cyclists, twitching their front wheels to bisect the tramlines at a safe angle.

Walk down the stairs to visit the furniture departments on the lower floors: the clean lines of elegant couches, chairs, furniture for home and office, fabrics and linens, gifts and oddments on the ground floor, glass, porcelain and kitchenware in the small, brick-arched rooms of the basement.

Out on the ornately railed bridge (Piet Kramer, 1921), look back at the Metz building. It was erected in 1891 for the New York Life Insurance Company in a baroque-Classical style, and faced with caryatids. The dome by Gerrit Rietveld was added in 1933, and the café-restaurant, almost brand-new, opened in 1986.

Moving along Leidsestraat, look out for the Berkhoff Tea Room which sells delicious biscuits and chocolates. Make up your own selection from seductive trays of *Aardbeien canach, Wodka Rhum canach, Mokka Melk*, etc. Next door, fine cheeses and delicatessen at Eichholt.

On the other side of Prinsengracht, the canopied windows of Dikker & Thijs announce a famous delicatessen with adjoining brasserie. Several bookshops along here: on the right, Moderne Boekhandel is both spacious and well-stocked.

You will also come across a number of shops selling Delft china. Or is it Delft? The distinction is actually quite simple: real Delft is expensive, in the order of Fl 400–600 for a dinner plate. Souvenir shops are therefore not selling Delft but what is sometimes known as 'Taiwan Delft'. Some of it is pretty, and people buy it for the design and the colour. Look closely, and the quality of the painting gives the game away.

Since 1854, only one factory in Delft is authorised to make authentic Delftware: the Royal Delft Ware Manufactory. If you buy one of their pieces, it should be accompanied by a certificate which includes a reproduction of the mark that every genuine item must carry.

The approach to Leidseplein is crossed by two streets famous for cheap and middle-range restaurants: Lange Leidse Dwarsstraat and Korte Leidse Dwarsstraat. They are very tourist-minded, predominantly Italian, Greek, Chinese and Indonesian, but good value if you are on a pizza-and-ice-cream budget.

On the right, at No.64 Lange Leidse Dwarsstraat, is the Bamboo Bar, the most agreeable jazz bar in Amsterdam, open every night of the week with live modern jazz from 22.00 to 02.00, and drinks at ordinary bar prices. The house band is the excellent Rinus Groeneveld Quartet; catch them mainly on Thursday. Check *What's On* for details of other performers, though the band advertised may not be the band on the stand, man.

Leidseplein

The second of the cross-streets, Korte Leidse Dwarsstraat, runs across the top of Leidseplein which is not so much a square as a rambling open space extending to the Singelgracht and sprinkled with various attractions. The two most interesting buildings are the Stadsschouwburg and the American Hotel.

The Stadsschouwburg (Municipal Theatre) is the huge 1894 porticoed red-brick pile on the right. Popular more by virtue of what goes on inside, the theatre has a quick-changing programme of plays from Shakespeare to Dylan Thomas, opera, ballet, or a night with the Dutch Swing College Band. Look in *What's On* for details or, for a fuller outline, walk to the far corner of the theatre building and pick up a copy of *Uitkrant*, the monthly listings paper, from the AUB office and ticket shop.

Across Marnixstraat is one of the finest turn-of-the-century buildings in Amsterdam. The American Hotel was designed by Willem Kromhout and built in 1898–1901. An utterly confident Northern *castello* with a corner tower, broad arches spanning the lower storeys and a recessed upper block ascending vertically into five attic windows, it stands historically in glorious isolation somewhere between Art Nouveau and the Amsterdam School. Inside, the café-restaurant, with Art Deco additions, is a popular and stylish meeting-place. Service may be on the slow side but there is always plenty to look at: the leaded windows with brilliant tropical birds and medieval figures; the long newspaper table lit by brass lamps, more like a library than a café; Art Deco lights suspended from the vaulted ceiling – inverted parasols of glass patterned in creamy amber colours. Highly recommended.

The Leidseplein, above all else, is famous for its café and night life. The active night life happens in the surrounding streets – in discos and cinemas, at rock shows and other events at the Paradiso and the Melkweg, and in jolly drinking establishments like the Bastille Bar, where the footballers and basketball players go.

The square itself is more passive, though always crowded. As an assembly and departure point – served by six tram routes and a taxi rank – it swarms with life all day until three in the morning. Each evening hundreds gather in the cafés of what is now called the Piazza Marco van Basten, in tribute to the heavy-scoring Dutch striker. Of these, the best is Reijnders, a classic brown bar with a dark wood interior and a billiard table. Further along this row, beyond the piazza, is another good bar – Eijlders, similarly brown, entered through a covered terrace and filled at night with a large and faithful clientele. In winter the piazza becomes an artificial ice rink. Skates are for hire and all may have a go, including children who get their own afternoon spot. For hockey buffs, the local game is less than deadly, played with brooms instead of sticks.

At other times of the year, not much happens in the piazza, beyond meeting, talking and drinking. That is where the buskers come in. They feel you should be entertained, and have not allowed a generally outstanding lack of talent to hold them back. One of the most audaciously bad performers is someone I will call the Jolly Bagman. This bearded middle-aged ruffian wears a knotted scarf on his head, a matelot's smock and long orange shorts. He can't sing, can't play, can't dance, and his act consists of doing all three, jigging about to unmelodic bursts on a harmonica, shouting indecipherable words and cracking up with laughter at his own ineptitude. He may be followed by the blue-haired rocking guitarist, the flugelhorn-player, two folk guitarists with amazingly dirty feet, or a pair of bowler-hatted semi-clowns who play a portable barrel organ. These smaller acts can operate anywhere, occupying the alleys around the piazza and moving on to play the nearby terraces of the Bulldog Café and its neighbour, De Leydse Poort. Other acts, requiring a larger, more circular space, perform in the scruffy, down-market area between the tram stop and the Bulldog. There you find the balloon blower, the Ecuadorean folk band, the female fire-eater, and numerous puppeteers. While most are pretty bad, all are easily surpassed in this by the Dreadful Bloodstained Man. He has converted his life's hobby into a bizarre livelihood. His act consists of taking empty spirit bottles from a shopping bag and playing alcoholic conkers with them. A crowd three or four deep has formed at a safe distance around him. Smash! A gin bottle has just destroyed a vodka bottle. He holds out both forearms in triumph. See! no blood. Now the gin bottle goes forward into the second round, and is matched against a squat brandy bottle. Gin, going first, comes down on brandy with a fearsome blow – but nothing happens, only a hollow booming sound. Then it is brandy's turn. Smash! Brandy wins! Fragments of glass pile up on a rug beneath the feet of the Dreadful Bloodstained Man, and he is just about to thrust out his forearms again when he notices a small red cut opening just above his wrist. Oh, dear. But the act must go on – and on – until the bottles are finished or you walk away.

A strange place, in some ways, the Leidseplein. Not particularly stylish – in this capital of informality, not many places are – but a great success for all that; offering, in its haphazard way, something for all types, conditions, and individuals who defy classification. Somehow they all seem to enjoy it.

Walk 12 ☂

Modern Art and Vondelpark

At Museumplein are four art museums and this walk visits two of them, the Van Gogh and the Stedelijk, and offers the Overholland as an optional third. Take a walk along the fashionable streets of the Old South – Van Baerlestraat and P.C. Hooftstraat – and enjoy the grassy banks and lakes of Vondelpark, home of the National Filmmuseum and adjoining Café Vertigo.

Allow   4–5 hours.

Best times   Not Monday, when Van Gogh and Overholland Museums closed. Museum section of Filmmuseum closed Saturday, Sunday and holidays, but cinema open all week showing 3–4 different films a day.

ROUTE

Begin at Concertgebouw. Trams 3, 5, 12, 16. Walk up through open space of Museumplein towards Rijksmuseum and take 1st left to **Van Gogh Museum**, entrance at 7 Paulus Potterstraat ☞; open 10.00 to 17.00, Sunday and holidays 13.00 to 17.00, closed Monday. *Admission, takes Museum Pass*.

Next door, on the Rijksmuseum side at 4 Museumplein, is the **Museum Overholland**, specialising in contemporary works on paper, i.e. drawings, watercolours, gouaches, collages; open 11.00 to 17.00, Sunday and holidays 13.00 to 17.00, closed Monday. *Admission*.

After a suitable break – see essay for suggestions – visit the **Stedelijk Museum**, 13 Paulus Potterstraat ☞; open 11.00 to 17.00. *Admission, takes Museum Pass*. Look round the sculptures in the museum garden, entrance in Van Baerlestraat.

Walk N along Van Baerlestraat and take the 2nd right into **Pieter Cornelisz. (P.C.) Hooftstraat** and look round smart designer shops for up to two blocks, then return to Van Baerlestraat. Keep straight ahead to entrance to **Vondelpark**.

The Route map shows a sample loop through the eastern side of the park, taking in the Vondel statue, the Round Blue Tea Room, the bandstand and the **Filmmuseum** ☞; open 10.00 to 17.00, closed Saturday, Sunday. *Admission, takes Museum Pass*.

Walk ends here. Nearest refreshments at Museum's Café Vertigo with, in summer, restful views over park from 1st-floor terrace. Trams 2, 3, 5, 12.

Museumplein

Ever since its opening concert in November 1888, the Concertgebouw Orchestra has had a high reputation. Its international standing was much enhanced under the conductorship of Bernard Haitink, who made his début with the orchestra in 1956 and took over as sole chief conductor in 1963. The orchestra performs here several times a month for most of the year, and there is a busy summer concert season featuring visiting orchestras. Concertgebouw brochures are available at the box-office, or look for details in *Uitkrant*; tickets can also be reserved at the AUB ticket shop in Leidseplein.

A short walk through the green open space of Museumplein, followed by a left turn through the trees, brings us out to Paulus

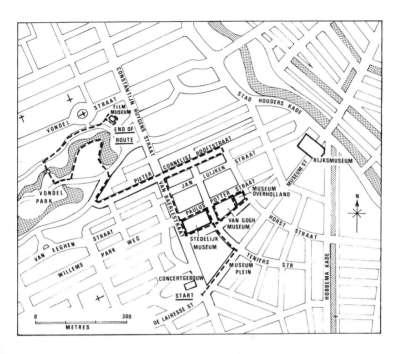

Potterstraat and the front entrance of our first museum.

Van Gogh Museum

There may be trouble with the cloakroom arrangements. A notice at the entrance bans all varieties of 'Back Pack, Handbags, Suitcases and Hand Luggage'. These must somehow be stored in little boxes on the cloakroom wall (insert Fl 1, returnable, like at swimming pools) or left on the floor.

The other storage device on offer is a coathanger and garotte. To operate, hang up coat, run garotte down through one sleeve and pass through numbered lock at bottom. The white piece is a key, and you pull it out to lock, and press it back in to unlock. I hope that is all clear, because, should you have the misfortune to get stuck, no one on the museum staff is likely to be available to tell you these things.

The museum was designed by Gerrit Rietveld and opened in 1973. It is arranged on five levels. In detail the layout may vary, but in general the ground floor introduces Van Gogh to the visitor. Here, too, there may be a special Van Gogh exhibition of either his letters, Japanese prints, or drawings; all three categories are fragile and difficult to show, and the museum rotates them.

The first floor is devoted to the works of Van Gogh. The second and third floors are used for temporary exhibitions, often about Van Gogh's contemporaries such as Emile Bernard, the Nabis, Toulouse-Lautrec, Jan Verkade and so on. The basement and part of the ground floor may also be used for another special exhibition, such as the photographs of Paul Huf, recording scenes associated with the painter. In 1990, the centenary of Van Gogh's death was celebrated with a series of special exhibitions.

This museum has the world's largest collection of Van Goghs. The principal source was the collection of the artist's brother Theo, amounting to some 200 paintings, 500 drawings and 700 letters.

Van Gogh lived from 1853 to 1890. Up to the age of twenty-seven he produced almost nothing. At the age of thirty-two he enrolled at the Antwerp Academy, staying for three months. His mature style, which has now made him a world record-breaker in the auction room, first appeared in spring 1887 and was in full bloom by December 1888. Less than two years later, he was dead. This museum presents the man and the pictures he produced in the last six or seven years of his life: an extraordinary, rocketing progression from the dull muddy landscapes of 1885 to light and brilliant works such as *Vase with Sunflowers*, painted in January 1889.

On the ground floor are paintings by some of his contemporaries – a Guillaumin (born 1841), a Signac (b.1863), a Toulouse-Lautrec (b.1864). Then compare and contrast a selection of flower paintings: a Fantin-Latour of 1877, a *Bowl of Pansies* by Van Gogh (1886), and a *Vase with Gladioli* (1886) also by him, then others by Georges Jeannin (b.1841) and Adolphe Monticelli (b.1824). That Van Gogh was about to erupt, and shower an indifferent world with his blazing images, is further signalled by the *Self-portrait at the Easel* from Arles, painted in summer 1888. Compare this with a dark, gloomy self-portrait which he produced in Paris in spring 1886, and one gets another glimpse of the devastating forces at work in the artist's mind.

On the first floor we follow Van Gogh's last six and a half years. First at Nuenen, at the vicarage where his parents lived, and where he painted still-lives, landscapes and figures. Of these the figure paintings show the way forward, the artist experimenting, close to caricature, pulling out noses, enlarging lips and exaggerating the slope of a jaw – producing *The Potato Eaters* in April 1885 and moving on to the brighter, more sketchy manner of *Peasant Woman with White Cap* (May 1885).

Three paintings only represent his brief Antwerp period, then from March 1886 to February 1888 he was in Paris, where his patient and devoted younger brother, Theo the art dealer, introduced him to Toulouse-Lautrec, Emile Bernard, Gauguin, Camille Pissarro, Seurat and others. He began to work with lighter colours and a dabbing technique, as in the view from his room in Rue Lepic. Another flash of the future is seen in the Japanese-style background and fruit forms in *Lemons on Plate and a Carafe* (Spring 1887). Then *Woman at a Table in the Café Tambourin* (February-March 1887). Then a series of pictures in his Japanese manner.

In February 1888 he moved to Arles, staying until May 1889, and in that period painted more than 200 canvases. The settled, mature Van Gogh style is seen in *Portrait of Camille Roulin* (December 1888). In this section the presentation is not chronological but grouped by theme – a series of portraits, another of landscapes. It matters little; his final evolution happened so quickly, and so erratically, there is no smooth line of progress. Just marvel at the paintings – *The Sower, Gauguin's Armchair, Vincent's Bedroom in Arles.*

In Arles, Van Gogh rented a studio and worked briefly with Gauguin. After a quarrel he cut off part of his ear, then in May 1889 admitted himself to the mental home at St Rémy. He stayed for a year. In this period there was an extraordinary oscillation between wild visionary pictures such as *The Raising of Lazarus (after Rembrandt)* (May 1890) and the tightly controlled *Branches of an Almond Tree in Blossom* (February 1890).

In May 1890 he moved to Arles to stay with the homeopathic Dr Gachet. In July he painted the virtually abstract *Roots and Tree Trunks*, and the same month two very different wheatfield pictures. *Wheatfield under Thunderclouds* is calm, simplified, but *Wheatfield with Crows* is dark, fatally disturbed: the black line of crows falling out of the black of the upper sky. On 27 July 1890 he shot himself; two days later he died.

etime Van Gogh sold only one painting and was tormented by his sense of failure. One hundred years later his paintings change hands in an artistic super-league which puts the rest of the world in torment lest these wonderful pictures vanish from public view into some billionaire's dugout.

Time Off

A break is now in order. The Van Gogh self-service café is all right, but I have a thing about institutional cafés. All those tables in neat rows, like a works canteen, a filling station for art travellers. The terrace is better, weather permitting, if you don't mind saucy sparrows trying to share your plate.

An alternative is to turn left at the exit and walk up to the Small Talk café-restaurant in Van Baerlestraat. It calls itself 'The Loveliest Eating House in Town', which is also pretty saucy. However, the décor and upholstered seats beat the museum's facilities, and the soups, salads and *stokbroods* are quite adequate.

Museum Overholland

Unlike the Van Gogh, which is a state or 'Rijksmuseum', the Over-holland Museum is private and does not accept the Museum Pass. It specialises in works produced on paper – drawings, water-colours and collages – and usually features one artist per exhibition. Not all the artists are star names, though many are: Lichtenstein, Stella, Cézanne, Ellsworth Kelly. Well worth a visit if you have time.

Stedelijk Museum

From the outside it looks too old and red-brick to be the city's foremost museum of modern art. It was built in 1885, its collection based on an original donation by Sophia Augusta Lopez-Suasso, to which other collections have been added and subtracted. Today it specialises in art from the mid-nineteenth century, and since the last war its airy whitewashed rooms have been a major venue for large-scale special exhibitions. The museum devotes much of its annual programme to these special shows, which have an international reputation and can take up most of the gallery space in the main building.

I recently saw an excellent show on Kazimir Malevich – a particularly important event because it marked a breakthrough in cultural relations between the USSR and the West. The Stedelijk has its own large Malevich collection, and to it were now joined numerous works from the Tretyakov Gallery in Moscow and the Russian Museum in Leningrad. Together they formed the first major retrospective of this prolific Russian artist. The other side of such ventures is that the Stedelijk's permanent collection cannot then be seen; at most, highlights of it are shown from time to time as space permits.

The best 'slot' occurs each year in July and August, at the Summer Exhibition, when the museum shows a large selection of its modern masters and recent acquisitions. To find out what is on view, collect a plan at the entrance.

A logical route through the ground floor may thus take you from the entrance hall (1) through Rietveld's furniture (2–7). Nos 8–11 are seldom open, so retrace to (13) and (12), the latter occupied by Edward Kienholz's *Beanery*, a walk-in Los Angeles bar where you mingle with a rough bunch of wax customers whose faces are clocks. Continue through the museum café to (25) and follow back to the entrance hall. Artists and works may include Claes Oldenburg's giant hinged *Saw (hard version II)*, and paintings by Lichtenstein, Warhol, Mondriaan, Braque, Picasso, Léger, Delaunay, Severini. I came upon a room with five Chagalls – the orthodox *Ida à la Fenêtre* (1925) next to the hugely famous *Le Violiniste* (1912-13) and *The Circus Rider* (1931). After German Expressionism comes Van Gogh, Cézanne, and a sketch for Manet's *Un Bar aux Folies Bergère*. Next to the entrance is the *Appelbar* (1951), a railed-off snack bar decorated by Karel Appel.

Go up to the first floor. One way to cover the rooms is to turn right into (213), then by a series of hairpin turns work down to (201). Continue across to (215) and repeat the process through the other half of the floor, finishing at the Malevich room (226, I hope). Artists and periods are furiously jumbled – a selection of Breitners (1880s and '90s) hanging next door to Anselm Kiefer's giant sand map *Märkischer Sand* (1982) and other painted structures. Artists may well include Judd, Newman, Rothko, and the neon messages of Bruce Nauman and Joseph Kosuth. You may also find Matisse's gigantic *The Parakeet and the Mermaid* (1952).

Return to the ground floor, and maybe pause for a drink-stop on the café terrace overlooking the sculpture garden. For security reasons, which means to stop people sneaking in the back without paying, you cannot reach the sculpture garden from the museum. Go out via the New Wing – usually showing very new, annoyingly silly work – or through the front entrance and turn down Van Baerlestraat. Henry Moore's *Reclining Figure* (1957) is on the grass by the road. A little farther along, just past an unmarked tubular sculpture, there should be a gap in the holly hedge and you can get in there. In truth, there is not much to admire that could not be seen from the café terrace – but there you are, you have found it!

P.C. Hooftstraat

Pieter Cornelisz. Hooft was a poet and playwright who came to the fore around 1600. The street named after him is now remarkable for being the only street in Amsterdam to offer uninterrupted chic from Azzurro on the corner of Van Baerlestraat for all of two blocks. Fashion shops to note are Jacques d'Ariège, Lisser, Mexx, Edgar Vos, leather at Arma Pell'. Abundant refreshment and lunch stops include Hoffmanns Bar Bodega, Patricia's Coffee Shop, Oldenburg's *pâtisserie*, Coffee Shop P.C., and Caffé Fiorito on the corner of Honthorststraat, with tables outside.

This is where the smart people moved when shops in the city centre took a downturn, and places like Kalverstraat opted for the guise of a high-street bazaar. It is also fashionable, and reasonably good value, to live in this part of the Old South. The result is a quietly stylish street with well-heeled local patrons, possibly the nearest equivalent of London's Sloane Rangers and the *BCBG* of Paris.

Vondelpark

The western arm of P.C. Hooftstraat, on the other side of Van Baerlestraat, is dingy and dull. Pass quickly along it to the park entrance.

This long, narrow, pretty and popular park is named after Amsterdam's most famous poet and dramatist, Joost van den Vondel (1587–1679). It was designed and laid out in 1865–77 in a relaxed 'English' style by the landscape architects J.D. and L.P. Zocher. Their evident fondness for water means you sometimes have to trail farther than you may wish in search of a bridge, but the visual effect is pleasant and widely appreciated by Amsterdammers.

Wander across to the statue of the poet, crowned with laurels, by L. Royer (1867), whose Rembrandt is the centrepiece in Rembrandtplein. Then follow the path to the Round Blue Tea Room, a flat-topped Thirties pavilion. From here I have suggested in the Route section that you go past the old island bandstand and turn back towards the Filmmuseum. However, in summer you may now be drawn by the sound of African drums, Latin trumpets or Cajun fiddles. Investigate the path ahead and it will shortly bring you to the open-air theatre (Vondelpark Openlucht Theater), a graffiti-sprayed steel shell covering a stage and fronting a large fenced enclosure with banks of bench seating. It's all very informal, and free, a place you drop into for a while, get a beer from the stall behind the seats, and amble off again when you feel like it.

The summer festival in Vondelpark runs from early June to the end of August; very keen on world music, it features bands at various times during the afternoon and evening, Wednesday to Sunday. Check timings in *Uitkrant*.

Festival or not, Sunday is the big day in Vondelpark. On a warm day it is as though the Sixties had never gone. Hippie folk drape themselves all over the grass, impromptu markets set up beside the paths, selling the same old boring handicrafts – beads, necklaces, etc. – plus T-shirts and the means to roll yourself a big fat joint then sit cross-legged under a tree and puff it. Always allowing, of course, that you are into that kind of thing. I am rather against it myself, and struggle sometimes to be tolerant.

Filmmuseum

The Nederlands Filmmuseum is housed on the ground floor of a late nineteenth-century pavilion. Its first-floor terrace is one of the joys of the park: a wonderful place to sit in summer with a drink and contemplate the slow arrival of evening, looking out towards the lake and the trees. At other times, try the Café Vertigo downstairs, a vaulted room with an art-school atmosphere.

The Filmmuseum does indeed possess a museum, though its more important function, I would say, is to show films in its cinema. It puts on a first-class programme of movies from all periods and nations, with three or four different films a day. Each month the museum publishes a free *Programma*; pick one up at the desk. Films are also listed in the diary section (*van Dag tot Dag*) of *Uitkrant*. A word, by the way, about movies in Amsterdam. All cinemas show films in their original version, with sub-titles for foreign-language films. In other words, no dubbing – hurrah!

The museum at the Filmmuseum consists of a small but interesting collection of early devices for portraying movement – a zootrope, praxinoscope, the photographic experiments of Marey and Muybridge, the stereorama which showed depth and the Kaiserpanorama which was a de-luxe version of a stereo viewer. There is also a reconstruction of a film set of the early Twenties, with ancient-looking arc lights, fat cables and a period-piece switchboard panel. In one corner is a tiny eighteen-seater cinema/video room, showing films about the history of the cinema and the restoration of old nitrate stock. Some films have an English version.

The Riding School

If you leave the park by the gate next to the Filmmuseum, you shortly come to Vondel Church (Vondelkerk). Standing at the centre of an oval circus, it was designed by P.J. Cuypers and built in 1872–80 and impressively closes the view along Vondelstraat. It was unoccupied between 1979 and 1985 and the interior was vandalised. Since then it has been restored and converted to offices, a change of use that I continue to find disconcerting, as when, for instance, I walk up to the tall west door and find a small printed sign on it which says, 'Dulmers & Partners'.

Finally, this street contains one unmissable curiosity, the indoor riding school. Turn left at Vondelkerk, then at No.140 walk through the archway. Follow the passage to the vestibule and the magnificent Hollandse Manege (1881), a long dignified hall with high open iron roofing. In the sandy arena half a dozen horses and riders slowly circle under the stern eye of a mounted instructor. No one speaks unless a fault is detected. Stillness and rhythm are all, the rider fusing his body to the movements of the horse – giving the onlooker the fascinating spectacle of fierce concentration masquerading as effortlessness. Round and round they go, oblivious to being watched, so utterly preoccupied are they with watching themselves.

More or less spellbound, we observe all this, then steal away to the tram stop.

Walk 13

Beer and Diamonds

An unlikely combination in any other city, but entirely natural in Amsterdam. This walk takes in the Heineken Brewery, the Albert Cuyp street market, and finishes with a tour of Costers diamond factory.

Allow 5 hours.

Best times Monday to Friday. Tours of Heineken Brewery currently begin at 10.00 and 14.00, closed Saturday and Sunday – but this may well change, for reasons described below; to check, telephone 70-91-11.

ROUTE

Begin at **Heineken Brewery**, Stadhouderskade ☞. Trams 16, 24, 25; also 6, 7, 10 (Wetering Plantsoen). Entrance is on left of building in Eerste van der Helststraat. Arrive 10-15 minutes early to be sure of getting a ticket. *Admission (nominal)*.

Follow tour and enjoy hospitality afterwards. At exit, turn right into Eerste van der Helststraat and walk down to **Albert Cuypstraat market** ☞; open Monday to Saturday, 09.00 to 16.30, closed Sunday. Market extends to left and right. Wander to left for a while, then turn about and continue W to end of market at junction with Ferdinand Bolstraat.

Continue along Albert Cuypstraat. If pressed for time, you could take a diamond tour at A. Van Moppes & Zoon, 2-6 Albert Cuypstraat, though I feel that Costers, our eventual destination, is a little swisher. If a café/lunch stop is called for, try Café Willy on corner Frans Halsstraat.

At end Albert Cuypstraat, turn right along Ruysdaelkade. Cross to W side and near top turn left by swimming baths (Zuiderbad) into Hobbemastraat. Follow round to rear of Rijksmuseum and look for corner house on left marked **Coster Diamonds**, at 2-4 Paulus Potterstraat ☞; open 09.00 to 17.00. Security at entrance a touch forbidding, but just say you want to see round and doors will open. Staff on hand to tell you about diamonds; see polishers at work, and then drift critically through showrooms as if you own it all.

Walk ends here. Nearest refreshments in fashionable Pieter Cornelisz. Hooftstraat (continue along Hobbemastraat and take 2nd left). Trams 2, 3, 5, 12.

Heineken Brewery

I was sitting in the Bamboo Bar, Amsterdam's friendliest jazz venue, drinking beer with three Yugoslav friends – Zoran, Zvonko and Stevan. It was our last night in Amsterdam and we had dined well on steaks, char-broiled Argentinian-style. The band was already into its stride when, to our joy, a tall sinuous redhead rose out of the audience and took the microphone. She started to sing, and sway a little, and soon the long dark room blazed with the glamour she had suddenly brought to the driving music.

I looked at Zoran and pulled a face. 'We must stay three more days,' I said.

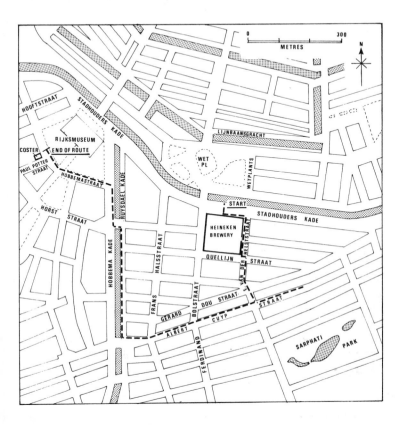

He smiled briefly, and passed the message along the bar. Soon he had an answer. 'Zvonko says, we stay *one* more day, and go to Heineken Brewery.'

The fame of the Heineken tour has travelled to many lands, and deservedly, for it is good fun, especially if you have a degree of enthusiasm for the product. In 1989 up to 320 people went round the building each day, and in 1991 a new kind of tour will begin, with an enlarged capacity of 600 visitors per day.

The old brewery is not what it was, though that is not to signal any decline in the beer. It is simply that the big building on Stadhouderskade, though prominently labelled 'Heinekens Brouwerij', is not a *brouwerij* any more. In January 1988 the company gave up making beer in Amsterdam. The city's traffic problems had increasingly conspired against the efforts of their fleet of trucks to service the bottling plant. Demand, meanwhile, had grown too rapidly for the old brewery to be able to keep up. It could manage 80,000 bottles an hour, but the need was now in millions. Today production is concentrated elsewhere, chiefly at Zoeterwoude, near The Hague, where they can rattle out one million bottles per hour, and at 's-Hertogenbosch which produces 350,000 bottles an hour.

A new Brewing Museum is being built on the old brewery site, and future tours will be channelled through it, replacing the old tour which went first round the white-tiled former brewhouse, with its two sets of huge brewing coppers, and on to a small museum located under the old malt silos. Visitors then eased their way into a large reception hall and sat round tables laid with check gingham cloths, and waiters promptly arrived with trays of beer and a bowl of crunchies per table, then brought more beer and further plates of salami and cheese. A video was shown, extolling the company founded by Gerard Adriaan Heineken, a genial side-whiskered gentleman whose portrait we had seen in the museum. Time passed and then, as the mood of geniality mounted, our hostess with the microphone sought and found a birthday girl and presented her with a blue china Heineken mug. Later, some while later as I recall, she announced:

'We always have trouble getting you to leave, so we make a bargain with you. If you promise to finish your beer in ten minutes we will bring you another glass. Do you agree to this?'

A hundred and sixty voices roared assent.

Albert Cuyp Market

From the brewery it is a short walk down Eerste van der Helststraat to the famous market, open daily except Sunday, in Albert Cuypstraat. You reach the market to a heady whiff of freshly baked bread flowing from the corner shop of Broodje van de Bakker. Next door is W. Noom's Slagerij (butcher's shop). Next to them is Pinto Mode, a one-stop clothes shop selling *'In-en Verkoop, Overhemden, Sweatshirts, Kolberts, Broeken, T-Shirts'* (On sale together, shirts, sweatshirts, jackets, trousers, T-shirts).

In the roadway a double row of stalls stretches far into the distance in either direction, leaving a broad central passage for the customers. The stalls offer an unrelenting and brash mixture of fruit, lingerie, cheap clothes, handbags, and random general goods such as a stack of bottles of nail varnish next to another of salt and pepper mills.

It does not matter which way you go, though our ultimate direction is westward, or to the right from our point of entry. In the other direction is a row of wet-fish stalls, each with a great wriggle of *Spiering* and rows of neatly overlapping *Wijting, Makreel, Schol,* the inevitable *Haring, Harder, Poon, Sepia, Kabeljauw, Schar* and shellfish too, *Gambas* and *Noorse Garnalen**. To keep them gleaming and beautiful, an assistant with a bucket walks up and down, dipping a paintbrush into the water and flicking it over the fish.

Stand outside the spice stall and let your nose do the work – a warm blend of more than a hundred spices, each in its own hand-labelled box. Selected boxes carry a second label describing what the spice can cure – *Laxeer, Bronchitus, Griep, Zenuwen, Rheuma, Migraine* and so on. You can no doubt guess what those all mean, except perhaps *Zenuwen* – nerves. Oh, and over there, just about every kitchen gadget you could ever want, hanging in lines from the front of the stall and piled on the trestle top.

But what is this? What is going on? Here we are, a hundred yards into the market – and no cheese stall. By this time I could have bought a sack of olives, an entire wardrobe for two hundred people, a cat basket, a bunch of asters, bales of cloth and a string of five-guilder wristwatches. But no cheese. Are the cows on strike?

The mystery was later solved. There *were* cheese stalls in the market, but on this particular stretch the stallholder had been late on parade. Moments later I came upon a rival cheese seller, and goggled at the variety of what, at first glance, had seemed a disappointingly uniform display. Everywhere the cheese was hard and Dutch. Then I began to see how infinitely it was graded, by age, number and size of hole, and by colour, from grey-white to deep buttery yellow. A friendly lady in a white coat stood by with her wicked curved cheese knife, as big as a scimitar, while customers peered and speculated on the merits of

*Sprat, whiting, mackerel, plaice, herring, grey mullet, gurnard, cuttlefish, cod, dab, king prawns, Norwegian shrimps.

the Goudse, the Hollandse Emmental, Texelaar and Maasdam, Feta and Leerdammer.

For much of last year bright yellow banners were stretched at intervals across the street, attached by cords to the first and second storeys of the houses. The message they carried was not, unfortunately, 'Welcome to Albert Cuypstraat' but a police warning: 'Beware of Pickpockets/*Let op Zakkenrollers* . . .' in four languages.

I sometimes wish they would not go on about it so much, unless it is to deter the thieves, to make them feel they are being watched. Surely the average shopper, native or visitor, is smart enough not to do the silly naive things that people once did with their wallets and handbags. Or must we still be treated like children?

I cannot leave this market without paying tribute to the brilliant displays of fruit and vegetables. Here are a few more Dutch names to conjure with, and maybe sharpen your powers of menu-reading: *Komkommer, Suikermais, Peulen, Paprika, Wortels, Zomerbiet, Perziken, Aardbeien, Wijnpruimen, Aalbessen, Frambozen.**

The pedestrian-only part of the market comes to an end at Ferdinand Bolstraat, which from Monday to Saturday is closed to traffic, except for loading and unloading, between 06.00 and 19.00. By way of farewell, treat yourself to a *Broodje Haring*, a fresh herring roll spiked with gherkin or pickled onion.

Continue past Van Moppes diamond factory, or go in if time is short (see also Route). Our next destination is another, I think smarter, diamond factory situated near the back of the Rijksmuseum. Our route to it follows the Ruysdaelkade, quieter than the big canals and almost provincial in feel. After the South Pool (Zuiderbad) it is a short distance to Costers, which consists of two sizeable villas joined by a modern bridge.

Costers Diamond Factory

'What is so hard, it can only be cut by itself? So brilliant that it is the most popular of all gemstones, the symbol of steadfast love *and* a girl's best friend?'

---

*Cucumber, sweetcorn, mange-tout, pepper, carrot, summer beet, peaches, strawberries, red plums, redcurrants, raspberries.

'Yes, yes. But what is actually so *special* about them? I mean, they are so tiny. Can anything that small be truly beautiful?'

'Buy me one and I'll tell you.'

It is probably no more than further proof of my incurable vulgarity, but I find diamonds oddly unexciting until I see a big one. In an effort to appreciate their singular characteristics a little better, I asked at Costers if I could get closer to some of the merchandise. They kindly showed me into a side room and locked the door.

The atmosphere inside the room was not unlike a gaming room. Four people sat expectantly at a table. An assistant unlocked a cabinet and drew out a clear plastic envelope containing a small number of extremely small diamonds. As they were laid out on a dark blue tray one of the four visitors, an elderly American who had played this game before, said: 'I hope you aren't going to pull the same trick as you did last year. You showed me a row of diamonds and one of them winked at me.'

The girl assistant smiled, her male colleague didn't get it. The first batch were too small to be capable of serious winking, though the price of each was impressive enough. A second batch arrived, a little larger, and their characteristics were described. First the cut: brilliant, with 58 facets; then the weight, in carats (1 carat = 0.2 grams or 100 points); the colour, white; then the clarity, judged on a scale from Internally Flawless – and having no inclusions or foreign particles when examined under x10 magnification – down through VVSI (very very small inclusions) to, eventually, three levels of Piqué, where the inclusions are visible. After the description came the price, punched out on a calculator and announced in every relevant language.

This went on for a couple more rounds, and I was getting the hang of the grading system but felt quite unmoved by the stones, still no bigger than a silver dragée on a cake. Then something larger arrived. Ah. This was different. I looked down with a fresh eye. Now for the first time the facets were large enough to wink, and to allow the cutter's skill to be seen and admired. Here at last was a stone with a hint of magic about it; sparkling and desirable. 'My' diamond was a brilliant cut, with 58 facets; it weighed 1 carat 24 points; its colour was Top Wesselton (clear white, 2nd top in value); and its clarity was rated VSI (very small inclusions, 3rd top quality).

My diamond was still not exactly huge. In fact, you could have fitted six like it on your thumbnail.

My diamond was none the less not cheap. They wanted £7,000 for it, or $10,500. I had neither, so thanked them and asked if they would unlock the door.

If you feel that asking to be shown some of the stock is going a little too far in your case, there is still plenty to see in the polishing room – where charts explain the niceties of cut, carat, colour and clarity – and in Diamond Land, as they call the showroom upstairs. Young ladies in pinstriped suits march about, but there is no pressure on the casual visitor to buy anything. The showroom is interesting for the sheer variety of diamond objects on view. Not only brooches and rings, bracelets and wristwatches, they will even set your diamond(s) in a pair of clogs. Then, surely, you would have everything.

Costers is one of the better known firms in an industry for which Amsterdam is world-famous. In 1986 it was exactly four hundred years since the first Jewish diamond merchants, refugees from Antwerp, settled here. The industry has changed since the Second World War, and today is focused more on tourists, with dozens of shops around the city and factories like Costers where they cut, polish and grade diamonds, and the public is invited to come and watch.

I have described my brief meeting with a 1.24 carat diamond. At the other end of the scale, the largest diamond ever found, the Cullinan, was cut here in Amsterdam. It weighed 3,106 carats and was cut into 105 stones. And at Costers they cut the famous Koh-i-noor diamond, the 'Mountain of Light', which in its polished form weighed 186 carats. In Amsterdam they definitely have a way with diamonds.

To round off this walk, try the agreeably up-market cafés of P.C. Hooftstraat. Choose from the Caffé Fiorito, the Oldenburg *pâtisserie* and Patricia's Coffee Shop.

Walk 14

To the Woods

A jolly outing by antique tram to the Amsterdam Woods (Amsterdamse Bos). Stroll along by the rowing lake to the Bosmuseum, and return past the Open Air Theatre to catch another old tram back to town.

Allow   6 hours/all day.

Best times   The Elektrische Museum Tramlijn operates on Sunday from approx. end March to end October. Some afternoon-only services on other days. Brochure with full timetable ('N Rijdend Trammuseum') available from VVV and many hotels.

ROUTE

Begin at **Haarlemmermeer Station**. Trams 6, 16. Bus 15. Follow sign 'Naar Tram' through old booking hall and bookshop to station yard. Climb on board next tram (every 20 minutes) and buy return ticket to Station Amstelveen from conductor.

At Amstelveen terminus, stretch legs and take tram back to **Amsterdam Woods**; get off at stop by crossing with Van Nijenrodeweg. Cross tracks, walk round circus and bear right towards rowing lake (Bosbaan/Roeibaan). Walk across terrace above boathouse and check out refreshments at Auberge Aquarius or Café-Restaurant De Bosbaan (changes scheduled here, see essay).

Continue along *fietspad* (cycle path) towards far end of lake. After white drawbridge follow lakeside path. At end lake, where rowing races begin, bear right and fork right, following sign to *'Pannekoeken'* (pancakes) which brings you to a soothing lunch stop at the **Boerderij Meerzicht**, open in summer 10.00 to 19.00. The **Bosmuseum** is in next-door building, with impressive displays about the park and how it was laid out in the early 1930s ☞ ; open 10.00 to 17.00.

At exit, turn left and return towards rowing lake. At junction of paths just before lake, take 1st right which turns back and loops away behind lake. Keep straight on to large glade where cars park, and cross metalled road (Nieuwe Meerlaan). Cross stream, then bear right on gravelled footpath (rather than black cycle path) and keep straight on to Open Air Theatre (Openlucht Theater). Walk across in front of stage and bear right. Keep on beside road round top of lake (Grote Vijver) and cross yellow railed bridge. Go past kiosk to end of long field, turn left at bottom and this path (use the right-hand footpath, with occasional benches) will bring you eventually to the circus next to the tram stop. Take a seat on bench by plane trees and wait for next tram back to **Haarlemmermeer Station**.

Walk ends at station terminus. Nearest refreshments in station buffet. Trams 6, 16. Bus 15.

Note If tired and unwilling to walk back from Bosmuseum, a No.70 bus will run you almost to the tram stop from end of lake (Bosbaan); service once an hour.

Electric Tramway Museum

This brilliant institution has brought new life to a group of old and

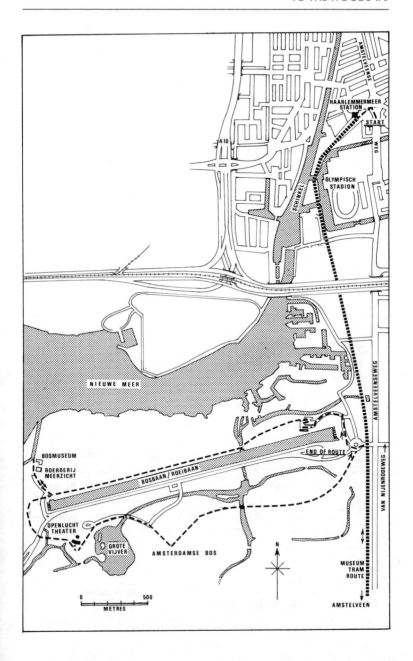

redundant tramcars, and antiquarian bliss to all who ride them. The cars were built between 1910 and 1950 for regular service in Amsterdam, The Hague, Rotterdam, Groningen, Kassel, Vienna, Graz and Prague. When their working days were over they were brought to the sheds at Haarlemmermeer Station, restored and put to work on the museum's own tramline which runs out through the southern suburbs to Amstelveen.

The museum *is*, in effect, its trams. In the old station building – until 1950 the head of the steam railway to Amstelveen, Aalsmeer and Uithoorn – there are one or two treasures on show: some finely made model trams, a signal, pieces of track, and also a bookshop. But what everyone really comes for is a ride on an old tram. They are what some might call *real trams*, from the days of high-varnished wooden seats, leather straps for standing passengers, posters from a slower, more naive age, an old bow collector on the roof, and a uniformed conductor who walks up and down selling tickets.

Climb aboard your tram in the station yard. *Bong, bong!* go the bells and away it rattles. *Bong!* as it crosses the points and *Bong, bong!* and *Bong, bong, bong!* at the approach to a road crossing. The conductor, a volunteer enthusiast like all the tramway staff, has much more to do than just sell tickets. At each passing loop along the single-track road he must jump down and change the points by hand. And at every road crossing not controlled by traffic lights, he gets down, stops the cross-traffic with a red flag, blows his whistle to tell the driver the way is clear, and blows it again when he is safely back on board.

After curving past the station tramsheds, the line is more or less straight thereafter, cutting between fertile allotments and the backs of quiet houses and gardens, each with its boat moored on a small green canal that runs parallel with the track. Look out for the entrance to Amsterdam Woods, through a broad tree-lined avenue on the right, but if you are enjoying the ride stay on the tram all the way to Amstelveen Station. After a five-minute halt the tram sets off back up the line. Leave it, this time, at the Woods – the name of the cross-avenue is Van Nijenrodeweg – and walk up to the circus or large roundabout and bear right to the rowing lake.

The lake, a long thin rectangular strip, is laid out as a six-lane regatta course, 2000 metres from start to finish. Make your approach over the roof of the boathouses and head for the grandstand and cafés on the far side, an area known collectively as the Tribune.

The course is the headquarters of the Okeanos Rowing Club, and regattas are held here through the season which ends in early July. The best oarsmen then go on to compete in national and international events, though most weekends crews will be out here training.

The future of the grandstand is currently under review. Some of the brickwork is crumbling and it may have to be pulled down. If it does go, the present bar and restaurant will have to go with it – a pity, because it is comfortable inside and offers prime views of the races through the glass front, just a few metres short of the finishing line. Inside, the tables are filled with rowing fans, and among them pass young men in battered but enormously prestigious-looking braided blazers, dropping a word here and there to a girlfriend. Although the future is a little vague at the moment, the demand for beer and food will probably remain eternal among rowing people and so, if necessary, a new bar-restaurant will have to be provided.

From here our route lies close to the water, the early part through pleasant woodland on the cyclists' and joggers' path, and then beside the rush-lined lake, where pairs and fours and eights battle past, screamed at by cycle-borne coaches and colleagues. At the end of the lake, we bear right through the trees to a former farmhouse, now a restaurant, the Boerderij Meerzicht, known for its outdoor barbecues and indoor pancakes, the latter served through a sort of cottage window let into the wall of a thatched octagonal buffet. Next to it is a self-service counter selling soup of the day, filled rolls, gooey pastries and drinks. Plenty here for the hungry walker.

After lunch, walk through the yard where peacocks stroll and visit the Bosmuseum. The Bos is entirely man-made, and Amsterdam is very proud of it. Work began in 1934 to provide the city with a handsome, new recreation area, large enough for people to find solitude as well as a place to exercise. Teams of men and horses dug out the rowing course and the ornamental lakes and ponds, laid roads and prepared the polder for tree planting. The rowing course, known as the Bosbaan or Roeibaan, was opened by Queen Wilhelmina in 1937. The work was done in the Depression years, and the use of machinery was rejected in favour of letting unemployed men tackle the work, and do it with their own hands.

The museum gives a painstakingly precise account of the Woods and their inhabitants, documenting everything down to the last stuffed squirrel, mole, blackbird, robin and titmouse. Children, and some grown-ups I know, will enjoy the schmaltzy Diorama, entered through a dark tunnel that seems to burrow past tree roots and emerges in a tiny clearing. Wait then for night to fall, the 'sky' above turns purple and stars come out, and the animals begin to call to each other.

From the Bosmuseum, follow the Route (see above) back to the tram stop. I have chosen a path which passes through the Open Air Theatre (see *What's On* for their summer programme), turns past a small lake, the Grote Vijver, and then becomes a gentle stroll along tree-lined paths with broad vistas of well-mown fields and clumps of woodland. There are plenty of toilets, refreshment kiosks, playgrounds and paddling pools, and benches to sit on. There is peace and order, and no litter anywhere.

I feel a sermon coming on about London's scruffy parks, though to be fair both scale and location are different. The Amsterdamse Bos is an out-of-town park, more like, say, Richmond Park than Hyde Park, sharing the former's breadth and openness. At the same time, the Bos manages to promote a host of leisure activities, from canoeing to fishing, camping and horseriding, as well as run a series of sports fields and a hockey stadium. It does so, what is more, with discretion, leaving the lone stroller plenty of space to explore by himself. To design all that, and make it work as smoothly as it evidently does, is something of a triumph.

OUT OF TOWN

I sometimes think of the unknown Englishman I met outside the Barbizon Hotel, waiting for his afternoon coach trip to, as he put it, 'Marken and somewhere'. He looked at me unhappily. 'We have to go on these coach trips,' he explained. 'Round where our hotel is, there isn't much to do.'

His trouble was, poor chap, he had been brainwashed by his tour operator into thinking that, no sooner had he arrived in Amsterdam, his first duty was then to leave the city, and dash off on a series of inane excursions.

I am not against all coach trips, only most of them. All that time spent cooped up in a bus, listening to a tired guide going through her tired routine in up to four languages, when you could be out there in the open, discovering the place for yourself.

However, there is one out-of-town coach trip I do recommend: the Bulbfield Tour. I can't make a Slow Walk out of it, because it needs some form of flexible transport to take you to places inaccessible by train: first to a grower's establishment, where you can order your own daffodil, tulip and hyacinth bulbs, and on to the Keukenhof, the marvellous gardens near Lisse, at the heart of the bulb-growing world. The season lasts for only seven weeks, between early April and mid-May. To book a trip, ask at your hotel or go to one of the excursion companies in the Dam.

Most other coach trips consist of mad eight-hour sweeps round the whole of Holland, with no time to see anything except as it whizzes past the window, or those essentially bogus excursions that fill me with dread about the aspirations of some tourists. These trips go to pretty-pretty villages where the natives still happen to wear traditional costume, and tirelessly demonstrate clog-making and cheese-racing. Cheese-racing? Yes, it says so here in the brochure: 'Watch four teams from the Cheese Carriers' Guild compete for the fastest, most faultless timing while handling tons of tender produce.' Oh, right.

It can be refreshing, none the less, to spend a day travelling out to one of the nearby provincial centres, so full of interesting sights and museums, and very different in character from Amsterdam. I have chosen Haarlem, Leiden and Utrecht, all of which are within a half-hour train ride from Centraal Station – and Haarlem is only fifteen minutes away. Services are frequent – at least three trains an hour – and punctual.

All three cities have two walks each, the second beginning where the first ends. Between them they may contain too much to fit into a single day, but if you return for a second visit you can easily pick up where you left off the first time round.

Walk 15

Haarlem A: Market Square and Frans Hals Museum

A walk into the heart of old Haarlem, calling at the marvellous Frans Hals Museum and passing several historic *hofjes* (almshouses) on the way back to the market square.

Allow 3–4 hours.

Best times Any day (but see *Walk 16* if you plan to do both in one day).

ROUTE

Begin at Haarlem Station. Exit platform at rear of train from Amsterdam. Walk through tunnel to booking hall and turn right in street to VVV information office, then turn left round bus station into Kruisweg.

Continue along Kruisstraat past high-street shops. At Hema, on corner, bear left into Smedestraat and continue to corner of **Market Square (Grote Markt)**. Many good café stops here.

Cross square and walk S between church and Vleeshal into Lepelstraat, then on to cobbled Warmoesstraat. Continue along Schagchelstraat, crossing filled-in canal of Gedempte Oude Gracht to Groot Heiligland. **Frans Hals Museum** is at far end ☞ ; open 11.00 to 17.00, Sunday and holidays 13.00 to 17.00. *Admission, takes Museum Pass.*

At exit turn right into Gasthuisvest, then next right into Klein Heiligland. Take the next left into Cornelissteeg. At end, bear left across Grote Houtstraat to **Proveniershuis**. Look in at courtyard.

Continue S and take 1st right into Kerkstraat, closed by stern Classical front of **Nieuwe Kerk**. Turn right into Lange Annastraat, past Guurtje de Waal *hofje* at No.40. Keep straight on to Tuchthuisstraat and larger Brouwershofje on left. Further on in Gasthuisstraat, at No.32, is the **Kloveniersdoelen**, hall of the Civic Guard of St Adriaan (a much-admired Hals portrait).

Turn right at end into Zuiderstraat. A quick left-right at Oude Gedempte Gracht brings you to Jacobijnestraat. Walk past former monastery garden in Prinsenhof to SW corner **Grote Markt**.

Walk ends here. Nearest refreshments in square.

Into Town

As you leave Haarlem Station via the blue and cream tiled tunnel, look at the yellow departures board for trains back to Amsterdam. As you will see, there are at least six an hour, and the service continues until after midnight.

In the vaulted booking hall are huge tile pictures of ploughmen and horses and foundry workers. Haarlem is also 'Chocolate City', where the Droste company has its factory. The front of the station is most impressive: a turn-of-the-century Castle of Transport with towers and a great semi-circular window. Walk along to the VVV office at the far

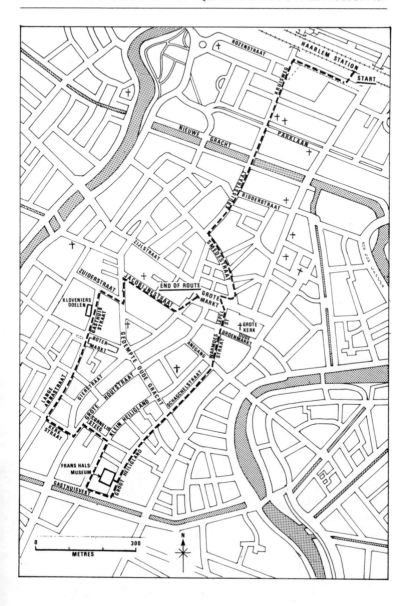

end, for supplementary maps and news of current events (available in the day-by-day section of *Toer-in Krant*).

After Amsterdam, Haarlem is quiet, small and low, with few buildings more than three storeys high. Kruisstraat leads past a mixture of chainstore names and small specialist shops. Look for the richly ornamented step-gabled house, now the Austral Gems shop, and Haarlemmer Halletjes where they sell Droste chocolates. At Hema, bear left into Smedestraat and walk towards the spire of the late Gothic Grote of St Bavokerk (Great or St Bavo Church) which dominates the market square.

The cobbled Grote Markt is roomy and picturesque, little changed from when Berckheyde painted it in the late seventeenth century. Turn right at the extremely pretty police station – the Hoofdwacht, one of the oldest buildings in Haarlem, which from 1755 until *c*.1900 served as the civic guardhouse. To rest awhile, and collect your bearings, take a seat on the shaded terrace of Brinkmann. Service is a trifle dozy but we are in no rush.

Now spread before you is a sumptuous panorama. On the left is the Great Church, and next to it the long pavilion of the converted Vishal (Fish Hall), used for art exhibitions. Also on the left is the statue of Laurentius Costers of Haarlem (*c*.1370-*c*.1440), here claimed as the inventor of printing with movable metal type. (In Mainz, they will tell you it was Gutenberg.) On the far side of the square is the old Vleeshal (Butchers' Hall), built in 1602-3 by Lieven de Key, surveyor of public buildings, and currently under scaffolding. With the Vishal, the Vleeshal forms part of the Art Centre 'De Hallen', a contemporary adjunct to the Frans Hals Museum. To the right, across the end of the square, is the sixteenth-century Stadhuis (Town Hall), originally a thirteenth-century hunting seat of the Counts of Holland. On Saturday there is an antiques market in the square.

Now aim south between the Great Church and the Butchers' Hall. In cobbled Warmoesstraat the shops quietly trade in bygones, china, old books, new books, smart clothes – and on the left is a puppet theatre, the Poppentheater La Condola; performances on Wednesday, Saturday, Sunday at 14.30; tel. 32-40-21 to reserve seats.

Keep straight on to Schagchelstraat, where the emphasis, in a pleasant, laid-back way, is on crafts – clock and watch repairs, violin making, theatrical make-up, and succulent chocolates at Bonnette

(No.32). We continue to the Frans Hals Museum, situated in the southern part of the old city known as the Holy Lands (Heilige Landen).

Frans Hals Museum

To clear up a common misconception, this museum is not dedicated to Frans Hals alone but deals with Haarlem painters of various periods since the sixteenth century. The emphasis is on the 'Golden Age' of the seventeenth century, and the museum serves also as a monument to Frans Hals and Lieven de Key, the architect of the original Old Men's Home (1608) in which it is located. The museum opened in 1913, and statues of the artist and the architect were added at that time when the monumental entrance gate was built.

The museum is pleased to call itself 'the Monday museum' which means that unlike most state museums it does not close on that day. At the entrance, turn right through the passageway to a covered cobbled yard. 'Old Masters' begin through the archway dated 1679.

The collection is a delight, enjoyment of it made all the greater by the quiet and modest setting. Move through a long series of rooms to Room 8. Highlights for me are Jan Mostaert's extraordinary version of a West Indian landscape, and *St Luke Painting the Madonna with Child* (1512) by Maerten van Heemskerck; *The Knightly Brotherhood of the Holy Land* (*c*.1530) by Jan van Scorel, the figures presented in the old-fashioned 'team photo' method, each man carrying a palm branch to testify that he had made the pilgrimage. Then the strange Bosch-like vision of Jan Mandijn – *The Temptation of St Anthony*; and the great sea painting of 1621 by Hendrick Cornelisz. Vroom, *The Arrival at Flushing on 29 April 1613 of Frederick V, Elector Palatine, and Elisabeth Stuart*. Revel next in the amazing cheesiness in Floris van Dijck's *Still Life* (1613).

On to winter landscapes by Isack van Ostade, Jan Josephsz. van Goyen of Leyden and the Amsterdammer Pieter van Santvoort. Van Ostade's *Slaughtered Pig* (*c*.1640–45) is all blood and tripes hung up to view. Then sensitive portraits by J.-C. Verspronck. At the end, turn left to the Renaissance Hall, the refectory of the former Old Men's Home. So far no paintings by Frans Hals have appeared, but will do so shortly. In Room 11 is a fine collection of silver on loan from the churches of Haarlem, made by the gold- and silversmiths of the city, whose quarter we visit in *Walk 16*.

In 1990 a major Hals exhibition was held at the museum with paintings gathered from all over the world. Before its arrival in Haarlem, the exhibition appeared in Washington DC and London.

Under normal circumstances the museum has eight large civic guard portraits by Hals. He lived from c.1581–85 until 1666, a long and productive life, and the civic guard portraits span a considerable middle period. One of the best-known and most highly regarded is the *Banquet of the Officers of the St George Civic Guard of Haarlem* (1616). Many reveal his distinctive 'fast' sketchy brushwork, pinning down the elusive moment in an impressionistic manner; his mastery of lace ruffs and cuffs, and sashes, and his way of suggesting character in figures that are the very opposite of frozen – eyes darting to one side, mouths open in conversation, heads tilted and turned. The museum also has some of his later, more severe work, when his groups bring out the solitude of the individuals: an example is *The Lady Governors of the Old Men's Home at Haarlem* (1664).

After the Frans Hals Room, go through to the pretty garden in the old almshouse courtyard – a classical layout of clipped hedges and sea-shells in place of gravel (the seaside is only just down the road, at Zandvoort). In the courtyard beyond the coffee shop, where we came in, are further rooms of twentieth-century paintings, including brilliant canvases by Jan Sluyters, Jan Toorop and Leo Gestel.

Proveniershuis and Almshouses

After several turns through narrow streets, we arrive on Grote Houtstraat by the Proveniershuis. This is now a somewhat drab building, but it is well worth going through the arch to look at the brick courtyard beyond, occupied by almshouses. From 1577 the Proveniershuis served as the headquarters of the St George Civic Guard (St Jorisdoelen) whose members were painted on several occasions by Frans Hals.

Walk on to Kerkstraat, dramatically closed by the flat-topped east façade of Nieuwe Kerk, designed by Jacob van Campen and built in 1645–49. Behind it, the twirly Renaissance steeple is earlier, the work of Lieven de Key (1613). As you approach, you have the curious spectacle of the steeple sinking rapidly out of sight behind the disproportionately bulky east front. Van Campen's Revenge?

To the right is Lange Annastraat. Keep heading north to find more of the almshouses (*hofjes*) for which Haarlem is famous. At No.40 is Guurtje de Waal (1661), and in Tuchthuisstraat is the larger red-and-white shuttered Brouwershofje (brewers' almshouse). At No.32 Gasthuisstraat, crossed muskets announce the Kloveniersdoelen of 1612, now a public library. Step in through the arch to see the large, well-proportioned hall of the civic guardsmen, the place where they met and banqueted.

The route back to Grote Markt goes past a leafy monastery garden in Prinsenhof; the building at the far end is now part of the Town Hall complex. As you emerge into the square, you may catch a wedding group arriving at or leaving the Town Hall. Best of all, they will have hired a string of horse-drawn carriages for their transport, each pair of horses commanded by a coachman in grey topper, red coat and black boots.

It may now be lunchtime, in which case the cafés of Grote Markt await your decision. If you have already been to Brinkmann and seek a change, try one of the others on the far side of the square, such as Café Mephisto.

Walk 16

Haarlem B: Great Church and Teylers Museum

Enjoy the medieval splendours of the Great or St Bavo Church with its towering organ, and the Teylers Museum, a Neo-Classical treasury of the arts and sciences. Includes also a secret wartime hideout in the Corrie Ten Boom House, the Amsterdam Gate and the Begijnhof.

Allow 3–4 hours.

Best times Tuesday to Saturday. Great Church closed Sunday, Ten Boom House closed Sunday and public holidays, Teylers Museum closed Monday.

ROUTE

Begin in main square (**Grote Markt**, described in previous walk). At NW corner, walk up Barteljorisstraat to No.19 and visit the **Corrie Ten Boom House** ☞; open Monday to Saturday, 1 April to 31 October 10.00 to 16.30, 1 November to 31 March 11.00 to 15.30, closed Sunday and public holidays. *Entry free but donation requested.*

Return to Grote Markt and visit **Great or St Bavo Church** ☞; open Monday to Saturday 10.00 to 16.00, closed Sunday. *Admission.*

At exit, turn left to Damstraat and walk down to Spaarne. Turn left to **Teylers Museum** at No.16 ☞; open Tuesday to Saturday, 10.00 to 17.00, Sunday 13.00 to 17.00, closed Monday. *Admission, takes Museum Pass.*

At exit, turn left and cross white lifting bridge (Gravestenenbrug). Walk through Wijdesteeg and turn left into Spaarnwouderstraat. Continue across narrow Burgwal canal as far as old city gate, the **Amsterdamse Poort**. Return along lane opposite De Drie Kemphaantjes café to Spaarne canal and turn left along Houtmarkt. Cross bridge at Burgwal and walk beside canal back to lifting bridge.

Cross bridge, bear right across road and follow quayside of Bakenessergracht. Turn left down Korte Begijnstraat and right to **Waalse Kerk**, former chapel of the Begijnhof and the oldest church in Haarlem. Walk round church and head N towards another church (St Joseph's), arriving in Donkere Begijnhof.

Turn right to old **goldsmiths' quarter**. Plaque on wall marks *'Goutsmitscamer'*, former seat of Haarlem's gold- and silversmiths. Walk on to little square, Goudsmitspleintje, then turn back and walk ahead to Jansstraat. On right is Roman Catholic Church of St Joseph. Opposite, the pretty Janskerk and Municipal Archives, open 09.00 to 16.00, closed Saturday.

Turn left along Jansstraat to **Great Church and Grote Markt**. Walk ends here. Nearest refreshments all around. Try Brinkmann in main square or Café Mephisto at 29 Grote Markt. Return to railway station either along Jansstraat or via Barteljorisstraat and Kruisstraat.

A Question of Tactics

If you have already been on *Walk 15*, you may wonder if you have time to complete another walk in the same day. The major visit in *Haarlem B* is to the Teylers Museum, which closes at 17.00 and deserves a good

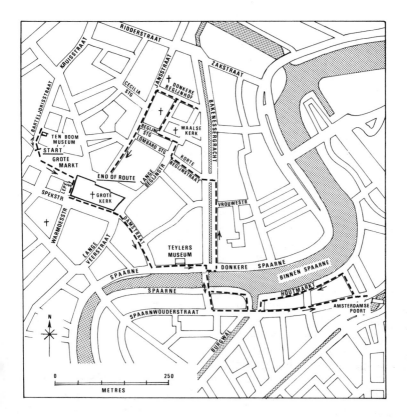

hour of your time. I would suggest, if time is short, that you keep the Corrie Ten Boom House for another day.

At the end of the walk, returning to Amsterdam is no problem at all. There are regular trains until after midnight, so it is perfectly feasible to dine in Haarlem, perhaps take in an organ concert at the Grote Kerk (currently on Tuesday at 20.15) and catch a train later. In August, you may run into the Haarlem Jazz Festival (*Jazzstad*); gigs take place all over town, making it quite difficult to leave early.

Corrie Ten Boom House

The tour begins, usually on the hour (see notice on door), in the clock shop at 19 Barteljorisstraat, and lasts about 45 minutes. During the Second World War this house, known as the BéJé, became a refuge for many who needed to go into hiding – Jews, students and members of the Dutch Resistance.

The Ten Booms were a devout Christian family who saw their non-violent resistance as an act of faith. In February 1944 they were betrayed. The Gestapo raided the house and arrested six members of the family, four of whom died as prisoners or from exhaustion after the war. The Germans were convinced that Jewish fugitives were hiding in the house, and they posted guards to keep watch. They failed to uncover the false wall in Corrie Ten Boom's bedroom. Behind it, six refugees stood without food and water for two and a half days, and then were rescued by the Resistance.

Corrie Ten Boom survived Ravensbrück concentration camp, and after the war travelled the world to spread her message that God's love triumphs over all human experience, even the severest cruelty and oppression of wartime. She died in 1983, and in April 1988 the house was opened as a memorial to her and the Ten Boom family, and to their spiritual courage.

Great or St Bavo Church

The origins of this fine cathedral church go back to 1313, when a Church of St Bavo stood here. It was badly damaged in a fire of 1328 and the present enlarged building was constructed around it, beginning with the choir (1390), then the transept (1455) and nave (1481). The elegant tiered tower, made of wood covered in lead, was designed by Michiel Bartssoen in 1518. Inside the church there are memorials to see – to the artists Frans Hals and Pieter Saenredam – and the famous Christian Müller organ, played by both Handel and Mozart (who was aged ten at the time).

The entrance is through the lodge at 23 Oude Groenmarkt (Old Vegetable Market) at the south-east end. Go through an oak door to the Southern Ambulatory where, on the left, is the tombstone of Pieter Saenredam (more legible than some). Walk round to the front of the choir to the finely wrought brass screen by Jan Fyerens (1517). In the floor of the choir is the tombstone of Frans Hals, indicated by a lantern.

The choir is separated from the ambulatory by a carved oak screen with painted panels. On the pillars of the choir and transept are fifteenth-century tapestry designs discovered during restorations in the nineteenth century.

Look up to the great vaulted timber ceiling, and walk down the north transept past the Lady and Christmas Chapels to the curiously named Dog Whippers' Chapel, separated from the rest of the church by a cast-iron grille. This is dedicated to the men responsible for removing troublesome dogs from the church; the left-hand console, supporting the arch, features a dog-whipper in action.

The Christian Müller organ (1735–38) dominates the west end. Nearly 30m (100ft) high – the crowning lions and shield almost scrape the roof – it has 5,068 pipes and releases a quite awe-inspiring sound. Beneath it is a group of large white marble figures carved by Jan-Baptist Xavery in the mid-eighteenth century: Poetry and Music dedicate their art to Piety and so attain Eternity (the angel hovering above them). To the left of the organ is the Holy Ghost Bench, where members of the Holy Ghost Guild distributed bread to the poor of the town after the church service.

In the Brewers' Chapel next to the southern transept, now also a coffee shop, is a final curiosity. Marks on the central pillar show the respective heights of two unusually built local men. Daniel Cajanus, a giant of 2.64m (8ft 8in) died in Haarlem in 1749, aged 46; Simon Paap, a dwarf of 84cm (2ft 9in) died in Zandvoort in 1828, aged 39. (Six feet between them!) Look behind you to see, hanging between two pillars, three models of Dutch warships: a seventeenth-century frigate, a pinnace of the same period and a yacht of the sixteenth century.

Teylers Museum

This is the oldest public museum in Holland. It is based on the collections of Pieter Teyler van der Hulst, a wealthy Haarlem merchant who died in 1778. As you walk down Damstraat from the Great Church, look for the unnumbered house after No.19. Above its ornate doorway the word 'Teyler' indicates the original home of the collector. The museum, considerably enlarged since its foundation, occupies a number of interconnecting buildings which lead back from the entrance round the corner in Spaarne.

The Teylers Museum breathes the spirit of the Enlightenment.

Above the pediment at the entrance, the bronze figures of Art and Science are united by Fame. In the circular hall, mellow oak doorways, marble columns and recessed statues convey a powerful mood of eighteenth-century learning and scholarship.

The collections begin with Palaeontology, and include many animal skeletons and some important fossils. The museum's first director, Martinus van Marum, was a man of encyclopaedic interests and a distinguished scientist. Even he, however, made the occasional error.

In 1802 he acquired a famous fossil – No.8,432 in the end bay on the left – said to be the remains of 'a man who had witnessed the Great Flood'. However, exploring further, scientists in 1811 found two short limbs, one on either side of the 'spine', and the human fossil turned out to be not an 'old Sinner' from Noah's time but a giant salamander.

In the next room is an enormous electrostatic generator, built for Van Marum in 1784, the largest ever made; also Stirling's hot-air engine (1816), an ancient gramophone, a telephone of 1861, telescopes, resonators and other nineteenth-century apparatus.

Next is the magnificent galleried Oval Hall of 1784, the first room in Holland to be purpose-built for a museum. It is naturally lit through panels set in the sides of an oval dome. In the centre of the hall is a long oval display case with rock specimens. In cabinets around the walls are more scientific instruments: magnets, scales, models of water mills, corn mills, electrometers, microscopes, orreries, celestial spheres, and a 1785 model by Adams of London showing Jupiter and her four largest satellites, as discovered by Galileo in 1609.

At each end of the Oval Hall, some 15m (50ft) apart, two parabolas face each other; at the centre of one of them, a ticking watch is held on cross-wires. Put your head in the bowl of the far dish and you can still hear the watch (the sound reflected from the curve of the 'sender' dish). Here too is a monster magnifying glass, 1 metre in diameter, set at a suitable angle for startling young visitors.

Among the treasures in the cabinets of the gallery, not open to the public, is a set of Diderot's famous *Encylopédie* (completed in 1772). From the ground floor of the Oval Hall a corridor leads through to the old house of Pieter Teyler; in nearby rooms are a lecture theatre and music library.

Next is the Medal Cabinet, with a valuable collection of Dutch coins and medals from the fifteenth to the twentieth centuries; magnifying glasses on long strings are thoughtfully provided. Continue into the first of the Art Rooms.

Thanks to an inspired purchase in 1790, the Teyler Foundation acquired part of a collection of drawings that had belonged to Queen Christina of Sweden, including works by Michelangelo, Raphael and Guercino. The first room is less exciting: rather staid Dutch landscapes of the nineteenth century predominate, though there is a good Breitner – *Two Serving Maids on a Bridge at Evening*.

The special treat is in a small room at the end. The museum's priceless drawings are shown here in traditional style, mounted on the wall but each behind its own small curtain. Pull back to reveal a Michelangelo (*Three Men at Prayer*), then others by Goltzius, Raphael, Bassetti, Van Ostade, Claude Lorrain, Rembrandt, Watteau. This marvellous collection is rotated to protect the drawings from undue exposure; for the viewer, there is always the extra thrill of not knowing what lies behind the next curtain.

In the adjoining gallery are eighteenth- and nineteenth-century paintings. These too are displayed in a traditional manner. In a group of five, the outer two are landscapes, winter on the left, summer on the right; in the centre is a history painting, and on either side of it are still-lives of fruit and flowers. The paintings are lit, moreover, by natural light. A curved glass roof beams the light down on to the paintings, and on a bright day gives them an extraordinary lustre. There is no glass in the picture frames, and the difference can be astonishing. The colours, for example of Kokkoek's *Winter Landscape* or flowers by Van Os, are stunningly bright.

There is much to be said for the methods of this excellent museum, demonstrating the spirit of the Enlightenment by the way they organise themselves.

Amsterdamse Poort

Follow the Route (see earlier) into Spaarnwouderstraat and keep straight on to the last surviving city gate, dating from the fourteenth century. You may already have seen a painting of it in the Frans Hals Museum, by Isaac Oudwater (*c*.1785), showing the view across the water from the Amsterdam side.

Beyond this turreted outpost of the medieval city are modern flats, a

noisy ring road and factory belt. Turn back and return beside the canal to the white bridge. This eastern quarter of Haarlem contains no other buildings of great note, but many charming small houses with decorative gables. A wise houseboat owner has turned his home into a flower garden, placing a gazebo at the entrance and crowding decks and quayside with leafy plants, and geraniums and hyacinths in tubs.

Begijnhof

Going back across the bridge, look over to the Neo-Classical façade of Teylers Museum, then bear right to a straight and narrow canal, the Bakenessergracht. This part of the city is crowded with churches, tucked away along narrow lanes and in tiny squares. The Renaissance spire of the Bakenesserkerk rises on its brick tower to the right. Above the roofs the Grote Kerk is never out of sight for long. Through herringbone-cobbled alleys we reach the neat brick Waalse or Walloon Church, until 1586 the chapel of the Begijnhof and the oldest church in Haarlem. I have never managed to find it open, though a plaque on the wall enticingly mentions frescos in the choir of c.1400, and wooden Gothic vaulting in the sacristy.

This is the Begijnhof, and on the left of the Waalsekerk is the Begijnhof chapel. Two quaint neighbours live in this peaceful backwater of almshouse cottages – the green-painted brothel alleys of De Poortje and Het Steegje, a red lamp at the entrance to each. In the screened-off hinterland, girls in de-luxe wooden cabins pose on chairs in the windows, and a ragged procession of cross-looking men passes up and down.

Arriving in Donkere Begijnhof, turn right to find the old goldsmiths' quarter. On the right is their *'Goutsmitscamer'*, in the Middle Ages part of the Begijnhof and between 1614 and about 1800 the seat of Haarlem's gold- and silversmiths. Around the corner in Goudsmitspleintje, the same house is decorated with a gold pot and the inscription *'Dit is de Gout Smits Camer'* (This is the Goldsmiths' Chamber).

Return along Donkere Begijnhof to Jansstraat. On the right is the Neo-Classical Roman Catholic Church of St Joseph. Opposite is the pretty brick Janskerk, once the cloister of the St Jans Order of Monks formed in 1310, and now part of the Municipal Archives complex.

Continue along Jansstraat to Grote Markt. On the right, at No.54, is the charming if decrepit gateway to the former St Barbara Gasthuis for women. This is the last vestige of a hospital founded in 1435. Above the entrance is a coloured relief of the interior of the hospital: it shows a white room with a green and orange tiled floor, and bed-recesses ranged along one of the walls.

Our walk ends shortly in the market square. Refreshments all around. To reach the station, go along Jansstraat, or retrace via the approach route of *Walk 15*.

Walk 17

Leiden A: Lakenhal to Hooglandse Kerk

A gentle introduction to a gentle place. Moving just slightly faster than the torpid currents of the Old and New Rhine, we visit the excellent Lakenhal Museum, the medieval market-place, the Burcht – the restored ramparts of a 12C castle – and the Hooglandse Kerk.

Allow 4–5 hours.

Best times Not Monday, when Lakenhal Museum and Hooglandse Kerk closed. Market days are Wednesday, Saturday.

ROUTE

Begin at Leiden Station. At exit, cross road into Stationsweg. (If required, VVV information office is in row of shops facing station.) Continue into Steenstraat, and at Beestenmarkt, with boat pier (*Rondvaart*) on far side, turn left to Oude Singel. Here visit the city's historical museum, the **Stedelijk Museum de Lakenhal** ☞ ; open 10.00 to 17.00, Sunday and holidays 13.00 to 17.00, closed Monday. *Admission, takes Museum Pass.*

At exit, turn left and walk to next bridge. Cross here, under beautiful dome of Mare Kerk, and walk down Lange Mare and Stille Mare to river. Cross tubular bridge facing old Weigh-house (Waag) and turn left. At **Visbrug** turn left, stopping maybe for a drink at one of the floating cafés moored here. Keep straight on and turn right to Oude Rijn (S bank).

At next narrow bridge, turn right through iron gate into Van der Sterrepad. This brings you to the **Burcht**, a restored 12C castle ☞. Turn right through 1st gateway and climb path up grassy mound to entrance. Inside, steps on right lead up to ramparts for fine all-round views over city.

Exit and walk down steps to courtyard, where old coach-house, the Koetshuis 'de Burcht', makes a most agreeable drink or lunch stop.

Turn left past Central Library and go through iron gateway to Nieuwstraat. Ahead is vast **Hooglandse Kerk**, entrance on S side ☞ ; open May to September, Tuesday to Saturday 11.00 to 15.30, Monday 13.00 to 15.30, Sunday service 10.00.

At exit, turn right and take 1st left along Beschuitsteeg to New Rhine (Nieuwe Rijn). Turn right and cross next bridge, Koornbrug, with market pavilions spanning river. Walk straight on past rear courtyard of **Town Hall (Stadhuis)** and turn right into Breestraat. Cross road for view of Dutch Renaissance façade of Stadhuis (1575).

Take next left into Pieterskerk Choorsteeg and continue to courtyard of **Pieters Kerk** (even larger than Hooglandse Kerk). Walk ends here. For nearest refreshments, turn right along Pieterskerkstraat and 1st left into Lokhorsstraat. On small terrace of Belgian café 't Gerecht you can relax opposite step-gabled Latin School at No.16, where Rembrandt was once a pupil.

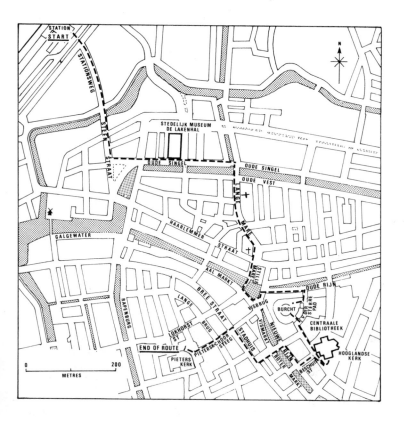

Advance to the Beast Market

At Leiden Station, either on the platform or downstairs, check the return trains to Amsterdam. Currently there are two to three Inter-City trains an hour to Centraal Station and two an hour to RAI Station. Walk into town along Stationsweg and at the canal bridge look left to the windmill – the 'De Valk' or Falcon museum which is the last calling point on *Walk 18*, as we return to the station.

There is so much to see in Leiden, it would be as well to think of the two Slow Walks as needing almost a full day each. To try and telescope the pair into a single Increasingly Rapid Walk might be a cause for regret.

The Beestenmarkt is now an unremarkable car park with a boat pier

offering round trips on the canals (*Rondvaart*). In the summer season boat trips depart on the hour – or are cancelled if not enough people turn up (business seems to be particularly slow in the morning).

Leiden stands at the junction of the slow-moving Old Rhine (Oude Rijn) and New Rhine (Nieuwe Rijn). The inner city is ringed by two concentric canals, so a stretch of water is never far away (and there are plenty of bridges). References to certain historic events and individuals occur in Leiden with unusual frequency, and below I have summarised the main ones:

Siege of Leiden (1574) The medieval city, famous for its cloth-making and brewing industries, joined the Dutch revolt against Spain and was besieged. Disease and starvation were widespread before William I the Silent, Prince of Orange, broke the dykes, flooding the land to allow Admiral Boisot's rescue fleet (the 'Sea Beggars') to sail across the inundated countryside and relieve the city.

University of Leiden William rewarded the town for its bravery against the Spanish by setting up the country's first Protestant university, which became a prestigious centre of learning.

Famous artists Rembrandt was born here in 1606. Other eminent Leiden artists are Jan van Goyen (1596–1656), Gerrit Dou (1613–75), Jan Steen (*c*.1626–79) and Gabriël Metsu (1629–67).

Pilgrim Fathers In 1608 a group of Puritans, refugees from England, formed a community in Leiden led by their pastor, John Robinson. Here they prepared for their journey to North America in the *Mayflower* (1620).

Museum 'De Lakenhal'

Above the front gateway a carved fulling-mill announces this building's old association with the cloth trade. From 1640 until 1800 the Governors of the Cloth Hall met here to examine and grade bales of cloth before they were sold and shipped away, stamping each bale with a lead seal.

Cross the forecourt, decorated with gablestones and architectural fragments, to the museum, which through a series of fascinating rooms illuminates Leiden's history and artistic heritage. The building, by Arent van 's-Gravensande, dates from 1640 and is in the Dutch Palladian style. At the front desk a brochure is available. Getting from one numbered room to another is not clearly explained, however, and I suggest the following route.

From the main hall (a thin collection of arms and armour), enter L3 – the Tile Department, a brilliant display of Flemish and Dutch tiles from *c*.1580 to the nineteenth century. Delicate and pretty animal and plant designs on the border tiles, and bolder scenes on the unglazed hearth-tiles used to reflect warmth from the fire, then large tile pictures in the Old Dutch Room.

Turn left after the last tile room and right, not ahead, into a corridor of archaeological finds (L6). This is the easiest way to find L7, the Old Dutch Kitchen, once part of the caretaker's premises, a red-tiled room with a twin pump for rainwater and wellwater, and a fireplace with an iron haul for cooking pots.

Turn right and right at the end, and go upstairs to the Great Press (*Grote Pers*). On the way up, see Van Bree's huge painting of Van der Werff's heroic act. Leiden's burgomaster during the Spanish siege, he offered his own body as food to the starving townspeople, and is here shown dramatically pointing a sword to his stomach. What happened next? In fact the burghers rejected his offer, but were inspired to carry on resisting the Spanish.

To reach the Great Press, go through the door on the landing (P28) and turn left through the Surgeons' Room (L14). Here see the cupboard of early surgical instruments, finely made but forbiddingly thick, intimating the awesome pain suffered by contemporary patients. The Great Press is chiefly decorated with eight large civic guard groups by Joris van Schooten and with banners from their messroom. The monumental fireplace is from the old Town Hall (Stadhuis). Various guild relics are on show in nearby rooms. L9 is the Stamp Room, with dies and presses used to stamp the cloth-seals. The Brewers' Room (L13) has splendid large murals of hop-picking and brewing, originally painted c.1772 by Hendrik Meijer for the old Brewers' Guildhall.

Next room to visit is L15, the Pavilion. Return to the landing and turn right. The entrance is via P29, a charming small gallery with views of the city, among them the St Annahofje and a panorama, dated 1600, of the Fish Market – a little dark but the sloping stick figures of the customers and stall-holders are full of urgency.

In the Pavilion are large paintings of the wool industry and two which portray Amazing Events in the town's history. On 12 January 1807, snow lay on the ground when a gunpowder barge carrying 37,000 pounds of powder exploded on the Rapenburg. The blast killed 151, wounded 2,000, completely destroyed 68 houses and left 80 others in ruins. The painting, in the manner of a newspaper photograph, shows the bleak aftermath. Next to it is a model barge made from a plank of the real vessel.

The other painting, comical by comparison, shows the plundering of a house on the Aalmarkt in June 1748. The owner was apparently an unpopular landlord, and the people of the neighbourhood are seen taking their revenge, dropping objects from upstairs windows and flinging them into the canal. Also here is a vigorous painting of *The Siege and Relief of Leiden*, and the *Lanckaert Tapestry* which shows the route taken by the 'Sea Beggars' who sailed in to relieve the city.

Take the stairs down to the picture galleries (the S series of rooms). Turn left to S17 (Hartevelt Gallery). Ahead is one of the most cherished pictures in the collection, the triptych of *The Last Judgment* (1526) by Lucas van Leyden, painted for the baptismal chapel of St Peter's Church (Pieterskerk). In S18 is an early Rembrandt, *Palamedes before Agamemnon* (1626). See also the immensely detailed pen-and-ink drawing by Willem van de Velde the Elder of the Dutch fleet, made in 1645, and Van Goyen's *View of Leiden* (1650). From the side of S18 go into the passage (S19) for more views by Van Goyen. In S20 are Gerrit Dou's *Astronomer* and genre scenes by Jan Steen and Frans van Mieris the Elder.

Turn right and right through the corridor of the Pape Wing, containing eighteenth-century furniture and sculpture, and return via L6 to the front entrance.

To the Market

Refreshments are available nearby, but hang on for ten minutes and the choice improves. Continue along Oude Singel to the next bridge, looking across to the elegant dome of the Marekerk (Waterway Church), designed by Arent van 's Gravensande and built in 1638-48, the first Protestant church in Leiden. The octagonal brick drum, with the compass points lettered over the windows, rises above the canal houses, supporting a shallow ribbed dome in the form of a half-grapefruit. Look up past the four clocks, set at the cardinal points, to the slender domed lantern surmounted by a gilt burning bush, the cross-keys of Leiden and a slender wind-vane.

Turn into Mare, until 1953 a canal. Continue across Haarlemmer-straat, a pedestrianised shopping street, to Stille Mare, busy with cafés. Cross the tubular bridge to the old Waag (Weigh-house) and turn left. Arrive at Visbrug, where the Old and New Rhine meet. On Wednesday and Saturday market stalls stretch away on both banks of the Old Rhine.

Take a break, maybe, at a table on one of the barges moored by the bridge. This is where, in the Middle Ages, the town's fish cargoes were unloaded and stored. Underneath the bridge, the low vaulted cellars now serve the cafés as inner rooms and kitchens.

The Castle

Cross the bridge to the Old Rhine and turn right. At the first narrow bridge turn right through a gateway to Leiden's twelfth-century castle, the Burcht, built by the Counts of Holland. The town grew outwards from this fortified mound which nestles in the confluence of the two rivers, an admirable stronghold.

It is always a surprise to come upon it. After walking along flat streets between canals, with no prospect of a break in the horizontal pattern, suddenly you turn a corner and begin scaling this sizeable man-made mound to the restored keep. Steps inside the enclosure lead up to the ramparts for excellent views of the city. From here you are at roof-level with the rest of Leiden, topped only by the Town Hall steeple and the cliff-like façades of the Hooglandse Kerk.

Be warned that there is no safety rail on the inner side of the ramparts. If this makes you uncomfortable, stay within the railed area close to the steps – better this than be assailed by altitude panics halfway round the circuit of the wall.

At the main gate, walk down the flight of steps to a courtyard, where a most pleasant place to stop for a drink or early lunch is Koetshuis 'de Burcht'. Inside the spacious hall, sit at a table on the cobbled floor of the old coach-house. Try the *Huzarensalade*, a *'burcht'* of chopped potato with mayonnaise, surrounded by salad.

Hooglandse Church

Turn past the Central Library and go through an ornamental gateway to Nieuwstraat. On top of the gate a flamboyant sword-waving lion guards the shield of Leiden above the motto 'Pugno Pro Patria' (I fight for my country).

Ahead is the vast Hooglandse or St Pancras Church, the late Gothic nave rising behind the west tower. This is the only surviving part of the original fourteenth-century church. The rest came into being between 1380 and 1515.

The entrance is on the south side, leading to the transept. It is astonishingly large and barn-like, the columns a fierce cream colour, and almost entirely lacking in spiritual atmosphere. In the transept are special exhibitions and artefacts on loan from the town's museums. On the south-east pillar at the crossing, horn-blowing cherubs frame the memorial to Pieter Adriaansz. van der Werff, the heroic burgomaster.

Corn Exchange Bridge and Town Hall

Traverse the irregular cobbles of Beschuitsteeg to the New Rhine. Turn right to the next bridge, the Koornbeursbrug, covered on each side by attractive open-sided pavilions built in 1825. Continue through

Koornbrugsteeg to the front of the Town Hall (Stadhuis).

Most of the building was destroyed by fire in 1929. The main façade, on Breestraat, survived and is a magnificent example of Early Dutch Renaissance architecture. Designed in 1595 by Lieven de Key, a refugee from Antwerp who also worked extensively in Haarlem (see *Walk 15*), the main entrance, the gables and steeple are unusually rich in strapwork, pinnacles and ornamental statues.

It was from these front steps that, on 3 October 1574, the town clerk announced that the Spanish siege was over. He called upon the citizens to go immediately to the Pieterskerk and give thanks for their miraculous relief. We now follow the route they took, along Pieterkerk-choorsteeg. On the right, look for the tiny brick-arched entrance between Nos 17 and 19. In the house in the alley William Brewster, a Pilgrim Father, ran the Pilgrim Press which printed tracts promoting their movement and criticising the attitude of the Church of England.

We arrive in the courtyard of St Pieterskerk, where this walk ends. For refreshments, seek out the Belgian café 't Gerecht (see Route). From its small terrace you face the step-gabled Latin School, where from about 1615 to 1619 Rembrandt was a pupil. He was then aged 9–13 and not keen on Latin. His reluctance to study eventually persuaded his parents that he should follow his natural talent for painting and drawing. In 1619 he left the Latin School and began a three-year apprenticeship with the Leiden painter, Jacob Isaacz. van Swanenburg. Still less than fourteen years old, he had found his vocation.

Walk 18

Leiden B: The University Quarter

Enjoy the quiet academic mood surrounding Holland's first Protestant university and its pioneering Botanical Gardens, and trace the story of the Pilgrim Fathers who settled here before sailing to New England.

Allow   3–4 hours.

Best times   Afternoon, Tuesday to Thursday, when University Historical Museum open (13.00). Pieterskerk not open until 13.30. Not Monday, when Archaeological Museum and Windmill Museum closed. Pilgrim Fathers Collection closed Saturday, Sunday.

For historical notes about Leiden, see *Walk 17*.

ROUTE

Begin at **Pieterskerk** ☞ ; open 13.30 to 16.00. *Admission*. At exit, turn left and walk round churchyard to **Jan Pesijn Hofje**, built on site of house where Pilgrim leader John Robinson lived. Push door open and look at courtyard.

Turn W along Kloksteeg to Rapenburg. Cross Nonnenbrug and turn left, then follow bend of Rapenburg and turn right at River Vliet. At bottom on right is **Pilgrim Fathers Collection (or Documentation Centre)** ☞ ; open 09.30 to 16.30, closed Saturday, Sunday. Ring bell.

At exit, turn left and 1st left into Bakkersteeg. Turn right into Kaiserstraat, passing two almshouses – Jeruzalemshofje at No.49 and Bethaniën- or Emmaushofje at No.43. Return to Rapenburg, and at No.73 turn left to **University Historical Museum** ☞; open Tuesday to Thursday 13.00 to 17.00.

Turn left to **University Botanical Gardens (Hortus Botanicus)** ☞; open 1 April to 30 September 09.00 to 17.00, Sunday 10.00 to 17.00; 1 October to 31 March same hours but closed Saturday. *Admission*. Booklet, in Dutch only, contains useful map (see essay for further details). Be sure to visit glasshouses (*Kassen*), then wander round paths and exit across bridge to **Clusiustuin** ☞; open 1 April to 30 September, 10.00 to 12.30 and 13.30 to 16.00, closed Saturday, Sunday and winter months.

At exit, turn right on 5^e Binnenvestgracht and 2nd right along Nonnensteeg to Rapenburg. Turn left past University building and cross next bridge, Doelenbrug. At 28 Rapenburg visit excellent **National Museum of Antiquities (Rijksmuseum van Oud-heden)** ☞ ; open 10.00 to 17.00, Sunday 12.00 to 17.00, closed Monday. *Admission, takes Museum Pass*.

On leaving, turn right and at next bridge turn left past war memorial to Noordeinde. Cross Oude Varkenmarkt and take next right up Weddesteeg to river and **Rembrandtbrug** (painter born nearby). Cross river and bear right past windmill to 1^e Binnenvestgracht. On left at the Morsstraat crossing is one of the old city gates, the Morspoort. Turn right along Morsstraat, cross bridge to Turfmarkt and turn left.

Keep straight on via Nieuwe Beestenmarkt to **Windmill Museum (Molenmuseum 'de Valk')** ☞; open 10.00 to 17.00, Sunday 13.00 to 17.00, closed Monday. *Admission*. Go up ladders to see exhibits on six levels, including outdoor viewing platform.

At exit, turn right on road and walk along 2e Binnenvestgracht to

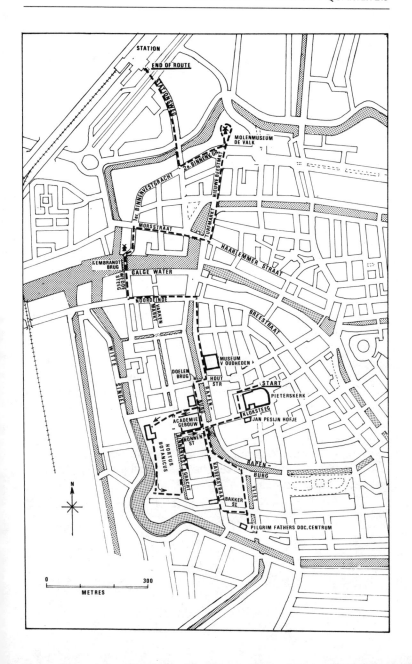

Stationsweg. At Grand Café Restaurant (good refreshment stop, if time before train), turn right and return to railway station. Walk ends here.

St Peter's Church

Although desanctified in 1975, the Pieterskerk has retained much of its old warmth. The pale red brickwork, arching above the pillars of the tall nave, can still inspire a feeling of wonder. A church on this site was consecrated to SS Peter and Paul in 1121, and thus the foundation served more than 450 years – until the Alteration of 1578 – as the oldest and largest of Leiden's three Roman Catholic parish churches.

The present late-Gothic basilica was completed about 1500. In 1512 its tower collapsed and was never rebuilt; there is a view of the old tower in the Lakenhal Museum. Since the church is now an educational and cultural centre, the great nave may be filled with school desks or an art exhibition. All the same, the wooden choir screen and richly polished organ are worth a closer look, also the various guildboards which hang from the pillars. See also the exhibition on the history of the church, in the south aisle, with stones from the original structure and the great bell, the 'Bonaventura', made by Willem Moer in 1490. Here too is the Leidse Mummy, the skeleton of a man aged about fifty, discovered in 1979 when the floor of the nave was dug up. There he was, lying in a wooden box with a cushion under his head. Three teeth projecting from the lower jaw help to remind us of his humanity – and calm the wish to run away in horror.

The pastor of the Pilgrim Fathers, John Robinson, is buried in the south-west corner of the church, and an external plaque on the south wall bears this inscription:

THE MAYFLOWER, 1620
IN MEMORY OF
REV. JOHN ROBINSON, M.A.
PASTOR OF THE ENGLISH CHURCH WORSHIPING OVER AGAINST
THIS SPOT. A.D.1609-1625. WHENCE AT HIS PROMPTING WENT FORTH
THE PILGRIM FATHERS
TO SETTLE NEW ENGLAND

IN 1620
BURIED UNDER THIS HOUSE OF WORSHIP, 4 MAR. 1625
AE^T XLIX YEARS.

On the way round the church you will pass a large pedimented building in the north-west corner of the churchyard, the tympanum containing lions and the cross keys of Leiden. This is *Het Gravensteen*, one of a group of buildings that furnished the medieval Counts of Holland with a castle and a prison. It is now part of the University Law School.

The Pilgrim Fathers

Facing the Robinson plaque, at No.21 Kloksteeg, is the Jan Pesijnhofje, an almshouse built in 1683. The door may look shut, but give it a push and walk through the porch to the tree-shaded courtyard. The present almshouse is attached to the Walloon (French-speaking Calvinist) church. Before it was built, John Robinson lived here between 1611 and 1625 in a house called De Groene Poort (The Green Gate). Other English Separatists had small houses built in the garden, which became known as 'The English Close'.

At the end of Kloksteeg we reach the Rapenburg canal. Across the Nonnenbrug is the Academy building of the University, which we visit shortly. For now we are in pursuit of Pilgrims and follow the bend of Rapenburg to the sleepy backwater of the River Vliet, fringed with water-lilies. It was from here that, in 1620, the Mayflower Pilgrims sailed to Delfshaven on the first stage of their voyage to America. Here, too, in 1574, when the Spanish siege was lifted, the Prince of Orange's relieving troops arrived with boat-loads of herring, bread and cheese for the starving population.

The Pilgrim Fathers Collection is in the end house on the right. Ring the bell, and be admitted to the exhibition room. A fifteen-minute slide show (in English) is worth seeing as much for background on Leiden itself as for its account of the Pilgrims. Here, for example, I began to appreciate better the extreme hardships of the Spanish siege. At the time, Leiden was one of the most successful towns in Holland, with a population of 12,500; the siege claimed 6,000 of them, victims of hunger and disease. After the siege, Leiden received a large influx of refugees from Belgium, especially after the fall of Protestant Antwerp in 1585.

Thus, as the University was beginning to establish itself in the city, raising scholarship and learning to new levels, Leiden also became host to a dozen or so religious groups. Among them were Roman Catholics, Eastern Orthodox, Jews, Lutherans, Dutch Mennonites, English Separatists (the Pilgrims), Muslims, Quakers, Moravians, Huguenots, and members of the Reformed Churches of England, Germany and Holland.

The English Puritans (Separatists) arrived in Leiden from 1609 escaping from religious persecution directed at them by James I. About a hundred settled in the town, getting all sorts of jobs in the textile industry and other trades. When they decided to leave, to form a more ideal community in America than they could achieve in Leiden, they bought a ship, the *Speedwell*, and chartered another, the *Mayflower*. The departing group left the Netherlands on 31 July 1620. Among them were Philippe de la Noy, ancestor of President Franklin Delano Roosevelt, and John Jenney and Sarah Carey, ancestors of President George Bush.

John Robinson remained in Leiden with some of his flock, hoping to travel to America with a later group. He died in Leiden in 1625, and within a few years all the Pilgrims who wished to leave had done so. The others were assimilated into Dutch society.

University of Leiden

On the way to the Academy building we pass through Kaiserstraat. At No.49 is the Jeruzalemshofje, the oldest almshouse in Leiden, founded in 1467. It was renovated at the beginning of this century and is now a neat courtyard of pantiled cottages. Further along, at No.43, is the Bethaniën- or Emmaushofje, another fifteenth-century foundation, renovated in 1907. Altogether Leiden has thirty-five *hofjes*. Some abide by their original conditions of use, being limited to women only, or married couples, or elderly people suffering from chronic diseases. Others have been renovated and turned into accommodation for students.

When the Prince of Orange proposed the foundation of a university in Leiden, in December 1574, he stated his wish to create a place where young people could learn 'the right knowledge of God and all sorts of good, honest and free arts and sciences that serve the legal government of the lands'. The training of Protestant ministers clearly took first priority, and a large Faculty of Theology came into being, whose members studied religious doctrine. They were supported by philologists from the Faculty of Arts who specialised in the study of the Bible. The University was also eminent in Literature, Law, Physics and Medicine, establishing itself as a humanistic centre which attracted scholars and philosophers from many countries. It became especially strong in practical applications for the sciences, setting up a pioneering anatomical theatre in 1592, a botanical garden in 1594 and an observatory in 1632.

The small but fascinating University Historical Museum is located on the ground floor of the Academy building, which until 1581 was the chapel of the Convent of the White Nuns. It has displays on the work of the various faculties, and panels on some of the great thinkers who came to Leiden, among them Descartes who enrolled at the University in 1630 – not to study but because he sought a quiet and appropriate atmosphere in which to pursue his thoughts.

There are entertaining records, too, of student life, including the costumed processions which after 1825 became grandly organised masquerades, and the University militia companies who served their country in several campaigns. Upstairs is a small room where students, waiting to be examined, covered the walls and table with their names. Above the door to this Chamber of Autographs is a charcoal inscription, quoting Dante's version of the entrance to Hell: *'Lasciate ogni Speranza voi che entrate'* (Abandon all hope, you who enter).

Botanical Gardens

Founded in 1594, the Hortus Botanicus is one of the oldest botanical gardens in Europe. It was founded as an aid to the Faculty of Medicine, for growing medicinal herbs and studying their application. Stroll through these seemingly wild gardens, cross the lily stream and head for the large greenhouse with the cockerel windvane on top. Turn right at the first greenhouse and left past the lawn to reach the public entrance. On the lawn to the right, four expressive standing stones are trapped in the endless dispute of dons.

In the wonderful Palmhouse, a damp and joyous riot of exotic greenery, wander beneath immense palms from Madagascar, Bengal, Burma, Sri Lanka, Malaysia and Indonesia. Somewhere here, try to pick up the signposted route (*'Looproute'*) which with luck and application will bring you to a sliding door at the end of a passage. Go upstairs to the *Victoriakas*, where gigantic lilies with spiky rims (*Victoria amazonica*) float in their pond.

Then wander the paths outside, aiming to find the Hortus Clusianus which lies just outside the main gardens, reached by a bridge halfway along the eastern side. Cross the narrow waters of the 5^e Binnenvestgracht to a door in the wall opposite. Inside the walled garden is a grid of slender brick-lined beds which reproduce the original Hortus plan of 1594. This was designed by the first prefect or keeper of the gardens, Carolus Clusius, whose bust stands at the far end.

Museum of Antiquities

If you began the day with *Walk 17*, you may now be running out of time. Never mind, you must have seen a lot already and may feel like giving

Leiden a second day. One of the problems of devising walks in this town is that both the Pieterskerk (13.30) and University Museum (13.00) are late starters, and so it is always a bit of a scramble to fit everything in. An immediate solution is to return to Rapenburg and retire gracefully to the terrace of the Café Barrera, opposite the Academy building, and watch the students come and go.

At 28 Rapenburg, the Museum of Antiquities (Rijksmuseum van Oudheden) is the national museum of archaeology. Its design and presentation are excellent, handling anything from a full-sized temple down to tiny Greco-Roman terracotta figurines.

The star attraction faces you in the entrance hall: the Egyptian Temple of Taffeh, dating from the first century AD. It was dismantled in 1960 and presented to the Netherlands by the Egyptian government as thanks for their role in supporting archaeological works along the Nile.

The temple is from Nubia, and from the fourth century was adapted for the worship of Ibis; it later became a Christian temple. Its somewhat glowering presence has been toned down by the museum's designers who have clad the surrounding walls of the gallery in panels of matching sandstone.

To the right of the main hall is part of the museum's fine Egyptian collection, a major assembly of steles and sculptures in red and black granite, limestone and red sandstone. Among the sarcophagi is the great black basalt tomb of Wah-ib-re-em-akhet, son of the Greek Alexikles; from Saqqara. On the first floor are more Egyptian treasures – painted coffins and canopic jars, wooden sarcophagi, mummies and masks, and shabtis: burial objects to serve the dead in the after-life, in the form of kings and ordinary people, in wood, terracotta and faience. Also on this floor are collections of glass, Classical vases, and the national collection of coins and medals. On the second floor is a survey of archaeological finds made in the Netherlands – prehistoric, Roman and medieval.

Rembrandt Quarter

Walk along Rapenburg through the old patrician sector, the double-fronted houses now mainly in the hands of university departments. This is the last of sleepy Leiden. The border with noisy Leiden is at the war memorial spanning the canal. In Noordeinde, look for the turning on the right called Weddesteeg. Although the old buildings have gone, this was the street where Rembrandt's parents lived and where he was born.

The painter's father, Harmen Gerritsz. van Rijn, was a miller and his mother, Neeltgen, was the daughter of a baker. Two of Rembrandt's grandparents owned windmills close to the Rhine on this side of the river.

Cross the steep bridge, the Rembrandtbrug – in the centre it is rather like negotiating a pitched roof – and look across to the right. The large Renaissance house dates from 1612 and is one of the few in the district that Rembrandt would recognise. It is the Stadstimmerwerf or Municipal Carpenters' Yard.

Walk through to Morsstraat. On the left is the domed 'Morschpoort', built in 1669, one of the two surviving city gates. Go through the gate and across the bridge, then look back to see how this old west gate appeared in the seventeenth century to travellers arriving at the city.

Windmill Museum

Follow the Route (see above) to the centre of town and arrive at the Molenmuseum 'de Valk' (the Falcon). The last miller to work this eighteenth-century cornmill, Willem van Rijn*, died in 1965 and the building was then converted into a museum.

On the ground floor, the miller's house has an agreeable turn-of-the-century atmosphere. On the first floor is a slide show (Dutch or English) and the exhibit on the second floor tells the history of windmills in Leiden. The patron saint of millers is St Victor and the Guild of St Victor in Leiden was founded in 1485. On the third floor are models of mills and guild medals. This brick-built mill dates from 1743, replacing an earlier wooden one. Mind your head on the stairs up to the viewing platform. Step outside for panoramic views, and a close-up of the sails whisking past.

You can go up two more levels, among the blocks and pulleys of the sack hoist, to where the action began. The sacks of corn were hoisted up here through trapdoors, then the contents were poured through a shute and hopper to the stone attic, where the corn was ground between pairs of millstones. Rather a jolly visit to round off a day in Leiden. Even I (Supremely Non-technical Man) was able to grasp the mechanics involved.

From here it is only a short walk to Leiden Station. Refreshment facilities are not great at the station, so if you have a train-time in mind, stop off at the Grand Café Restaurant on the corner of Stationsweg.

*No relation to the painter, though he searched long and hard to find a connection.

Walk 19

Utrecht A: City Centre and Cathedral

In the medieval centre of Utrecht, stroll by the 'sunken' canal, visit the jolly Museum of Musical Boxes and Street Organs, the Pieterskerk with its Romanesque treasures, and the choir of the Cathedral and its gigantic tower, tallest in The Netherlands.

Allow   3–4 hours.

Best times   Not Monday, when museum and Pieterskerk closed.

ROUTE

Begin at railway station. From platform, go up to main concourse and walk through to **Hoog Catharijne shopping centre**. Bear left and follow signs to 'Gildenkwartier', 'VVV' and 'Vredenburg'. On right, just before the 'Uitgang Vredenburg', is the VVV information office.

Outdoors at last, turn right and next right at Smits Hotel. Walk through Vredenburg market-place (general on Wednesday, antiques and junk on Saturday) and turn left into Drie Haringstraat. At pretty **Oude Gracht**, turn right and walk along upper level beside canal, or sample a wharfside café down below.

Take 5th right into Hekelsteeg. Cross Steenweg into 1e Buurkerksteeg and arrive at the Buurkerk, now the **Museum 'From Musical Box to Street Organ' (Nationaal Museum Van Speelklok tot Pierement)** ☞ ; open 10.00 to 17.00, closed Monday and some public holidays. Guided tours on the hour until 16.00. *Admission, takes Museum Pass.*

Leaving the museum, turn left and left up Choorstraat to **Town Hall (Stadhuis)**. Turn right across bridge into Oudekerkhof.

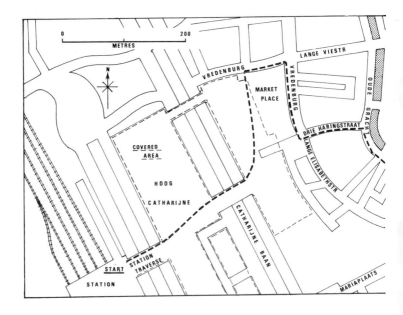

Diversion Take next left and 3rd right and visit neat little **Grocery Museum** at 6 Hoogt. It's a combination of working shop, selling dry goods and old-fashioned sweets from jars, with upstairs a room full of non-edible groceriana – covetable tins, boxes and tools of the trade; open 12.30 to 16.30, closed Sunday, Monday.

Continue to Achter St Pieter, take 2nd left into Pieterskerkhof and visit **Pieterskerk** ❧ ; open June to September, 11.00 to 16.30, Saturday 10.00 to 13.00, closed Sunday, Monday. Opening dates vary from year to year; ask VVV for details. *Admission*.

Return to Achter St Pieter and turn left, passing Provinciehuis and arriving in square called Pausdam. On corner is 16C **Paushuize**, the papal residence built for Adriaan VI, the only Dutch pope (he never lived there). Nod politely to gateman and he will not mind you looking in at courtyard.

From Pausdam, follow Achter de Dom up to E end cathedral. Turn left into cloisters. On far side, walk through to Domplein where

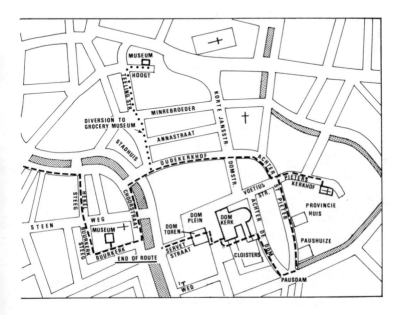

entrances to **Cathedral (Domkerk)** and separate **Tower (Dom-toren)** face each other ☞.

Domkerk open May to September 10.00 to 17.00, October to April 11.00 to 16.00, Sunday 14.00 to 16.00.

Domtoren open late March to 31 October 10.00 to 17.00, Saturday and Sunday 12.00 to 17.00; November to March 12.00 to 17.00, Saturday and Sunday only. Carillon recital Saturday 11.00 to 12.00. For climbers to the dizzying upper levels, guided tours usually depart on the hour. *Admission*.

Walk under the tower and turn through arch on left to **Flora's Hof** (1634), a quiet garden with reliefs on far wall illustrating life of St Martin, patron saint of Utrecht. Continue down Servetstraat to Oude Gracht.

Walk ends here. Nearest refreshments all around. Recommended: Opoe's Eethuis in 't Wed (next street parallel with Servetstraat).

Out from the Station

Utrecht is *the* railway city in the Netherlands, and in 1989 hosted a grand exhibition to celebrate 150 years of Dutch railways. The station is sparkling and new, and the citizens of Utrecht are proud of it.

They have rather more mixed feelings about the neighbouring Hoog Catharijne Centre, completed in 1983, through which you must walk to reach the city – a gigantic covered shopping and business centre with bus stations and car parking beneath. Follow the Route instructions past innumerable fast fooderies and trinket shops until you reach the VVV office, conveniently located close to an exit.

Call in at the VVV for supplementary maps and information should you need any. Nearby is an entrance to Music Centre Vredenburg, perhaps the most creditable enterprise in the Hoog Catharijne. This is a major venue for live music and currently puts on about four hundred concerts each season.

Ten to fifteen minutes after leaving the train, you find yourself at last in the open air. So this is Utrecht! Well, not quite. This is a rather anonymous market-place, better on Wednesday (food market) and better still, and larger, on Saturday when it's antiques and junk. To find the old centre of the city, which is altogether more attractive, turn along Drie Haringstraat and emerge on Oude Gracht.

This is much better. Below is the leafy 'sunken' canal and the lower wharf or quayside. Ahead the great tower of the fourteenth-century Cathedral dominates the view. To the left are two medieval tower-houses (*stadskastelen*). At No.99 is Oudaen, dating from 1320, now a high-ceilinged restaurant; in the eighteenth century it was a home for the elderly, and statues above the door of the adjoining house relate to that period. Across the canal is the impressive step-gabled Draken-borch, built in 1280. Somewhere here, take the steps down to the quayside and wander along. Several outdoor cafés have long terraces beside the water. Try Café Eethuis 'The Ostrich', open from 11.00.

Utrecht seems to abound with paradoxes and contradictions, one of which is that the sunken canals are not sunken at all. After the Oude

Gracht was dug in the twelfth century, the land beside the canal was allowed to rise naturally, through a combination of soil, manure and waste. When the land had risen some 3m (10ft) above the present quayside, houses were built on the upper level, creating a system of double streets that is unique in Europe. The deep cellars on the lower level, formerly used as warehouses and domestic stores, now serve as restaurants and shops.

Another interesting use of the lower quayside was to lock up drunks and short-stay offenders, in cells built inside some of the bridges. The cold and damp of those medieval lock-ups must have been a powerful deterrent to committing the same offence twice, to say nothing of the company provided by the swarms of bugs and rats also lodging there.

Utrecht now prospers as an industrial and business centre, though most of this activity is confined to the outskirts of the city. In the middle, around the 'sunken' canals, there is an air of lassitude, even stagnation, as time extends the gap between the present day and Utrecht's greatest period of power under the medieval bishops. In the early Middle Ages the bishops' sphere of influence reached as far as Groningen in north Holland. It was they who built Utrecht's many churches and cloisters, and attracted merchants from far and wide to establish themselves in the city.

By the sixteenth century, Utrecht had been surpassed by Amsterdam, and thereafter settled for a smaller role as capital of the province of Utrecht. Its geographical position at the centre of the country kept it for some time at the political forefront. As you will no doubt remember from your schooldays, the Union of Utrecht was signed in the chapter house of the Cathedral. In 1581 this alliance between some of the country's northern provinces formed the basic constitution of the Dutch Republic (the United Provinces of the Netherlands).

In 1713–14 two series of treaties were signed here, known as the Treaties of Utrecht or the Peace of Utrecht. One series reordered France's relationships with Britain, the Dutch Republic, Prussia, Portugal and Savoy. The other series put an end to the War of the Spanish Succession (1701–14).

Musical Boxes and Street Organs

We are in the thirteenth-century Buurkerk, the oldest parish church in

Utrecht, where each of the medieval craft guilds had its own altar. Here a Sister Bertken, unbearably ashamed at being illegitimate, had herself immured in a cell in the wall of the choir and remained there for more than fifty years until her death in 1514. In 1586 the choir was demolished and a new street, Choorstraat, took its place. Since 1984 the Gothic hall of the church has housed the quaint and amusing Museum 'From Musical Box to Street Organ' (Nationaal Museum van Speelklok tot Pierement).

The tour begins with the musical boxes, the guide introducing and playing some of the star exhibits. A French table clock plays three melodies and has flying and singing birds which perform in a tree. A child's chair plays when sat on. A large coin-operated precursor of the jukebox (c.1900), loaded with ten melodies, plays 'O Susannah' – and most of the elderly Dutch visitors know the words and join in. Then we see and hear various pianolas, one with built-in violins and another, an amazing belt-driven machine made in 1932 for a Belgian café, which plays organ and percussion. Then, dear to Dutch hearts, a room full of street and fairground organs. Deafening, especially the Belgian Hooghuys which hits you with a rolling, bounding boogie-woogie.

St Peter's Church

Wander past the Neo-Classical Town Hall (Stadhuis) and cross the Oude Gracht to Ouderkerkhof. Turn down through quiet cobbled streets to the eleventh-century Pieterskerk. This was the first of two Romanesque churches built by Bishop Bernold, who planned a cross of four churches centred on the Cathedral, the others being the Janskerk, Mariakerk and the Paulus Abbey.

The Pieterskerk, consecrated in 1048, is a wonderfully atmospheric place, with several Romanesque treasures. The striking nave pillars of red sandstone were cut from one great block and brought here by ship from Germany. On either side of the raised choir is a pair of Romanesque bas-reliefs (c.1170), discovered in 1965 beneath the old tiled floor. Those on the left show the Crucifixion and Pontius Pilate on his throne; those on the right depict an angel sitting on the empty sepulchre and the three women approaching the tomb with their jars of balsam. See also the baptismal font, from Maastricht. The four heads represent the four streams of Paradise.

In the semi-dark of the crypt, lit by candelabra and tiny circular panes of coloured glass, stands the sarcophagus of Bishop Bernold, who died six years after the church was completed. The six decorated pillars with Romanesque capitals are particularly fine.

The Bike Cycle

At the Union of Notaries building next to the Pieterskerk they auction off bicycles and household goods. On *Kijkdag* (viewing day), would-be buyers wander round the hall, no doubt hoping for treasure but finding mostly ancient saucepans and radios, and white goods on their last legs.

Best value are the bicycles. Such is the theft rate, not just here but throughout the country, it is now only possible to insure a new bike. Stealing has become a commercial operation, carried out in bulk with the aid of heavy metal-cutters and a getaway van. The life expectancy of a bicycle in the Netherlands, by which I mean the time you can expect to hang on to it, is measured in weeks rather than years. You can post-code it, shackle it to a lamp-post with a length of ship's anchor-chain, paint it pink with yellow spots – there always seems to be someone else who needs it more than you do.

The Only Dutch Pope

We stroll along Achter St Pieter, past the provincial council building (Provinciehuis) to Pausdam. On one corner of this attractive square is the step-gabled Papal Residence (Paushuize), built in 1517 for the only Dutch pope, Adriaan VI.

Adriaan Florisz. Boeyens of Utrecht was born in 1459 and educated at the University of Louvain, where he became Professor of Theology. Erasmus was one of his pupils. The Holy Roman Emperor Maximilian I then made him tutor to his grandson, the future Charles V. He was created cardinal in 1517 and elected pope in 1522. He died, however, the following year before he was able to live in the house that Utrecht built for him.

In 1959 the building was made over to the provincial council. If you step through into the courtyard there is nothing much to see but a car park, though the scale of the council buildings is impressive – a reminder of the existence of the 'other' Utrecht, the province which shares the same name as its capital city, and is governed from it.

The province of Utrecht is the central and smallest province of the Netherlands, extending southward from the South Flevoland polder of the IJsselmeer. Its other principal town is Amersfoort. The residence of the Queen Mother (Princess Juliana), in the village of Soestdijk near Baarn, is also within the provincial boundaries.

Cathedral and Tower

From Pausdam walk up to the Cathedral along Achter de Dom, passing on your left the statue of François Villon. Soon you come upon the Cathedral choir, a quite awe-inspiring view up to its multitude of Gothic pinnacles and buttresses, with the top of the Dom Tower just visible behind. Turn into the charming cloister, where low evergreen hedges frame twenty-two tiny flower and shrub gardens. On the far side, walk through to the Domplein and the imposing statue of Count Jan of Nassau, brother of William the Silent.

The Cathedral and Tower now face each other across the broad expanse of Domplein. They were originally built as separate structures and joined by an elevated bridge. In 1674 a hurricane destroyed the nave, which was never rebuilt although the débris remained much where it had fallen until 1826, when the Domplein was laid out in its present form.

What remains of the Cathedral – the eastern fragment from the transepts to the choir – has been recently restored and functions as a church. The entrance is through the small part of the nave that was left standing. The present Cathedral replaced an earlier Romanesque building destroyed beyond repair by a great city fire in 1253. In 1254 the foundation stone was laid for the new Cathedral, and building continued until 1520.

If you enter a Gothic cathedral expecting grey stone walls, cobwebs and tattered banners, you will be disappointed by this Cathedral's interior which is light, bright and Calvinist white. Many of the fittings and decorations are relatively new – the pews, pulpit and transept windows date from 1926–36, for example, and the font was installed in 1978. Of the older memorials, the most imposing is the tomb of Admiral Van Gendt, a canon of the Domkerk, who was killed in battle in 1672; the great white marble mausoleum stands in place of the old high altar.

Across the square the huge Tower awaits your visit. It is 112m (367ft) high, the tallest in the Netherlands, and visitors can go as high as the upper gallery, a not-inconsiderable journey of 465 steps, 102m (335ft) above ground. I confess that I have not climbed the Domtoren. What finally unnerved me was not purely the height of it, but looking up to those far-away galleries and seeing people nonchalantly gazing down – and I could see their legs. Instant vertigo!

As a structure the Tower is a masterpiece of Gothic architecture. It was built in three tiers between 1321 and 1382, the top one an octagonal lantern rich in ornamental tracery. It is Utrecht's finest monument to its great medieval past.

Flora's Hof

Near the base of the Tower an arch dated 1634 leads into Flora's Hof, a quiet garden with reliefs on the far wall illustrating the life of St Martin. He is the patron saint of Utrecht and the Cathedral is dedicated to him. He is most commonly represented cutting off part of his cloak with a sword and giving it to a beggar.

The garden was formerly the Bisschopshof or Bishop's Court, attached to the Episcopal Palace. The entrance gate bears the provincial coat-of-arms and was built for the governor of the city.

A well-earned lunch stop might best be had beside the Oude Gracht, where many terraces beckon. Around the next corner, in 't Wed, is Opoe's Eethuis, which has a comfortable terrace, a pretty beamed room and a good menu – and is also a shade quieter than most.

Walk 20

Utrecht B: Centraal Museum

By drowsing streets and tree-shaded backwaters to the city's historical museum, past almshouses and the Catharijne Convent Museum, which records the story of Christianity in the Netherlands and has the largest collection of medieval art in the country.

Allow   3 hours.

Best times   Not Monday, when museums closed.

ROUTE

Begin on **Oude Gracht** at bridge between Vismarkt and Lichte Gaard, where previous walk ended. Turn S along Gaard (first Lichte then Donkere) and take 2nd left into Hamburgerstraat.

At Nieuwe Gracht, turn right to **Catharijne Convent Museum** ☞; open 10.00 to 17.00, Saturday, Sunday and holidays 11.00 to 17.00, closed Monday and New Year's Day. *Admission, takes Museum Pass.*

Diversion To see historic almshouses, walk up Schalkwijkstraat. On right at end is Gasthuis Leeuwenberg, a 14C hospital for victims of the Plague. Street on left is **Bruntenhof**, with a long row of 17C almshouses next to old city wall. No.5, the 'Governor's entrance', has an ornate porch decorated with symbols of mortality – a cherub holding a skull, another with an hour-glass. Most encouraging for the inmates!

Leaving Catharijne Convent, turn right and walk down Nieuwe Gracht to Agnietenstraat. Entrance to **Centraal Museum** is on left ☞; open 10.00 to 17.00, Sunday and holidays 13.00 to 17.00, closed Monday, Christmas Day and New Year's Day. *Admission, takes Museum Pass.*

Continue along Agnietenstraat, turn left into Nicolaas Dwarsstraat, and follow into Wijde Doelen. Cross main road into Bijlhouwersstraat and walk into park. Turn right along path beside canal (Stadsbuiten Gracht) and walk up to **Geerte Kerk**. Turn right through churchyard (Geertekerkhof) and left along Springweg.

Keep straight on past old almshouses to Mariaplaats, and turn left to railway station. Walk ends here. Nearest refreshments in **Hoog Catharijne centre**, or trolley service on Inter-City back to Amsterdam.

Quayside and Backwaters

This walk could well begin as you rise from your lunch table. Make your way next to the quayside known as Gaard, and turn south. In Donkere Gaard my attention was caught by the windows of a pet-shop, 'De Natuurvriend'. In one section were some sweet puppies and lop-eared rabbits – and next to them, the rabbits' natural enemy, a frenzy of about twenty ferrets, tumbling over each other with innocent vigour.

The ferret as pet has always seemed to me a subject for alarm, the

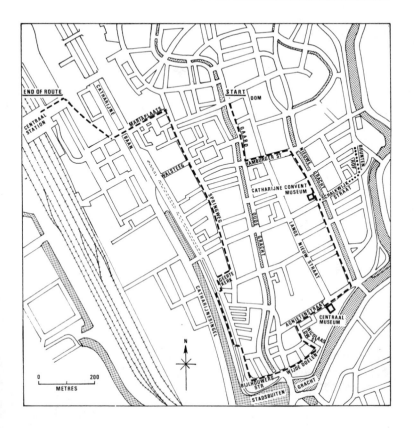

impression fortified by gruesome music hall jokes (ferrets down the trousers, etc.). They certainly look highly unsuited to domestic life with the average Dutch family, and yet in this shop they far outnumbered the other species on sale. The sight of them reminded me of a man I had seen in Leiden, a few days earlier, taking his pet weasel for a walk in the Fish Market. The wriggling beast hugged the ground, attached to its master by a red leather lead and matching harness, like a poodle's. It snuffled into doorways and around the toes of shoppers, but was so subdued or remote from its origins that it neglected to bite anyone. I felt immediately sorry for it, this naturally secretive animal transformed into a walking exhibition – and all to please its smug bearded master, who was probably an architect.

Continue beside the canal. On the lower quayside some of the lamp-posts are decorated with modern sculptures illustrating moments in the history of Utrecht. Turn down to Nieuwe Gracht, one of the sleepiest waterways you could wish to find. On the lower quayside flourishing weeds sprout between the cobbles, and a rusted and broken bike lies among them, having apparently committed suicide from the upper level. Never again would it be offered for auction at the Union of Notaries.

I have so far not mentioned the University, pockets of which occupy buildings all round this part of the city. It is the largest state university in the Netherlands; founded in 1636, it now has around 20,000 students. When they are in residence, they add fizz and life to these streets; when they are on vacation, a blanket of torpor descends.

Catharijne Convent Museum

This unusual museum, housed in a restored sixteenth-century convent, documents the history of Christianity in the Netherlands and has a stupendous collection of church art and regalia. At the entrance walk through to the café/bookstall where you can get a basic guide in Dutch/ English which outlines a route taking in thirty-two 'highlights'.

Locating all these may be more than you wish to do. If you prefer to float more freely, go anyway to the basement to see the vestments. Dating back to the early Middle Ages, they are well displayed in a room kept dark to protect them. In the next-door cellar are precious bindings, manuscripts and paintings. On the ground floor are statues and paintings, including *Christ as Man of Sorrows* by Geertgen tot Sint Jans and two portrait panels by Jan van Scorel.

Walk through to St Catharine's Church, founded by Carmelites in 1468 and completed in 1550 by the Knights of St John. It is now the cathedral church of the Roman Catholic Church in the Netherlands. To enter, press a button beside the glass door which silently opens and glides shut behind you. The main decorative elements are twelve polychrome statues of the Apostles in the choir. The Neo-Gothic rood screen now stands at the rear of the church.

On the upper floors are many fine paintings of religious subjects, priests and nuns. Among the seventeenth-century works are Frans Hals's *Portrait of Nicolaas Stenius* (1650); Rembrandt's *Baptism of the Eunuch* (1629) and a church interior by Pieter Saenredam, *The Great Church at Alkmaar* (1635).

Centraal Museum

Continue along sleepy Nieuwe Gracht. Moolenbeek – a bread and pastry shop – offers tempting smells, the only sign of life you may meet. Go past the University's Natural History Department and the entrance to their Botanical Garden, and in Agnietenstraat arrive at the Centraal Museum, which is concerned with the history of the town and has a pleasant mixed collection of paintings, furniture and applied art.

At present no guides in English are available, but all is fairly compact here. Below are some items to look out for.

I heard in advance about the Dolls' House. It is well worth trying to find. Turn right at the entrance, go through the costume gallery and turn left in the next room. It was made *c.*1680, and takes the form of a glazed cabinet made of inlaid olivewood. The rooms are displayed on three levels and filled with human figures of exaggerated height (about

23cm/9in tall) and furniture created in marvellous detail, down to the tiniest pieces of crockery, paintings on the walls and ornaments for the mantelshelf.

Another famous item is the Utrecht Ship. To find it, return to the front entrance and go downstairs to the crypt. The swooping lines of the great Viking ship (c.700) fill the long low room. Discovered in 1930, it is 14.3m (47ft) long and has a maximum width of 1.93m (6ft).

Go upstairs half a floor at a time to the *Tussenetage* (mezzanine) and *Etage*. On the right at the first landing is the Jan van Scorel Room. Van Scorel (1495-1562) was a widely accomplished man, and well travelled. He accompanied Pope Adriaan VI to Rome as his court painter and made a pilgrimage to the Holy Land. He was a writer and marine engineer as well as a painter and has been dubbed 'the Leonardo of the North'. Not all the works here are by Van Scorel, in fact the majority are copies or 'after Scorel' or 'Atelier of'. However, there are three excellent panels by him of the Utrecht Jerusalem Brotherhood.

The room opposite contains a most stimulating assortment of nineteenth- and early twentieth-century paintings. There is run-of-the-mill stuff too, but the list below will give an impression, I hope, of the range of good or anyway interesting pictures to be seen:

A bright Pointillist view by Theo van Rijsselberghe; an early Mondriaan landscape, c.1903; a Van Gogh woodland scene (1887); two good Breitners – *Reclining Nude* (c.1887) and *Horse Trams on the Dam, Amsterdam, at Evening* (c.1890-91); Fantin Latour's gentle *Ariadne in Naxos* (1901).

In the adjoining galleries are portraits and landscapes by Wim Schuhmacher and Charley Toorop, then bright abstracts by Karel Appel – *De Ontmoeting* (1951) and the collage *Drift op Zolder* (1947) – and abstracts by Wim de Haan, Willem Hussem and Jaap Wagemaker.

Up in the roof (second floor) are coins and archaeological finds, and displays on the history of Utrecht – well worth a look for early views of the city and coloured maps; a model of the Cathedral and two views showing how it looked before and after the hurricane of 1674.

A Walk in the Park

From the museum we make a loop that brings us to the pleasant open parkland beside the Stadsbuitengracht, which formerly skirted the old city walls. On the right, St Martinuskerk has recently gone the way of many Dutch churches, converted into thirty-eight apartment dwellings. Leave the park and turn through the pretty churchyard of Geertekerk to Springweg. In this quiet street, which leads us almost to the railway station, look for the step-gabled almshouses, the Huize Andreas founded in 1583, and the decorative gateway at No.104, formerly the municipal orphanage and now a children's day centre, 't Springertje, announced with suitably jumpy lettering. At Mariaplaats we turn left, cross the busy Catharijnebaan and spend the next ten minutes negotiating the raised alleys of Hoog Catharijne shopping centre.

Plenty of refreshment stops here, though fast trains to Amsterdam (Inter-City rather than *Stoptrein*) are frequent, and you can rely on someone coming down the train with a trolley full of snacks and drinks.

AMSTERDAM FROM A WALKER'S EYE-VIEW

WHAT TO WEAR AND CARRY WITH YOU

If something as innocent as a Slow Walk may be allowed a philosophy, it is that readers should spend as many enjoyable hours as possible at large in the city, forming their own considered view of the place. To do this in Amsterdam, no great feats of exploration are called for: this is one of the most friendly and hospitable cities in Europe, its natives famous for being only too pleased to show puzzled visitors the way, *and* joke with them in their own language. You will, however, feel better if you are comfortable and well supplied. Here are some reminders.

Your feet may hurt if you are not used to walking much, or if you wear unsuitable shoes. With the exception of the harbour walk (*Walk 3: City by the Sea*), no Slow Walk is more than a couple of miles in length, plus the distances travelled at stopping-places such as shops or museums. However, the walking surfaces of Amsterdam are surprisingly uneven. Canalside roads are cobbled, and elsewhere, even in a smart central thoroughfare, the paving stones may suddenly dip and undulate at surprising angles – the product of a soggy subsoil.

On such pavements, high heels and pinching uppers will not carry you far. My own preference is for classic stout walking shoes, somewhat heavy on the feet but good stayers. The important thing is to wear shoes that take good care of your feet, and do not leave you groaning when the sun goes down.

I would also put in a word for cotton socks. They keep the feet a lot cooler than other materials. To avoid chafing, put on a second pair; your feet will still 'breathe' normally, and be better protected from any jarring imparted by Amsterdam's eccentric pavements.

Another small snag is that it may rain. Amsterdam is on a similar latitude to Birmingham, Warsaw and Voronezh, and has a rainfall pattern similar to most of the west-facing coastal regions of Western Europe, with a special tendency to rain in the afternoon until tea-time then brighten sharply. A folding umbrella, or a good hat, and a rainproof jacket or coat are essential luggage at all times of the year.

Take a small bag on your walks, preferably one with a shoulder strap. Load it with: the umbrella; a camera and extra films; sunglasses; street map; tram pass or strip-ticket; Museum Pass, and, of course, your copy of *Slow Walks in Amsterdam*.

ON BEING A GOOD PEDESTRIAN

During a visitor's first day or so in Amsterdam it is not uncommon to feel, 'Yes, I am going to like it here, provided I am not mown down by a tram.' Trams swoop round corners at alarming speeds, and crossing any road laid with a tram track is a four-part operation.

In some places, usually near tram stops, there may be a central strip of pavement on which to break your journey to the other side. Try, also, to cross at traffic lights if possible, and follow the red and green pedestrian symbols. Wherever you cross, take special care until you have got into the rhythm of how the traffic moves, and be watchful ever after.

THE GEOGRAPHY OF AMSTERDAM

Maps of the present-day city clearly show a central area, shaped like half an orange slice and surrounded by the watery girdle of the Singelgracht. This area is called the Centrum, and it is here that most of our walks take place, most of the shops, sights and museums are situated, and nearly all the night life apart from concerts at the Concertgebouw.

This central part of Amsterdam was fully laid out with streets, canals and houses by 1650. Later expansion took place in the next surrounding areas, the Old West (Oud West), the Old South (Oud Zuid) and the East (Oost). Many of the buildings in those districts date from the late nineteenth century, when between 1875 and 1900 the city's population leapt from 300,000 to 550,000 (today it is about 700,000). In the 1930s the New South (Nieuw Zuid) came into being, a carefully planned suburb of broad boulevards and open spaces, and mansions and apartment blocks in the distinctive architectural style of the Amsterdam School.

Outside the Centrum, the most interesting areas for visitors are probably those between the Leidseplein and Vondelpark where many tourist hotels are located, and the neighbouring Museumplein. This runs between the Concertgebouw and the Rijksmuseum and is bordered by three other important art museums – the Stedelijk, the Van Gogh and the Overholland – and is close to the fashionable shopping streets of Van Baerlestraat and P.C. Hooftstraat.

The Centrum is admirably compact, ideal for exploring on foot. Along by the harbour (the diameter of the orange slice), the distance from the Haarlemmer Gate in the west to the De Gooyer windmill in the east is about 3.5 km (2.2 miles), and the distance from Centraal Station south to the Leidseplein (roughly the radius of the orange slice) is about 2.2 km (1.4 miles).

Although some parts of the Centrum are filled with narrow lanes and a profusion of cross-streets, it is actually quite difficult after the first day or so to lose your way. Just keep moving and the chances are that you will soon recognise some familiar landmark along the line of a canal or above the gables. Places such as the West Church (Westerkerk), the Harbour Building (Havengebouw), the Royal Palace (Koninklijk Paleis), the Rijksmuseum and the Old Church (Oude Kerk) loom with a regularity most comforting for the newly arrived.

If you need to ask the way, you can expect most Dutch people to answer you in clear, sometimes astonishingly colloquial English, which they learn as a second language from the age of ten or eleven and practise constantly, helped also by a large diet of English-language television. Amsterdam is a truly international city, and nowadays English is *the* international language. This does not stop many Dutch people from being briskly proficient in several other languages, French and German to the fore.

For all their linguistic talents, it is not a bad idea to buy a small two-way Dutch dictionary. This will equip you with a basic stock of 'please', 'thank you' and 'hello/goodbye' words, and also with a means of translating those words that continually pop up in a tourist's day, e.g. *toegang* (entry, admission), *geen toegang* (no entry), *duwen* (push) and *trekken* (pull). So much easier, when you know them, to get through doors.

Maps Each Slow Walk has its own Route map and this should be sufficient to guide you round the walk, bring you to a closing refreshment stop and direct you to the nearest onward tram route. For a broader and more detailed view of the city there are various reasonably priced folding maps on sale, and another set which is produced in book form with a ring-binder. Many of these tourist maps are published by Falk.

The folding maps in the Falk series have an index on the back, and although it is a little irritating to keep having to refold the thing each time you want to look up a street name, I prefer these to the ring-bound maps because the amount of ground covered by one ring-bound page is so small that I am continually walking off the edge.

VVV   A good place to go for your map, and all sorts of advice including hotel accommodation, is one of the Amsterdam Tourist Offices (VVV). Their main office is at 10 Stationsplein, in the Noord-Zuid Hollands Koffiehuis building opposite Centraal Station; open in summer 09.00 to 23.00, in winter generally between 09.30 and 17.30. They also have a small branch at 106 Leidsestraat, a few doors from the Leidseplein tram stop; open 09.00 to 22.30, in winter generally between 09.30 and 17.30.

The VVV publish the very useful *What's On In Amsterdam* (see *What's On*, below), and sell Museum Passes (*Museum Jaarkaart*). These are excellent value, admitting the holder to the national and municipal museums of Amsterdam and to more than 400 museums throughout the country. At a very limited number of these, e.g. for a special exhibition at the Stedelijk, you may be asked to pay a small supplement; otherwise, entry is free to pass-holders. The Museum Pass is valid for one calendar year, 1 January to 31 December. Take along a passport photo when you buy your pass; failing that, make sure you slot a photo into the plastic holder before you present it at a museum. Passes can also be bought at major museums.

TRANSPORT

Trams

A grasp of the tram network is more or less essential for getting around the city. All Slow Walks in Amsterdam begin at a tram stop, and there is a map of the system on the back cover of this book.

Services are frequent, and easy and cheap to use. Most trams are yellow, though you may find the odd blue one with a cobra painted on the side or some other gaudy device. Most run in three-car units, and clank along as fast as they can go, which in central districts usually leaves you plenty of time for a good look out of the window.

When you want to get out at the next stop, press one of the 'Stop' buttons along the side of the car; a red light goes on near the driver. To work the automatic door, press the *'Deur Open'* button. The bottom step controls the closing of the door. Keep your foot on it if you want the door to remain open.

Services run throughout the day, finishing around midnight. Then night buses run to many parts of the city, starting from Centraal Station. The GVB (municipal transport authority) issues a leaflet about night buses, available from their information and ticket offices. These are located opposite Centraal Station (next door to the VVV), open 07.00 to 22.30, Saturday and Sunday open 08.00; also at their head office in the Scheepvaartshuis building, 108 Prins Hendrikkade; and at Amstel Railway Station.

Tickets There are various forms of tram ticket on offer. By far the easiest solution is to go to a GVB office, collect their free leaflet which includes a map of the network, and buy a day ticket (*Dagkaart*) for however many days you want (up to a maximum of nine). This allows you to ride on all Amsterdam's tram, bus and Metro lines. All you then need to do is stamp the ticket in the tram *at the beginning of your first trip*. Yellow stamping machines are located at the rear of the tram and in the middle car. Push in the top of the ticket and stamp it along the white strip.

You can also buy a two-strip ticket, which allows you to ride in one zone (Centrum, Noord, Oost, Zuid or West), or a 'one-hour ticket'. The Centrum zone embraces most of the routes included in the Slow Walks, and is the only zone featured in the map on the back cover of this book.

Another method is to buy a strip ticket (*Strippenkaart*) – either a strip of 10 tickets from the driver or, for the same price, a strip of 15 tickets from one of the GVB offices mentioned above, or from a post office or certain tobacconists. Each journey in one zone costs two strips, plus one strip for every other zone entered during the journey.

To stamp your ticket, let us say for one journey in one zone, fold the ticket over so that the strip numbered 2 is at the top. Push it in the machine and collect a coded stamp within the margins of strip 2. For a journey going into two zones, stamp strip 3, and so on. On the right of the strip, the stamp will show the time of day. You can now take any number of rides – by tram, bus or Metro – within the hour and should not stamp the ticket again in that period. The same applies to the two-strip and one-hour tickets, though with the former you must stay in the same zone.

A strip ticket may be used by more than one person. It is also a *national* ticket, usable in other parts of the country. If, having bought your strip ticket, you are not sure how to stamp it, ask the driver to do it for you, telling him how many zones you are going into and how many persons are travelling on that ticket.

Make sure you keep your ticket, of whatever kind, until the end of your journey. Uniformed inspectors travel the network and can impose a nasty fine on anyone unable to show a valid ticket.

I have said that the day ticket is the easiest to use, and after digesting all that information about strip tickets you may be inclined to agree. But which of these longer-term tickets offers the better value? By my calculations, it is cheaper to buy strip tickets if you take only two rides a day. If you take four rides a day, the day ticket becomes notably better value by the third day and stays ahead thereafter.

Buses

Central Amsterdam is dominated by the tram network, and except for travelling along by the harbour, e.g. to or from the Maritime Museum, you may seldom need to catch a bus. When you do, the routine is similar to that for trams except that you get on at the front and either show your day ticket to the driver or ask him to stamp your strip ticket. Day tickets and strip tickets are also valid within the city limits on the yellow buses which serve the regional bus system. For details, see maps at tram and bus shelters, and in Metro stations.

Tickets   These are the same as for trams, above.

Metro

The Amsterdam Metro is chiefly for commuters and runs out to the south-eastern suburbs. It begins at Centraal Station, then goes down to Amstel via Nieuwmarkt and Waterlooplein. Beyond Amstel the line divides at Duivendrecht, one arm going to Gaasperplas and the other to Gein.

Carriages are functional and roomy, on the scale of the Paris Métro, usually with four or six carriages to a train. Doors at two points per train carry a big picture of a bicycle, and that is where cycling travellers should put their machine on board. As with trams, the doors open automatically when you press the *'Deur Open'* button. When the driver is ready to depart, a 'Ding dong' signal sounds a warning and you should not try to get in or out once it has gone off.

Tickets   These are the same as for trams, above. In Metro stations there are automatic ticket dispensers supplying one-hour tickets, two-strip tickets and day tickets. Stamp one-hour and strip tickets in the yellow stamping machine near the stairs to the platforms.

Taxis

Taxis are a little expensive but a useful alternative, especially after the regular tram and bus services have shut down for the night. Taxis may be hailed on the street, but drivers seldom stop, often because they are on their way to pick up a telephone fare. You can catch a taxi at one of the ranks on main squares such as Stationsplein and Leidseplein. Otherwise, telephone 77-77-77 and let the taxi come to you.

TELEPHONES

Public telephones are easy to use and a lot cheaper than making calls from a hotel. Most take 25c, Fl 1 and Fl 2.5 coins. To telephone the UK, insert coins, check for dial tone and dial 09; wait for a second tone and dial 44, then the STD code and number deleting the first 0. Thus the code for London is 09-44-1.

Another way to make a cheap international call is to go to the Telehouse, open 24 hours a day, at 46-50 Raadhuisstraat – about 200m west from the Main Post Office.

MONEY

The Dutch currency is the guilder (Hfl, Fl or F), and there are 100 cents to the guilder. Coins are 5c, 10c, 25c, Fl 1, Fl 2.5 and Fl 5. Notes are Fl 5, Fl 10, Fl 25, Fl 50, Fl 100, Fl 250 and Fl 1000.

A local bank should give you a better exchange rate than the change shops. The prevailing cash limit of Fl 300 per bank cheque may seem meagre, especially for families, but that is something we all have to put up with for the time being. If you need more than Fl 300, say for the weekend, ask if you can cash two cheques.

Most banks are open 09.00 to 16.00, Monday to Friday, and some are open on Saturday morning. Outside banking hours, several change shops are open until 22.45 or later, including the following:

GWK, Centraal Station, open April to October 07.00 to 22.45 Monday to Saturday, 08.00 on Sunday, November to March 08.00 to 20.00.

Change Express, branches at 106 Leidsestraat; 17 Damrak; 86 Damrak, 150 Kalverstraat; open every day until 24.00.

Travellers' cheques and Eurocheques are the easiest means of exchange (look for a bank displaying the EC sign), and most banks and change shops accept the major credit cards – American Express, Diners Club, Access, Mastercard and Visa. Take your passport with you for identification.

To pay for goods in shops and restaurants, credit cards are widely acceptable but ask first before you commit yourself, or eat anything. Eurocheques are also commonly used; make sure you have both cheques and encashment card with you. Travellers' cheques are not popular.

It is a good idea to buy some guilders before leaving home. This will accustom you to the glare of the colourful banknotes and allow you to pitch straight in as soon as you arrive and want to buy something, say at the airport, or tip someone, a taxi driver perhaps, or a hotel porter.

Tax-free shopping For visitors living outside the EEC, this is a way of reclaiming Dutch VAT (called BTW) on goods bought to a value of more than Fl 300. Ask the shop for an export certificate, or tax-free shopping cheque, which you then hand in at Dutch Customs. This goes back to the shop, or their tax-free representatives, and they forward the refund. Remember that goods above a certain value may also be liable to Customs duty on arrival in your home country.

EEC residents may claim a refund of Dutch VAT, but must still pay the VAT in their own country. Value of goods must be more than Fl 910. Ask for an import certificate which you present to Customs at your home point of arrival. You then pay your national VAT and claim back the Dutch VAT.

Clearly, this is not such a good bargain as that enjoyed by non-EEC residents, e.g. Americans, Japanese, Swiss, Austrians, Saudi Arabians and others. However, if your national VAT is less than Dutch VAT, you may think it is worth the effort.

Tipping The prevailing system in restaurants is a little complicated, and made worse by those waiters who seek to exploit it. This they do by saying, when you ask them, that service is not included. In fact, you can expect both a service charge and sales tax to be included in the bill. What is not included is the tip.

The usual practice is to round up to the next guilder on something small like a drinks order, and up to the next round number of guilders on something larger. Say lunch for two cost Fl 18.25; most people would then leave Fl 20.00. It is up to the customer, but usually a tip is in the range of 5-10 per cent.

For taxi drivers leave a similar amount. Give hotel porters and cloakroom attendants a small tip; in loos they may tell you how much they want, usually 25-35c.

OPENING TIMES

You are in a crowded club at 3 am on Sunday night. It then occurs to you to wonder what all these Dutch people are doing. Don't they have to go to work in the morning? Well, no doubt some do, but if they work in a shop they may well be free until lunch-time.

On Monday, shops open from 13.00 or 13.30 to 18.00. On Tuesday to Friday they open from 09.00 to 18.00, and on Saturday afternoon they close at 17.00. Late-night shopping in Amsterdam is on Thursday, until 21.00. On Sunday, basic shops such as newsagents are open, but few others.

Cafés and bars do not rush to open their doors in the morning. For many, 11.00 is quite early enough.

Banks are open 09.00 to 16.00, and some are open on Saturday morning. Change shops are open longer (see *Money* above).

Museum hours vary, so check with *What's On In Amsterdam* for the latest information. In general, state museums are open Tuesday to Saturday 10.00 to 17.00, closed all day Monday and Sunday until 13.00.

Opening times for all main places of interest on Slow Walks are listed in the appropriate chapter.

Finally, Dutch opening times can be hard to understand if they are described in Dutch only. For example:

Open di t/m za 10.00-17.00; zon- en feestdagen 13.00-17.00.

This means: Open Tuesday to Saturday 10.00-17.00; Sunday and public holidays 13.00-17.00. The expression *t/m* is an abbreviation of *tot en met* = up to and including. The days of the week (and their abbreviations) are as follows:

maandag (ma)	Monday	*vrijdag (vr)*	Friday
dinsdag (di)	Tuesday	*zaterdag (za)*	Saturday
woensdag (wo)	Wednesday	*zondag (zo)*	Sunday
donderdag (do)	Thursday		

LIST OF PUBLIC HOLIDAYS

All banks are closed on the days listed below, and most shops except where noted. State museums are closed on Christmas Day, Boxing Day and New Year's Day, and open Sunday hours (13.00 to 17.00) on other public holidays.

1 January: New Year's Day
Good Friday (many shops open)
Easter Sunday
Easter Monday
30 April: Queen's Birthday (many shops open in morning)
5 May: Liberation Day (public holiday every five years – 1990, etc)
Ascension Day: sixth Thursday after Easter
Whit Sunday: second Sunday after Ascension
Whit Monday
25 December: Christmas Day
26 December: Boxing Day (St Stephen's Day)

In addition, Labour Day is commemorated on 1 May, and Memorial Day on 4 May, remembering the victims of the Second World War.

CLOTHING SIZES

For Women

Dresses, knitwear, blouses, coats

Ned	36	38	42	44	46	48
GB	10	12	14	16	18	20
USA	8	10	12	14	16	18

Tights, stockings

Ned	35	36	37	38	39	40		
GB	8	8½	9	9½	10	10½		
USA	8	8½	9	9½	10	10½		

Shoes

Ned	35½	36	36½	37	37½	38	38½	39½	40½
GB	3	3½	4	4½	5	5½	6	7	8
USA	4	4½	5	5½	6	6½	7½	8½	9½

For Men

Shirts

Ned	36	37	38	39	40	41	42
GB	14	14½	15	15½	16	16½	17
USA	14	14½	15	15½	16	16½	17

Sweaters

Ned	46	48	50	52	54	56	
GB	36	38	40	42	44	46	
USA	36	38	40	42	44	46	

Shoes

Ned	39	40	41	42	43	44	45
GB	5½	6½	7	8	8½	9½	10½
USA	6	7	7½	8½	9	10	11

WATERING-HOLES

In every regular Dutch brain, and many Dutch brains are regular (and nothing wrong with that), there is a busy department which deals in 'Statistics'. The Dutch love to spray their foreign visitors with facts and figures: how many bridges, how many barrel organs, how many tulips per square metre, and so on. Thus the excellent *What's On* guide tells us that Amsterdam has, among other things, 700,000 inhabitants, 220,000 trees, 574 coffee shops (*koffiehuis*), 1,402 cafés and bars, and 755 restaurants.

Coffee shops need little explanation. They serve coffee, tea and soft drinks, and a useful range of snacks and lunch dishes – soups, salads, filled rolls (*belegde broodjes*), baguettes with a filling (*stokbroods*), open sandwiches of meat and cheese topped with a fried egg (*uitsmijter*) as well as traditional apple cake (*appelgebak*), etc.

Cafés and bars are either old or new. The old type is that famous Amsterdam institution, the brown bar (*bruine kroeg*). In nature it is akin to the almost-vanished English snug: a friendly dive with a wooden bar, bare floorboards and brown or ochre walls darkened by years of tobacco smoke. There may be newspapers on a stick, a coat stand, a pocketless billiard table, an armchair by an old chimneypiece. Only in the most bustling places would the staff dream of hurrying you over your drink. Some customers, and their dogs, more or less live in their brown bar. Catering habits vary, but most serve rolls or sandwiches and some are *eetcafés*, offering a full menu.

The new type is the international designer bar, available in Europe anywhere from Glasgow to Rome and therefore not so special unless your taste is for spindly black furniture, exposed steel and mirrors, loud music and cocktails in bilious colours.

In some bars and coffee shops the customers can buy and smoke marijuana. The bars are no longer allowed to advertise this facility by putting a picture of a cannabis leaf in the window, but can usually be picked out by their psychedelic frontages and/or giveaway names – Extase, Grasshopper, etc. (see also 'Red Light District' section in *Walk 2: Old Side*).

Other specialist bars and cafés cater for women only, and for gay men. The latter tend to cluster in Warmoesstraat, Amstel, Kerkstraat and Reguliersdwarsstraat.

Another type of drinking establishment is the *proeflokaal*. Formerly they were the tasting houses of *jenever* (gin) distilleries, and customers went to them to sample the goods before buying. Now they are spirit shops where people go for an apéritif. No beer is served. Glasses of old, young or flavoured *jenever* arrive full to the brim, and it is entirely acceptable to place your hands behind your back, lean forward and suck.

Amsterdam has an enormous range of restaurants at all prices. Dutch cooking is sound, not very imaginative and served in ample quantities. Indonesian restaurants are popular and widespread, and

Chinese, Japanese and Thai cooking attracts many customers. The other most familiar categories are Surinamese and Caribbean, French, Greek, Indian, Italian, Pancake places and Vegetarian.

The Dutch tend to eat early, and restaurants are at their busiest between 19.00 and 21.00. If, on your daily round, you see a place you fancy, it is well worth asking if you need to reserve. Last year, writing about Paris, I noted that nothing was worse than having to queue for a table. In Amsterdam there *is* something worse – to arrive in a half-empty restaurant and be turned away because all the other tables are reserved. It can happen in other cities, of course, but here diners seem to be heavily into the booking habit.

In the Slow Walks chapters I make a number of suggestions about where to eat in the evening. To supplement your personal list of places, look in the restaurant columns of *What's On* (see below), which are organised by speciality – Dutch, Indonesian, etc. Also, many hotels recommend nearby restaurants, which return the compliment by offering a free drink or discount of up to 10 per cent on the bill. These can be worth a try, though your compatriots will tend to gather there, which may not be to your liking.

TOILETS

This is really not a problem. Cafés and bars have loos which you can expect to be clean, fitted with a seat and the usual accessories. In larger establishments there may be a lady sitting at the entrance by a saucer who will expect a tip of 25–35c.

In tourist centres such as the Keukenhof, a toll may be exacted before they let you in, but the charge will not be unreasonable.

For men, a few iron *urinoirs* still adorn the quaysides.

WHAT'S ON

The VVV tourist office publishes a most useful fortnightly guide, *What's On In Amsterdam*, available in some hotels or from their offices in Stationsplein, opposite Centraal Station, and 106 Leidsestraat. It contains general information for visitors, news of current attractions, lists of exhibitions, museums, galleries, theatres, restaurants, and a day-by-day entertainments guide. References to it appear from time to time in this book, e.g. 'See *What's On* for details'.

Another useful source is *Uitkrant*, a free monthly newspaper published by the AUB (Amsterdams Uitburo), available from various outlets such as museums or from the AUB ticket shop in Leidseplein (corner of Marnixstraat), open 10.00 to 18.00, closed Sunday. This has good day-by-day listings for theatre, music, dance, film and children's entertainments, and further alphabetical sections organised by venue.

AMSTERDAM BY NIGHT

When your day's Slow Walking is done, the stamina test begins. Not immediately, in fact not for several hours. Plenty of time to return to base, take a shower or a nap, or both. Emerge refreshed for an apéritif, say between seven and eight o'clock. Take at least two hours over dinner. The late late things – discos, blues and jazz bars, rock clubs – don't begin till ten or ten-thirty, then go on until two or three in the morning. After the rave-up, home at three-thirty, in bed by four. Up again at eight, ready to begin the next Slow Walk by nine-thirty.

It *can* be done, of course it can. But perhaps it is best done every *other* night, with something more gentle for the evening in between. An organ concert in the Oude Kerk, the Amsterdam Baroque Orchestra at the Concertgebouw, a play at the Stadsschouwburg (many are in English), a new film at the Art Deco Tuschinski Theater, an old film at the Filmmuseum in Vondelpark, a candle-lit dinner on a canal cruiser, a Chinese meal at the floating pagoda in Oosterdok. Look them all up, these and many more, in *Uitkrant* and *What's On*.

A visit to some outpost of the sleaze industry is also possible. If you are in the mood, you can do more or less anything in Amsterdam. For respectable, old-fashioned striptease, try somewhere in Thorbecke-plein. For the full works, go to the Red Light district, preferably, after dark, with a couple of hefty companions. You probably won't enjoy it, people seldom do. Just don't ask me for your money back, that's all.

QUICK AMSTERDAM

If you have only a weekend or 3-4 days in Amsterdam, choose from this selection of Walks. Be sure to check all opening times (see 'Best times') before you set off.

Day 1	Begin outside Centraal Station. Buy tram pass from GVB office and copy of *What's On In Amsterdam* from VVV next door. Then take *Walk 1: New Side*, including a canal cruise. Near Centraal Station, Rederij Lovers have more comfortable boats than some. Follow with *Walk 2: Old Side*.
Day 2	*Walk 10: Rijksmuseum and Six Collection*. Follow with *Walk 11: Rembrandtplein to Leidseplein*, perhaps omitting Vijzelstraat section, i.e. at Muntplein go straight ahead to Floating Flower Market.
Day 3	*Walk 12: Modern Art and Vondelpark*.
Day 4	*Walk 4: Jordaan*. Halfway along, cross Prinsengracht and visit Anne Frank House (see *Walk 6*). Then resume *Walk 4*.
Day 5	*Walk 3: City by the Sea*.